It's Always Possible

One Woman's Transformation
of Tihar Prison

It's Always Possible

One Woman's Transformation of Tihar Prison

Kiran Bedi, Ph.D.

HIMALAYAN INSTITUTE®
PRESS
HONESDALE, PA 18431 USA

Himalayan Institute Press
952 Bethany Turnpike
Honesdale, PA 18431
www.HimalayanInstitute.org

Published by the Himalayan International Institute of Yoga Science and
Philosophy, 2006.
10 09 08 07 06   6 5 4 3 2 1

It's Always Possible:
One Woman's Transformation of Tihar Prison
©1998, Kiran Bedi
Originally published by Sterling; First Edition 1998
Reprint 1998, 1999, 2000, 2001, 2002

Bedi, Kiran, 1949—
It's always possible: one woman's transformation of Tihar Prison /
Kiran Bedi.
    p. cm.

Summary: "An account of the reformation and rehabilitation of Tihar
Prison, one of the largest prisons in Asia. With a foreword by the
Dalai Lama and input from the prisoners themselves, this book illustrates
Dr. Bedi's efforts to fundamentally change an entire prison system of
criminality to one of humanity."
—Provided by publisher.

Includes bibliographical references and index.
ISBN–13: 978-0-89389-258-6 (alk. paper)
ISBN–10: 0-89389-258-0 (alk. paper)
1. Bedi, Kiran, 1949–   . 2. Tihar Central Jail (New Delhi, India)
—Administration. 3. Prison administration—India—New Delhi.
4. Prisoners—India—New Delhi. I. Title
HV9795.N42T543 2006
365'.70954   2005035635

To my Mother and Father whom I love the most.
Together we believe it's always possible.

contents

THE DALAI LAMA

foreword

Serving humanity even beyond the responsibilities of one's duty calls for special human beings. Kiran Bedi is one of them. As a woman and as an officer, her compassion, concern, and total commitment toward social issues, whether in the fields of drug control or prison administration at Tihar Jail, have earned her unusual distinction.

I have myself believed deeply and strongly in the need to treat people who are imprisoned as part of our own society. Unfortunately, society in general, and prison authorities in particular, treat prisoners as outcasts. I, therefore, admire and laud Kiran Bedi's noble attempts to reinstate aberrant individuals into the mainstream of society by giving them a kind and considerate exposure to a more civilized environment, meditation, education, and better civic amenities.

I am confident that this book by Kiran Bedi will inspire readers and set a precedent for those who can wield authority to retain the human touch.

The Dalai Lama

acknowledgements

I am deeply indebted to:

- The Jawaharlal Nehru Memorial Fund for the Nehru Fellowship
- The United Nations, Governments and Embassies of the United Kingdom, the United States, Denmark, Germany, Austria, Slovakia, Italy, Holland, Switzerland, Japan, the Philippines, Sri Lanka, and Mauritius who facilitated my visits to the prisons in their countries
- Former Cabinet Minister P. Chidambaram, industrialist R. P. Goenka, Gopal Subramaniam and Aveek Sarkar of *Anandabazar Patrika*
- My colleagues Jaydev Sarangi, Tarsem Kumar, K. R. Kishore, D. P. Diwedi, and P. R. Meena, who led the movement for change in Tihar
- The large family of prison staff, non-governmental organizations, individuals, and thousands of inmates who made the impossible possible
- Shri Ajay Agrawal, Director General Tihar Prisons, who respected the initiatives taken during my tenure, and has carried them forward
- Shri Sunil Gupta, Law Officer Tihar Prisons India Vision Foundation, Navjyoti, Delhi Police Foundation, and my personal staff
- My family, whom I have always taken for granted
- All these who made the first edition of this book possible: Jyoti Sabharwal, Mr. S. K. Ghai of Sterling Publishers, Dolly Narang, Ajay Goyal, Achal Paul, Esha Beteille, and Amalin Cinegraphics

preface

The position of Inspector General of Prisons in Delhi had been vacant for many months. Prison postings are generally considered dead-end punishment postings, and no one, including myself, appeared to have been interested in the job. But some things are destined to happen. As a civil servant, I had been the Deputy Inspector General of Police in a community in northeast India, and had been waiting for nine months for a new appointment. The Government of India took its time, and apparently posted me to Tihar only after the auditor's office told them I couldn't be indefinitely carried on the payroll without an assignment. The orders came on Friday evening, effective immediately. Posting orders never state the duration of posting. I reported the following morning. I was now the official custodian responsible for over 7,200 inmates.

About this time, I happened to meet a colleague. He was happily perched on a high-back rocking chair behind a large glass-topped table, in a conference hall-sized office. Hearing of my appointment, he said, "Kiran, what are you doing? What will you do there? There is no work there!" He went on, "I was the Inspector General of Prisons many years ago. I received just two files a day. So, I used to clear them from my home, or at my other job. Get yourself out of this."

I knew that he was wrong, but I said nothing. My family was also worried. But deep down inside, I could see destiny leading me. I knew I was headed in the right direction, to a place where I could use all my years of experience in policing.

The posting to Tihar Jail was an opportunity for me to apply twenty-one years of experience in policing, and to reach out to people in need. When I was a Deputy Police Commissioner in Delhi, I worked with substance abuse treatment centers as a means of crime prevention. The program I developed then continued to grow, and one organization born from that work, Navjyoti, enjoys observer status with the United Nations. However, my experience with lawbreakers did not include looking after them. This I had to learn immediately. This book is the story of how I implemented my philosophy of reformation and transformation, and put the prison community on the road to holistic correction.

My personal habit of preserving and meticulously documenting events and situations served me well when it came time to write this book. I was also fortunate that as I left my post at Tihar, many released inmates came to see me either for a personal visit or to bid good-bye. Since they knew I was working on this book, they volunteered to go on record uninhibitedly.

I am grateful to the Jawaharlal Nehru Memorial Fund, for awarding me the Nehru Fellowship. This Fellowship, undoubtedly one of the most outstanding Indian scholarships, made it possible for me to research prisons around the world and to write this book. I visited prisons in London, Edinburgh, Copenhagen, Zurich, Frankfurt, Bratislava, Vienna, Washington, Philadelphia, San Francisco, Hawaii, Tokyo, Hong Kong, Manila, and Colombo. In those visits I did not come across even a single prison supervisor, governor, or warden handling a prison as large as Tihar. I met no woman heading a male prison. At first upon meeting me, almost no one really believed that a diminutive woman like myself was the head of the largest prison complex in India. And certainly, until I gave sufficient visual and written evidence, no one really believed that my prison complex was a riot-free, no-smoking zone with a *vipassana* meditation camp of over 1,100 inmates. Equally unbelievable was that 90 percent of the population in Tihar was waiting for trial, and in many cases, had been waiting for years.

I saw excellent infrastructures in these foreign prisons, and excellent facilities for education and rehabilitation. But I did not see a single prison with over three hundred non-governmental organizations (NGOs) working with prisoners as they did in Tihar. At the end of these visits, I envied their infrastructure, and they envied the voluntary acceptance and participation of Tihar prisoners in all the programs. I saw a mix of both only in the Grendon Prison in the United Kingdom that works with psychotherapeutic treatment of personality-disordered individuals.

These visits made me proud to be from India. Whatever we did stemmed from our inherent belief in non-violence, forgiveness, compassion, sacrifice, selflessness, and community participation. What gave me the greatest satisfaction was knowing we had reached out to the prisoners, and that it had worked. In 1994, when I was in Manila receiving the prestigious Ramon Magsaysay Award for my work in Tihar, over 10,000 inmates and staff back home celebrated the event inside the prison. Each one rightfully felt that the award was conferred as a result of his or her commitment to the transformation programs in Tihar. When I returned to Delhi with the award, the celebrations were repeated. That this could happen inside the largest prison in a liberal democracy anywhere in the world was indeed gratifying!

As you read, you will be joining in the pain and pleasure of the process by which India's largest prison was transformed. I hope that you will come to believe as I do, that it's always possible.

Kiran Bedi, Ph.D.
January 1, 2002

life in the
infamous tihar jail

My First Day in Prison

I came to prison unprepared like everybody else. I did not know what to expect, or what went on inside. The difference was that I was in charge. All I knew was that thousands of men and women were incarcerated behind the rusted gates and high walls topped by barbed wire. All I could see from the outside were tall poles topped with gleaming yellow floodlights. The sentries were faceless figures on the distant watchtowers.

It was May 1, 1993, and I was the new Inspector General of the infamous Tihar Jails, the largest prison complex in Asia Pacific. I had heard rumors of the terrible conditions and nefarious activities. I had heard stories of the gang wars, prisoners running extortion businesses from inside the prison, and tales of rampant corruption, violence, and tragedy. There was a whole other world in exile behind those high walls. This hellhole was now my duty.

I stepped out of the staff car and walked briskly toward my new office. In those few steps, I geared myself up to face the situation, determined to do my job. I was there to make Tihar a respectable human dwelling. I am a policewoman, but I am also deeply spiritual by nature. My spiritual beliefs have been an enormous source of strength and comfort to me throughout my career. I recited a short prayer and then moved to assume the Inspector General's chair.

My office was the worst I had ever had in all my years of policing. It appeared to have been built as an afterthought, and never intended to be occupied. It was a claustrophobic, viewless room 20 by 15 feet. The pale yellow walls were bare. My presence was no deterrent to the rats and numerous insects that obviously considered me an intruder.

Nonetheless, in that office I called my first meeting

The entrance to Tihar Central Jail, New Delhi, India

with the senior staff, the Deputy Inspector General, and the superintendents of the four jails. As they sat across from me at the prison-manufactured wooden table, I sensed their curiosity. Perhaps they were curious to see how I would speak and how I would conduct myself as a woman Inspector General. What was my agenda? Was I enthusiastic, or would I sulk about being posted there? Was I going to accuse my seniors of dumping me in an undesirable job and seek their sympathy? Was I a misfit posted to an obscure job?

As for my impressions, the staff did not appear enthusiastic or motivated. It appeared that they just happened to be there because of their posting. None of the officers were in uniform. They were all young, in their thirties. I was the oldest person in the office. For the first time, I felt a bit too responsible, not by virtue of my official position, but because of my years.

The staff was reticent and on guard, perhaps unsure about the extent to which they could share their thoughts with me. I provoked them by throwing out a few questions, and when I saw them looking at each other out of the corners of their eyes, I decided to take the initiative. During that short inquisition, I sensed who their leader was and decided to lead them through him. I told them I was primarily a team person. I set goals, but only after I understood both the task and the resources available. I made it clear that I respected experience and encouraged participation. I assured them that I would be learning from each of them. Once the goals were set and vision shared, we should all be in it together, through thick and thin. More importantly, I would take full responsibility for my acts of omission and commission. I would begin with trust, but a breach of trust would not be tolerated. Honest mistakes would be examined and decisions made on the merits of each case. Credit for good work would be made public.

As the meeting progressed, I tried to share some of my immediate thoughts about the prison. I recalled my days as a police officer trying to rehabilitate repeat offenders, and how I had wished that the prison would play a supportive role in reforming them. But since I did not have a relationship with the prison, and there was no system to provide one, that wish had remained a mere thought. Now it was possible to translate that personal desire into action, and we were going to be the people to bring about that reform. I told them that I looked forward to working with them without knowing whether they looked forward to working with me! I thanked them for coming and then drove home wondering what lay ahead.

On Monday morning I reached my office exactly on time, determined "to do my time" at Tihar. My personal assistants, P. V. Rao and C. B. Virmani, were already there. We went immediately for a round of Prison No. 1 (four prisons comprise the Tihar complex). Prison No. 1 was just a 50-foot walk from my office, but a monstrous prison gate barred our way and confronted me with a premonition of the difficulty of the task ahead. Protecting a secret world of retribution, the immense structure loomed over me under a thick layer of rust and peeling bottle-green paint. I felt dwarfed, and wondered if that giant gate would ever open for me. It did not. What opened was a faded green wicket gate, 2 feet by 4 feet. I had to bend over and leap over a low hurdle to enter the *deodhi*—massive hall between two big gates. Twenty steps ahead I noticed another huge locked gate. No one could enter the prison unless the main gate I had just come through was locked and this second gate was opened. Thus, we were in the *deodhi*, a complex between the two gates, which housed the administrative block with the office of the Superintendent, the record room, a closed-circuit television monitor for internal vigilance, and the visitors' gallery. The Warder directed me to sign in on the register kept for recording the time of every entry and exit. The register was kept on a sturdy wooden table made in the prison factory. Had the table been a few inches higher, I would have had to stand on my toes to reach it.

The prison had almost no modern electronic gadgets or devices. The system dated back to the colonial era, and the security measures could be traced back to an even earlier period. The gatekeeper, who had opened the wicket gate for me, kept the keys to the locks for both the iron gates and the wicket gate. He was under orders to open only one gate at a time. Therefore, this person, a constable by rank, spent his eight hours of duty walking between the two gates. Having recorded my entry, I waited at the second gate. Standing in front of the second wicket gate that opened into the prison, I was beginning to get the feel of a prison. Then the second gate closed behind me and I was inside.

It was like entering an organized and unique town. The first thing that struck me was the definitive and peculiar smell. The second thing I noticed were inmates waiting at the gate to enter the *deodhi* and exit the prison. They looked shocked, bewildered and silent—exactly how I felt. I saw only men and wondered when a senior woman officer had last been here. Wearing a uniform was not mandatory, so I deliberately wore a full-sleeved pastel pathan suit, topped by a waist-length Nehru jacket, and flat walking shoes, so even my toes were covered. I wanted to present a non-distracting presence. I was accompanied by a warder in uniform, but no armed guard. The jail superintendent soon joined me. I carried a notepad to record my observations. As I filed past the waiting prisoners, the warders, perhaps from force of habit, but without the slightest provocation, started to physically contain the prisoners. Some waved their sticks menacingly at the onlooking prisoners, and made disparaging sounds in a gesture to show concern for my security. I ordered them to stop.

My first visit was to one of the largest wards of the prison housing about 600 inmates. Prison No. 1, one of the four jails under my charge, had twelve wards, varying in size. The wards were further subdivided into barracks or dormitories. Inside the ward, I saw a sprawling mud compound and a few tall trees. No doubt it had been a long time since an Inspector General had visited the place. The inmates in the courtyard began to walk slowly toward me, but the staff abruptly signaled them with their *lathis* (sticks) to sit down at a distance. The word had apparently gone around that there was a visitor in the prison and it was none other than the Inspector General. I was taken aback by the blank stares all around me. I stood facing them, not knowing what expression would be most suitable for the moment. The prisoners seemed to be wondering why I had come right into their den. By being out of uniform, I hoped to signal my desire for informal communication, not authoritative distance. I had already begun to empathize with them, wondering if our criminal justice system was designed to help offenders and forgive those who were willing to mend.

Perhaps it was that thought that prompted me to break the silence by asking, "Do you pray?"

No one answered.

I repeated: "I am asking you, do you pray? Please tell me." I spoke in Hindi.

The men looked toward the warders as if to ask if they were permitted to speak. The warders seemed confused, and

I could sense their nervousness. I had obviously put them in a bewildering and perhaps unprecedented situation. In the past, an inspection by the Inspector General meant a head-count of all the inmates by loud roll calls, and locking the inmates back in their barracks well before the Inspector General's expected arrival to ensure that the visit went without a hitch. The warders would stand outside the locked barracks to show their own presence. A prisoner had bitten off a former Inspector General's finger during a round many years ago. And here I was asking them, "Do you pray?"

I moved closer to the bunch and directed the question to one randomly chosen inmate.

He answered, "Yes, sometimes," nodding his head.

"Very good. Who else does? You?" I pointed at another prisoner, again at random, getting even closer to the crouching men.

And then one after another, voices joined in saying, "Yes, I also do. I recite the *Path* (the holy prayers). Most of us pray on our own. . . ."

With some relief I thought that perhaps the first human contact had been made.

I probed on: "Would it be better if we say a prayer together? Would you like that?" I realized that I was becoming a part of that "we."

They fell silent again, and I wondered if they had a collective voice. They had never prayed together.

Then one of them, with one eye on the staff and the other on me, said hesitantly, "Yes. . . ." Others nodded their heads in agreement, wanting to be part of the prayer.

I said, "All right, which prayer should we sing together? Can you suggest one?"

Silence. I volunteered one from a popular film I knew they would all know.

This time there was an enthusiastic and instant positive response. I said, "Get up to sing together." They began to rise to their feet, but the omnipresent staff with their sticks stopped them. Raising my voice, I asserted, "I told you to stand up to sing."

The staff got the message and withdrew their batons. I told the inmates, "Close your eyes and sing with me."

And we sang. When we opened our eyes, all my fingers were still intact. I felt that we had together succeeded in creating the first sign of mutual trust, and the foundation of our work together. The words of prayer reflected the message of closing our eyes: "I am willing to trust you, you may try trusting me, and we could work together for the benefit of all."

Next I moved to the women's ward. I knew that the women would be waiting for me. As I entered, all the women in the courtyard rushed toward me, uninhibited and happy, cheering my visit, a total contrast to the men. Was this a homecoming? The women promptly sat around me, wanting to hear what I had to say. They had taken it for granted that I would visit them. Looking at their faces, I felt they were my children and I had indeed come home for them. I sensed that each one needed a comforting hand on her shoulder. Yet, in spite of their grief and agony, all of them put on a cheerful appearance for my sake.

I asked them, "Do you read and write here?"

"No."

"Would you like to?"

"Yes."

"Very good. We will study here, and before you leave, you will be literate." They applauded in excitement.

My prayer with the men gave me the joy of seeing hope and acceptance; but with the women, something deep within pulled at me. I was "imprisoned." Tihar was my destiny.

The Realities of Tihar Jail

I scrutinized Tihar Jails over the next few weeks. The experience was agonizing. I grew angry and frustrated. I could see who was responsible for this horrendous state of affairs, but I could not hold them accountable or make them see the enormous folly of their ways. The overwhelming hypocrisy, which characterized their administration, was tellingly revealed in Tihar Jail. The system that I had inherited was totally derailed, and the sordid reality was conveniently hidden behind the huge iron gates.

The officials responsible for the institution were preoccupied with numerous other pressing matters, and they seldom visited Tihar. An honor guard with full ceremonial uniform and a lot of fanfare, including buglers, heralded the rare visit. Subservience was the order of the day. The system spurred itself into action merely to receive them and show them only what they wanted to see. The appalling muck and filth and the subhuman conditions inside the cells were convincingly camouflaged behind a facade of temporary neatness imposed on a few public areas for the benefit of the VIPs. The prison barracks, stuffed beyond capacity with human beings herded in like animals in a cage, were out of bounds. The officials were invariably accompanied by a media team, which faithfully reproduced the lofty statements they made on prison reforms and rehabilitation of prisoners. I had heard many such statements during my career as a police officer. But after coming face-to-face with the overpowering and nauseating reality of Tihar, I felt nothing but contempt for such blatant exaggerations and hypocrisy.

Tihar Jail complex was designed to house 2,273 inmates. By 1993 the jail held over 7,200 inmates. Tihar was literally bursting at the seams. Only about 10 percent of the prison population had been convicted and sentenced to prison. The remaining 90 percent were undertrials, or on remand waiting for trials in various courts. There were about 300 women and about 50 children under the age of four, and around 1,200 inmates between the ages of eighteen and twenty-one. The 125 foreigners of 38 nationalities were incarcerated mostly under the Narcotic Drugs and Psychotropic Substances (NDPS) Act 1986. The inmates were lodged alphabetically in the four prisons of the Tihar complex, except for foreigners and women who were lodged in Prison 1. Prison 2 lodged most of the convicted prisoners. Prison 3 housed all those who were arrested for offenses under the Terrorist Activities Disruption Act, TADA (now repealed). Besides other undertrials, Prison 4 housed mainly substance abusers.

None of the prisoners had an effective spokesperson through which they could convey their problems and/or expose the miserable conditions in Tihar. None of their appeals reached the decision makers. Occasional headlines in the media on the conditions in the jail were of little avail, causing only fleeting embarrassment to the officials for whom prison was meant to be solely a means of punishment.

The prisoners' catalogue of woes seemed interminable. The first item in this catalogue was food. There was no breakfast. Lunch was served at 11:00 a.m. Those appearing in court early in the morning invariably went to court without a meal. Lunch consisted of five *chapatis* (a flat wheat bread) with watery *dal* (lentils), or vegetables. The richer upper layer of dal, sometimes containing oil, was skimmed off and served to the prison elite. The same food was served at about 5:00 p.m. as dinner. The quality of the food defied description. Meals were doled out from round rusted iron containers 10 inches in diameter and 2 feet deep. These same containers were used for other activities, such as washing clothes, storing water, and bathing. They were even used for collecting and carrying dry garbage. This misuse of food containers was due to administrative apathy.

"Why are we using such rusted old containers for carrying food? Why don't you replace them with stainless steel ones?"

"Madam, stainless steel containers break easily. They have no resale value either."

"So what?" I asked.

"Madam, stainless steel containers are also very difficult to procure."

"But we can buy these from SAIL (Steel Authority of India Ltd.)."

"We will have to place an order."

"Then who stops us?"

"Madam, it will take a very long time."

"How long?"

"Three to four months."

"Then what?"

"No, Madam, one thing more, these iron containers are very sturdy and durable. We bought them fifteen or twenty years ago. Still they are serving the purpose."

I could no longer control myself, and burst out, "Would you serve food to your own family in such durable containers? If yes, go on. If no, then let's be ashamed of what we are doing." The officer had no answer. His silence said it all.

The food was carried in these containers from the kitchen to the inmates. Occasionally the containers were covered with dirty towels belonging to the inmates; by the time the food reached the individual prisoners, it was invariably cold. Many enterprising prisoners devised ingenious ways of heating their food. Some smuggled in electric heating coils. Some burned paper or plastic. Some prisoners even burned dried chapatis to heat up the fresh ones.

Making chapatis in Tihar Jail

The aromas of such impromptu cooking along with smoke fumes added to the choking smell in the prisons. As far as jail food was concerned, quality control was unheard of. The items on the menu were insipid and as unappetizing as they possibly could be. Most of the inmates had no choice but to eat whatever came their way. Sometimes the food was so completely inedible that the prisoners were compelled to throw it into the already backed-up sewer.

Neither the food, the cooks, nor the prisoners were clean. Some prisoners had no plates or utensils and had to share them with others. There were no basic requirements such as clean hands and clean nails for cooks. Nail cutters were not allowed inside the prison. The majority of prisoners had long, filthy nails, unkempt hair, and filthy-smelling clothing. The cooking utensils were plated with chrome, and an element of metallic bitterness seeped into the food as the chrome wore off. The vegetables and dals were not washed properly, due to the shortage of water. On many occasions, I personally detected insects and other assorted unidentified particles floating in the vegetable broth. Moreover, the quality of the cereals and other food items was inferior, as they were not procured from reputed outlets. Government-sponsored stores were not preferred for reasons unknown. Milk was diluted by half with water and wasn't boiled, as it should have been for sanitation purposes. The menu was monotonous, based on the cheapest and the most easily available supplies. No one planned the menu for the week ahead. Chapatis roasted over the gas stove were strewn all over the floor of the cookhouse. Whatever arrived in the prison store went to the kitchen for cooking. Soap and towels as well as water were always in short supply. Moreover, the cook-convicts were never subjected to any medical checkups. Many of them suffered from tuberculosis and other contagious respiratory ailments.

The cook-convicts were not motivated by kindness or compassion. They adopted double-menu standards; one for their own cookhouse and the other for the rest of the prisoners. They enjoyed large helpings of the best well-cooked food. Pilferage was rampant. Those in charge of the kitchen had years of experience in this art and made money for themselves by siphoning food, raw vegetables, and milk to prisoners and also to some staff members who had the means to pay for them or who were powerful enough to demand special favors.

Water was the most precious item inside the prison. Whatever the condition of food, it would at least arrive, but there was no such guarantee for water. In summers especially, getting adequate water was the greatest anxiety of all prisoners. The crucial question was would they get enough water to drink? Never mind bathing or washing clothes, let alone cleaning the barracks. There were no flush toilets in the jail, and large quantities of water were needed to drain the pot properly. There were hand pumps in some wards for this purpose. The water level had dropped so low that it was very difficult to get any water out of the pump. The water from these hand pumps was not fit to drink, and the pumps were labeled "Water is not potable," but many prisoners were illiterate and drank from these pumps.

During the lockdown time (6 p.m. to 6 a.m.) the prisoners had no choice but to use the toilets inside the barracks. An outsider cannot even imagine the mixture of foul odors that emanated from the barracks where the toilets had no running water. When the doors opened in the morning, the inmates surged out in droves, desperately needing to relieve themselves in the toilets outside the barracks. These external toilets were also clogged for lack of water, and because the system could not cope with almost four times as many people as it was constructed for.

The existing infrastructure for water supply was completely inadequate, but even the existing system was neglected. The situation was so bad that the water pipes had become a part of the underground foliage. The roots of many trees and plants were sucking water directly from the pipes and impeding the flow to the barracks and toilets. Then there was the problem of timing. Water was available on a limited basis, and the timings fixed for water supply by the municipality were meant for free society. The prison rulebook strictly stipulated lockup by sunset. Unfortunately, the municipal water began flowing to the prison after this hour, and the taps were outside the barracks. It was truly agonizing to see water running to waste from taps that were defective due to negligence and could not be closed. From behind bars, thirsty inmates desperately wished that they had long arms so that they could fill their earthen pitchers, or even polythene bags.

The quantity of water that was supplied during the morning hours was woefully inadequate to meet the needs of the overcrowded prison. The aging and corroded water pipes just could not carry the necessary quantity of water. Sometimes in the summer, there was no water at all for three or four days. There were also frequent fights near the tap for water. The queue of assorted buckets, pitchers, and even plastic bags waiting to be filled was a scene typical of a crowded slum dwelling with acute water supply problems.

As a relief measure, the prison barrack compounds were dotted with a few hand pumps, but these pumps could not function to full capacity due to dropping water levels. The prison also had tube wells, but, again, they functioned erratically with little or no maintenance. There were no maintenance kits or provisions for making repairs in the prison. Every time something went out of order, which was

Rationing water in the courtyard of Tihar Jail

frequently due to misuse and overuse, the Public Works Department (PWD) had to come to the rescue. The PWD took its own time to rectify the defects. When things went from bad to worse, mobile water tankers were pressed into service at an exorbitant cost through the city municipal corporation. Many of these tankers had leaking taps and no covers.

Due to the serious water shortage and overcrowding, the sewers were invariably clogged. Consequently, the barracks were engulfed by stench. Also, gutters and manholes remained uncovered, providing a fertile breeding ground for mosquitoes. The huge accumulation of uncleared garbage at various places around the prison compounded the already intolerable situation. Neither the cookhouses nor barracks had screen doors or windows, or insect repellents. As a result, flies swarmed on the food, adding to health problems. During the monsoon, the contents of the clogged sewers would flow back into the barracks, and the stench and filth became intolerable. Epidemics of cholera and dysentery became serious possibilities.

Prisoners did make sporadic efforts to get rid of the garbage, which they had to carry in gunny bags because wheelbarrows were scarce. Astonishingly, there was not a single departmental sweeper for the compounds. Consequently, the inmates themselves cleaned the compounds, barracks, and toilets. Such a state of affairs bred corruption and acrimony. Some inmates were forced into these jobs as a punishment, and others because they could not afford to pay off the staff. At times, money was collected from the prisoners to pay an inmate to clean, and inevitably a middleman, called a *munshi* or a mate, pocketed part of the collection.

The summer months were extremely agonizing—an endurance test for the inmates. Conditions inside the barracks could only be described as inhuman. The massive ovens and the gas burners augmented the solar fury of the scorching summer months. Ventilation in the barracks was poor. The exhaust fans themselves were exhausted and hardly functioned. The vintage ceiling fans were ineffective. Everything was hot—the walls, the ceiling, the floors, and the temperament of the staff.

In the summer, in addition to the acute shortage of water, there were frequent power outages. Tihar Jail is located in the western part of Delhi, which suffers the most frequent blackouts. In the overcrowded barracks, fans stopped whirring and the circulation of air came to a standstill. The heat became suffocating. The prison had a generator, but it barely met the requirements and frequently broke down. Also, the diesel required to run the generator would not be available, and, if it were, there would be no one to pour it into the generator. Such was the power situation.

The Prison Administration was in a peculiar predicament. All work relating to planning, construction, purchase of materials or equipment, and their procurement and repair had to be done by the Public Works Department, more aptly known as the Public Woes Department. The PWD enjoyed a monopoly and was prone to all the flaws a monopoly enabled. The prevailing water, power, sanitation, and hygiene conditions were proof of their weak to non-existent service. The PWD did not even have a blueprint of the underground water pipes, or the electric conduits and connections. Only the Almighty knew how the machinery functioned at all in Tihar. Examples of the remarkable apathy of PWD officials were many. Scores of fans, which had gone out of order, waited for repairs for weeks. None of them was repaired; in fact, the practice was to procure new fans. What exactly happened to the old fans remained a mystery.

Meanwhile, electrical wires dangled all around the prison. It appeared quite incredible that no one was electrocuted. These wires were meant to provide electricity for TV

Watching TV in a barrack in Tihar Jail

sets, which were permitted inside the barracks, but since plug points were considered a security risk, the TV sets were connected directly to the bulb holders or hanging wires. These conveniently available wires also provided electricity for unauthorized coil heaters, which frequently overloaded the system and tripped the breakers. Such unauthorized heaters were either smuggled in or provided by the staff members who demanded money for this privilege. Thus the prison headquarters forked out huge penalties for excessive consumption of electricity. In fact, a large portion from the prison budget went toward meeting these expenses.

All the foregoing problems stared us in the face. The prison bureaucracy had earned a justifiable reputation for procrastination. "Never put off until tomorrow what you can put off indefinitely" appeared to be their motto. The PWD officials clung to their monopoly status. A couple of incidents will highlight their attitude. In the first case, jail officials suggested that the inmates could whitewash the barracks. I vividly remember the afternoon when I called the senior PWD officials for a meeting to plan whitewashing the prison barracks. I spoke about the unutilized labor of the prisoners, which could be put to use for this job. The opposition came from the lower ranks. I was astonished to hear what they had to say.

I asked, "What's the problem in having the prisoners whitewash their own barracks?"

PWD Junior Engineer: "It's not possible, Madam."

"Why?"

"Because they are not trained in the trade."

"No, we have trained manpower inside," said my colleague Jaydev Sarangi. Silence. PWD staff looked at one another.

Another PWD official spoke, "But we will have difficulty in measuring the area they have whitewashed."

"Don't you have a measuring tape with you?" asked Sarangi.

"No, no, but the problem is how we would show it."

"To whom are you supposed to show it?" asked another Jail Superintendent, D. P. Diwedi.

"In the register."

"Then it's very simple. You can write the measurements the way you always do. What's the problem if the prisoners do it?" I insisted.

"There may be some wastage."

"So?"

"How shall we show that?"

"Show it in the manner you show for your own workforce," I said.

"No, Madam, it will put the pressure on us."

"What type of pressure?"

"First, we will have to buy the material, then hand it over to the prison staff, take the measurement, and make the recording."

"This you do even when your own labor does the job," argued Sarangi.

"But that is a separate thing."

Then I understood the meaning of "a separate thing." The PWD refused to commit to doing the job, and refused to allow the prisoners to do the job.

In a second example, several community organizations were willing to offer a number of saplings to encourage hundreds of interested inmates to plant trees inside the prison. The horticulture department of the PWD would not allow any such free planting. Their one and only agenda was to buy and plant saplings at an exorbitant cost.

So the argument went:

Horticulture official: "Madam, these donated plants will not grow."

"How can you say that?" asked my colleague, D. P. Diwedi.

"It's my experience."

"Experience?"

"Yes, because their roots are naked."

We were getting a naked explanation of the root cause of our problems. It is rightly said that when supervisors do not solve problems, they become a part of the problem themselves. In Tihar, it seemed, everything and everyone was becoming part of the problem.

Medical Disservice

Tihar Jail was notorious for corruption, inefficiency, indifference and incompetence. The medical staff made considerable contributions to this reputation. The shocking health situation of the inmates made me feel helpless, perhaps for the first time in my career. I had gained sufficient experience to effectively deal with hardened criminals and other varieties of lawbreakers. I could also effectively handle recalcitrant or obdurate staff members. But, how was I to cope with the enormous suffering of a whole township of men, women, and children under my charge in Tihar?

The magnitude of Tihar's health problems was staggering. The majority of the prisoners came from underprivileged backgrounds, and they brought with them a plethora of medical problems. Apart from common ailments resulting from obvious causes such as malnutrition, unhealthy lifestyle, and cramped living conditions, avoidable maladies caused by alcoholism, heavy smoking, and drug abuse flourished.

The geriatric prisoners fell into a category all their own. Their problems related mainly to failing eyesight and decaying teeth. The small percentage of the prison population from the middle- or upper-income levels suffered from diabetes, hypertension, and heart problems. On top of that were the ubiquitous fevers, coughs, colds, and seasonal viruses responsible for malaria, cholera, or gastroenteritis.

The situation was complicated by the constant changes in the population. Each day, on an average, 200 to 250 prisoners left the prison, and by evening, an equal number had been admitted with a fresh set of health problems. The rule was that all new arrivals were to be inspected by the prison doctor on the day they were admitted. The doctor was required to record the state of health of each new inmate and note any serious ailments or injuries, as well as general health information. Since there was only one doctor for all four jails, and he or she also performed routine calls, emergency duties, and prison hospital duties, new inmates could wait for days before the doctor had time to do their entrance evaluation. In the meantime they huddled together in the inspection ward waiting to be sent to their lodging wards.

There was no segregation for inmates. Healthy prisoners were housed with those suffering from infectious skin diseases, leprosy, tuberculosis, and AIDS. We brought in one tuberculosis specialist who, after a preliminary survey, stated that 70 to 80 percent of the prison population either had tuberculosis or were at risk of contracting it. There was no provision for disinfected spittoons to be placed inside the barracks and cells to prevent the spread of infection. Prisoners spat anywhere and everywhere inside the barracks during the lockup time.

Similarly, at least a quarter of the inmates who entered the prison daily were addicted to drugs or intoxicants. Upon arrival at prison, they suffered from withdrawal symptoms. They could neither sleep nor allow fellow inmates to sleep. They would reel in pain and yell for the doctor. The single doctor on duty could not possibly cope with the hundreds of calls he received each night from all four jails. So, no matter what the complaint, he sent Parmol, an over-the-counter aspirinlike drug. It was, I later discovered, Tihar's panacea for all ills—from a fever to an upset stomach to any other unidentified ailment.

The effectiveness of Parmol for all and sundry could be questioned, but at least it was innocuous. At the other extreme were doctors who prescribed Sorbitrate, a heart medicine, for a minor disorder like a headache. Yet another doctor prescribed tuberculosis drugs at random to anyone who consulted him. He was an eccentric old man who had spent a number of years working in the jail. When we questioned his method, he refused to accept that anything was amiss. The situation came to a head when the inmates discovered what they were being given, and we removed him from his position.

For drug abuse and addiction management, I found that the doctors were only transferring the addiction from illicit drugs to synthetic pills. When I took charge, literally half the prison population was addicted to tranquilizers. The doctor-staff network in collusion with the inmates ran a thriving market of its own. Inmates who ran out of stock would yell for more, and the lone doctor would send more of the addictive drug. The evening or night doctor was much more concerned about getting through his shift than with the consequences of his actions. There was no organized drug-abuse treatment program inside the prisons. There was one non-government center in Prison 4 capable of handling not more than twenty patients at a time. Not fewer than a thousand needed help.

Tihar Jail was starved for doctors. There were only twelve doctors in May 1993, which worked out to one doctor for each of the four prisons in each of the three shifts.

The doctor who was on night duty would get a full day off the following day even if he prescribed only tranquilizers during his duty. One doctor was allotted for hospital day duty, and there was the Resident Medical Officer, who was the overall supervisor. There was one female doctor for all the women prisoners. Any doctor on leave meant that there was no doctor for the day for that particular prison. This meant there would be only emergency calls. This situation led to arrears for the next day, both in the inspection ward as well as the general prisoners' ward. No single doctor could possibly attend to such a huge population. Medical services in the jail remained in arrears all the time. Dr. Bishambar Das, the then Resident Medical Officer at Tihar was quoted in the *Delhi Mid-Day* on June 22, 1993:

> Tihar Jail is reeling under an acute shortage of medical staff. In blatant disregard of last year's enquiry report on Tihar, which recommended setting up of proper medical facilities within the jail compound, the jail authorities are functioning with just 11 doctors to look after 8,300 prisoners. In other words, there was only one doctor for 750 prisoners. This situation has persisted for almost seven to eight years now, say serving medical officials.
>
> "We have been repeatedly appealing to the administration authorities to give us more medical staff," says Dr. Bishambar Das, Resident Medical Officer, Tihar.

Many of the jail doctors had a habit of arriving to work late and leaving early. As a result, they saw some 250 patients in a two- or three-hour period. Essentially, doctors were inaccessible. Even if one somehow succeeded in gaining access to them, they were rude and indifferent. They refused to wear uniforms and would not prepare a report unless directed by the court. Whenever a night-shift doctor did not turn up, the prison went without one. If something serious happened, the same officials who were responsible for not providing more doctors to the prison in the first place would order a judicial enquiry. No wonder incidences of diseases such as TB, leprosy, scabies, and asthma only went from bad to worse.

The doctors themselves were a harassed lot. Gangsters inside the prison sometimes threatened them with bodily injury or death for not complying with their demands. The gangsters dictated the information they wanted in their medical sheets to secure legal favor from the courts. On the other hand, the doctors demanded payment for performing such favors. Decisions on bail orders or court detention were based on the content of medical reports. The only real interest of many doctors was the capacity of the prisoner to pay for a "doctored" medical report. They were more interested in the crime case details than the medical history of their patients. They were known for sending healthy prisoners to outside hospitals for treatment while keeping chronically ill prisoners in the Central Jail Hospital. The inmates knew this game. The dishonest doctors had an educated convict to act as a conduit for the flourishing business. This convict struck minor deals. No one would dare say anything against him. His job was to identify the healthy paymasters seeking bail on grounds of ill health, get them introduced to the right doctor, and pocket the percentage earned in the bargain. The price would depend upon the financial status and family background of the prisoner, including whether he paid income tax, how much property he had or would inherit, and how many cars he possessed. The gravity of the crime committed was also factored into the price. Sometimes, factors like age, lifestyle, children, and wife's affection also influenced the price.

A few petitions from prisoners will illustrate this aspect of prison life:

> I am ill. I have continuous pain in the stomach. I suffer blackouts. I am spitting blood. Doctors say I need to go to an outside hospital, but now, over three months have passed, I have not been sent.
> *Kalve, prisoner, Jail 1: June 7, 1993*

> I am imprisoned since April 1988. I am a TB patient. I am not getting regular medicines. Milk diet to me in the prison was sanctioned three months ago, but I am not getting it. I went to the court seeking the magistrate's intervention. The court directed me to ask my prison doctor to confirm that I have TB. The doctors here want money to write the certificate. If they get money, they are willing to write anything.
> *Akram Ali, prisoner, Jail 4: June 14, 1993*

> My four molars have decayed. I want them to be extracted and replaced. I could not eat anything for one whole year. I was sent to the hospital only once. There the doctor said that there was no X-ray film, that I should buy it and bring it. I told him that I was a poor man and in judicial custody. How could I bring it? I went back to the jail hospital and asked the doctor to provide me with the necessities. The doctor said that there was no provision. "So you stay as you are."
> *Prem Prakash, prisoner, Jail 1: June 14, 1993*

> I am suffering from severe backbone pain due to which I get fever. I can't eat or sleep. I am fed up

with myself. I am poor. It is money which gets referrals. It is always available for the rich but never for
the poor.
Jamaluddin, prisoner, Jail 3: June 16, 1993

It was evident that those who could afford lawyers filed
petitions in courts to direct the prison authorities to refer
them to medical services outside. It was also evident that
nothing happened without the sound backup of muscle
power or money, as far as medical services were concerned.

I was stunned and astounded to discover neither the
medical office nor the four dispensaries in the four jails
kept any records of a prisoner's attendance, his or her ailments, or prescriptions or medicines issued. There was no
internal audit system and no accountability whatsoever.
The entire medical system was sick to the bones.

An institution as large as Tihar obviously required hospitals. There was in fact one hospital in Prison No. 3, which
had to cater to all four jails. Prisoners from all four prisons
came to Central Jail No. 3 for treatment. But a majority of
them manipulated visits to communicate extortionist messages to their colleagues. Genuine patient-prisoners of
other jails rarely found their names in the referral list to
Central Jail Hospital. This hospital itself was not in good
health. There were around thirty beds in the hospital and
some medical equipment, but the resemblance to a hospital
ended there. Many prisoners were seen rolling on the floor,
as there were insufficient beds. Beds for the genuinely ailing patient-prisoners were a luxury to be had for a price.
The prisoners on the beds looked healthier than those
rolling on the floor. Toilets of the hospital wards were frequently blocked due to scarcity of water. The frequent fluc-
tuation of electricity voltage made the function of the
X-ray machines difficult. Instead of installing a stabilizer,

the doctors just didn't use the equipment, and the X-ray machine remained out of order, and the staff radiographer remained idle.

A laboratory assistant and the infrastructure for carrying out routine tests could help little in the absence of reagents. An EKG machine and a dental chair were left idle, and sophisticated eye-testing equipment gathered dust in the prison store. It was not the forlorn equipment, however, that gave me a feeling of unreality when I visited the hospital, but the complete absence of figures wearing white coats moving between the beds or sitting in any of the four dispensaries. The hospital had no nurses, I was informed, owing to vacancies that had lapsed because they had not been filled over the years. The convicts themselves doubled up as nurses in the hospital, and represented powerful vested interests. The hospital had no separate kitchen to offer a special medical diet. It had a blanket washer sanctioned by the PWD, but true to form, for years it had remained uninstalled. There was no provision for running water and no facility for prisoners to cart water for themselves. One can only imagine the state of hygiene and sanitation. Nevertheless, the gangsters managed to use the hospital as a place for leading an easy life with a special diet. By compelling doctors to exaggerate their ailments, they avoided court appearance and maintained special privileges.

The prison was bereft of any kind of specialists. A doctor from a government-run mental hospital visited the prison twice a week. But his trips were intended to provide legal protection to the authorities rather than to pay attention to the number of mentally ill patients who were left without help. Critical medicines were in short supply and poor in quality. Only those prisoners who could afford to dole out adequate amounts of money managed to get medicines.

The position of the Resident Medical Officer (RMO)

was a joke, since he was non-residential and totally distant. He was supposed to reside within the Tihar Prison complex but lived 10 kilometers away and refused to provide his residential telephone number to the jail staff, lest he be disturbed at night or after-duty hours. He exercised little control over the prison medical officers. According to the prisoners, he added to their woes by recommending the purchase of non-effective medicines for reasons best known to himself. He was always seen looking for opportunities to purchase medicines in bulk irrespective of their utility, even when he knew there was a dearth of funds to purchase needed life-saving drugs. He had to push his way through a bureaucratic maze of files to procure emergency drugs. The illness of the inmates, of course, did not wait for the files to move, and their condition often deteriorated, and some died.

Within the prison walls, there were 46 children up to the age of five staying with their mothers who were prison inmates. Some had been born in jail. There was no child specialist, no immunization program for the children, and no night female doctor to attend to them. At night, prisoners looked after themselves. In case of an emergency, the patient was sent to a hospital outside the prison. Even with so many children, there was no nursery school to isolate them even for a short time during the day.

A female doctor was on call until 2 p.m. She was reportedly insensitive and mercenary. Women's special gynecological needs were ignored unless an emergency situation arose. Any disease more serious than fever or influenza had to be referred to government hospitals outside the prison. Such treatment entailed added cost for the inmates, and even then, without muscle or money power, they were likely to be ignored or mistreated. The outside government hospitals were also overcrowded and hence, even there, proper treatment could not be guaranteed. Sometimes prisoners merely wanted to get out of the claustrophobic confines of the jail. If they could manage to get admitted to an outside hospital, they might be able to have their family stay with them and bring them food. If they could bribe the police guards, they could even arrange for more privileges.

A vehicle faintly resembling an ambulance was used to transport patients to outside hospitals. Like the RMO, the ambulance was also a misnomer. It was nothing but a rickety skeleton without seats that served a variety of purposes, such as transporting milk and vegetables from one jail to another. The jail staff also used it as their family car. The driver of the ambulance considered the vehicle his personal property and parked it at his residence during the night. Despite numerous complaints, it was not replaced because the administrators who could sanction a new vehicle felt it was not really necessary.

At the root of Tihar's health problems was an inadequate and inefficient infrastructure. The doctors were not completely under the administrative control of the prison authorities. The Delhi Health Services (DHS) decided personnel posting and transfers, whereas the prison department paid their salaries. The Inspector General of the prison wrote the annual confidential report only for the Residential Medical Officer, who, in turn, wrote the reports of the other doctors. The reports were then rewritten by the DHS. Such dual control resulted in a total absence of accountability. There was no coordination among the doctors themselves, and no interaction with the prison staff. The senior- and middle-ranking medical officers of the prison rarely ventured into the prison to identify the prisoners who needed medical care. This way, problems such as a death in custody could be blamed on lower-level doctors or the junior prison staff. The junior doctors could usually offer acceptable explanations, and the junior prison staff would be suspended. The senior medical and prison staff denied responsibility by claiming preoccupation with other important responsibilities.

In practice, the prison administration had effectively left the medical management of the jail to the convicts and high-security prisoners. Again the gangsters, as in other aspects of prison life, ruled the roost. They would go every morning from one ward to the next, listing the prisoners who did not want to attend court. These names were collected along with the requisite price, and the thugs would then ensure that the doctors issued the necessary medical certificates. The staff also facilitated this practice, besides making their own recommendations.

This incredible tale of the hospital and its doctors would be incomplete without a description of the less visible and smartly hidden Twenty Cells, located in Prison No. 3. Twenty Cells was the most gruesome part of Central Jail Hospital. The area was accessible only through a secret gate inside the jail hospital building. The gate and the cells looked deserted, as if no prisoners were lodged there. The lower ranks of the prison authorities kept the Twenty Cells area inaccessible to any visitor—official or non-official—including the Superintendent of the Jail. Prior to my posting to the Tihar Jail, jail superintendents rarely visited the jail. Either they were totally absent or visited once or twice a year.

A newly appointed, conscientious Superintendent, Tarsem Kumar, conveyed this about his experience with the Twenty Cells:

I joined as Superintendent Jail No. 3 on April 6, 1993. On April 7, 1993, I decided to have a round of the jail. My Assistant Superintendent advised me not to go inside the jail without full security. I insisted on going inside, as I was curious to know how the prisoners live and what the jail looks like. My predecessor did not brief me about the jail even after repeated requests. He only introduced me to an Assistant Superintendent, saying he was loyal, though he eventually proved to be exactly the opposite.

I went on the round with this Assistant Superintendent. After visiting the Central Jail Hospital, I headed unknowingly toward the Twenty Cells. Watching me advance in that direction, he questioned me:

"Where are you going, sir?"

I stopped at once, as his tone implied that I was heading toward some danger.

I asked anxiously: "What is there ahead?"

"Sir, it's better you don't go to that side."

"Why?"

"There are Twenty Cells ahead."

"Twenty cells?"

"Yes, sir."

"What's that?"

"Sir, they are the cells where violent, mentally deranged prisoners are lodged."

"Oh! But what is the harm in having a look at them too?"

"No, sir, you should not go there."

"Why?"

"Sir, they can harm you."

I was a little frightened but very curious.

I told the Assistant Superintendent firmly, "I want to take a look at these cells; please get the gates opened." A security guard came running with a heavy bunch of keys and opened the door. We went inside and looked around.

I saw prisoners suffering from mental disorders in solitary confinement. They were not released from the cells during daytime like the rest of the inmates. Some of the so-called mental prisoners wore nothing except dirty underwear.

"They do not have clothes?" I asked.

"Yes, but we don't give them the clothes," replied the Assistant Superintendent.

"Why?"

"So that they cannot commit suicide."

These so-called madmen were not only deprived of essential clothing but also of other necessities, such as slippers, towels, and toiletries. Their eating bowls were worn out. In one of these cells, a broken bowl had some liquid in it. I thought it was dirty water. A convict told me that it was dal. The chapatis were thrown to them from outside. The sane convicts on duty derived sadistic pleasure from mocking and tormenting them.

It was obvious to me that if a normal person was kept in one of these twenty cells even for a week, he would definitely go insane, to say nothing of a prisoner who had already lost his mental equilibrium. I was too disturbed to continue my rounds and went back to my office.

For the rest of the day, this encounter weighed on my mind. By the time I returned home, I was thoroughly upset. The sight of such utter human misery was deeply disturbing. I kept thinking how could human beings be put in such extreme misery? How could human beings live like this? No hell could be worse than this.

Life-Term Jailors

As the days rolled by, I was gradually getting to know the prisoners, but not the jailors, who somehow maintained a distance. To look at them, there was not much difference between the jailors and the prisoners. Many of the jailors were unshaven, unkempt, and shoddily clad. Most did not wear uniforms. There was no system for uniform and kit inspection. There was no pressure on the staff to be appropriately dressed. In fact, some staff members had been in service for several years but had yet to be issued an official uniform. I was amazed to discover the ill-maintained, erratic, and whimsical system of procuring uniforms. The procedure was so convoluted that only a few benefited. In winter, they performed their duties wrapped up in different kinds of blankets and mufflers as if they were trying to hide. The overcoats, which had been issued to them to wear on the job, were mostly reserved for off-duty social occasions. During the monsoon, the staff members turned up for duty without raincoats, ensuring excuses for taking shelter and relaxing rather than staying on duty.

The Tihar Jail administration consisted of warders, head warders, assistant superintendents, and deputy superintendents. Each of the four superintendents was head of the respective prisons, accountable to the Deputy Inspector General (DIG) who, in turn, was accountable to the Inspector General. The head warders and warders constituted the real backbone of the security system of the prison. The majority of them were barely literate. Warders, head warders, and even assistant superintendents were hired without even a simple written test of ability or aptitude. Many of them were unable even to count properly. Consequently, they were unable to do their primary duties, like taking attendance of the inmates and doing the final headcount (called *ginti* in

A staff member gazing through the gates of Tihar Jail

prison jargon). They were dependent on the help of literate prisoners called *munshis*. A few of the warders were literate and had finished the tenth grade. Such individuals were drawing lower salaries compared with their matriculate colleagues in equivalent departments.

The salaries of the staff members were grossly low in view of the rising cost of living. Some staff members had large families, and their standard of living could not be much better than that of the prisoners. Desperate for money, they often sublet their government accommodation, or diverted electricity from the overhead poles, or converted their compounds into cattle sheds. Water was scarce even for domestic use, and it was stored in crude containers in highly unhygienic conditions. The staff had developed a subculture of their own that bred delinquency and criminal tendencies. The staff-housing complex had no security checks and was frequented by released gangsters or relatives of persons inside the jail, all with ulterior motives. Many staff family members were involved in petty crimes. The local police station had rated the area as crime prone.

Tihar was seriously short of manpower. At the time I took charge, the available personnel were meant for about 2,273 prisoners—one-fourth of the number of actual prisoners. Therefore, the presence of every warder mattered, even if his mind was absent. The staff members worked in one long single shift, literally staying on call for twenty-four hours. The warders, head warders, and all others were on duty nonstop for twelve hours every day. The only way they could take leave was by producing a medical certificate that supervisors could not ignore. And they did that frequently. Absenteeism was high; so were alcoholism, drug abuse, spousal abuse, and domestic violence. All the deputy superintendents lived in the same complex. Family rivalries based on professional jealousy were not uncommon in the quarters.

Almost all the staff had marred service records for both minor and major infractions of the rules of law. Except for a few, most of the deputy superintendents were of doubtful integrity. Some staff members had been suspended and then reinstated by court orders or by the favors of prominent persons. They had no respect for anybody, and often acted with vengeance to inflict as much harm as possible. The majority of the deputy superintendents were facing suspension on corruption charges. For example, one deputy superintendent who was involved in a jail factory scam was fired for insubordination. The courts ordered him reinstated. His arrogant and violent behavior was a daily drama in the neighborhood. Another deputy superintendent was alleged to have been instrumental in a prisoner's escape from the jail. He faced suspension for four years but was taken back on duty.

The prison had no program for professional training for its staff. There was no visible motivation to work. Rewards of any kind were unheard of for the lower-level staff; the officers grabbed the goodies. There was almost no possibility of promotion, and nothing to look forward to. They were expected to stay at work in the same prison throughout their career. The system had crumbled to such an extent that the staff had to shell out money to get their names on seniority lists, obtain a raise, or get a loan. There were no meetings. There were no redressal forums. There were no facilities for recreation, library, or sports at either the workplace or the residential complex. Tihar Jail was an institution where prisoners could come and go, but the staff stayed on for thirty years or more. The only transfer available was from one prison to another within the jail complex. During the long hours of the day, they invariably saw only two sets of faces: those of the inmates and those of the cattle at home.

The staff members led a largely insecure life. Officially, they had no protection from the threats to their lives from the kingpins inside the prison. To ward off the danger, most of them befriended the criminal element. No wonder their residential complex was streaming with unsavory visitors.

Within the prison, the staff members resorted to violence, which begot more violence. They threatened the inmates and were threatened in turn. On the whole, their working conditions were tense, acrimonious, and unnerving.

The Inescapable Grip of Corruption

I have visited high-security prisons in the United States; prisons for young offenders in the United Kingdom, Japan, and the Philippines; women's prisons in the United Kingdom and Denmark; juvenile homes in Japan; and many other prisons all over the world. Nowhere have I seen prison management so heavily dependent on prisoners as it is in India. In almost all other countries, convicted prisoners work inside the prison. Some do cleaning and cooking. But under no circumstances are prisoners assigned to security and control duties. For internal correctional programs, staff was either hired on contract or on a full-time basis. The quality of these programs depended not only on the philosophy of the prison management but also on the resources available.

But India is unique. The prison system runs on the basis of the antiquated Prison Act of 1894. This archaic Prison Act, dating back to the colonial era, permits the deployment of life-term convicts for night-watch duties. With a population of over 9,700 inmates and barely 40 warders for internal security and management, using convicts for night guards was common practice. Their cells were not locked at night, and they could move about freely. They were expected to stand guard, make rounds, and inform the prison sentries of any problems. Gradually, these privileged convicts became a class apart who bullied other inmates, demanded sexual favors, and further corrupted an already corrupt system.

There was corruption in every sphere of the prison. From the moment the prisoner entered the jail to the moment he left, he had to pay for every need. The long-term prisoners knew the needs and the problems of the new prisoners and offered solutions for a price. Sometimes they mercilessly beat up another inmate at the Central Administrative Office right inside the prison in front of their prospective target to convey the message "Pay up, or else." The security staff would usually back them up. If the matter was reported to the courts by an audacious newcomer, the authorities portrayed the incident as nothing more than a minor scuffle between prisoners over the sharing of water or food.

The system for using inmates for cooking and cleaning in the prison was also a sordid state of affairs, a monumental logistics problem, and one of the major causes of ongoing corruption. Toilets needed to be cleaned frequently due to sustained overcrowding, and finding inmates for this dirty job was difficult. Inevitably the poor and the weak swept the toilets while the rich and strong watched with satisfaction. The warder-supervisor persuaded the inmates to do their job with the threat of violence. The inmate sweepers were rewarded with soap cakes and mustard oil while the officials and henchmen shared the money, which was collected for their services. This practice was unique to India. I did not come across anything even remotely similar anywhere in other countries.

The pattern of corruption devised by the staff was comprehensive and encompassed a wide variety of activities. The corrupt schemes were full of ideas and ingenuity. Being ill trained or illiterate did not seem to be a drawback. In fact, the lure of dirty money was the biggest motivation to report for duty. Officialdom was fully aware of these external incentives, but the top brass showed no interest in increasing staff allowances or putting a stop to the corruption. The dishonest prospered, and the few honest ones suffered. Some were forced to convert their houses into cattle sheds, and even to sublet their small houses to make ends meet. Deftly hidden behind the huge gates of Tihar, a corrupt world was flourishing.

To understand the complexities of the prevalent corruption, we begin at the moment a prisoner enters the jail. An inmate was not automatically housed. The officials exercised a great deal of discretion as to where and with whom a newcomer would be lodged, and his fate depended more on his social, economic, and political status than his professional and educational qualifications.

In Tihar Jail in particular and in Indian jails in general, there had been no objective system of lodging prisoners. The prison manual had only one rule on housing, and it pertained to classifying prisoners as class B or class C. Dormitory lodging is class C, and small-cell lodging is class B. Legally, there was no further distinction. Class B prisoners were entitled to more milk and better food. (This class distinction was struck down by the Delhi High Court in 1998, following a public interest litigation.) However, the corrosive cancer of distinction crept in on the basis of status, money, and coercion. If the inmate was without money or political or criminal backing, he was sent to the dormitory full of individuals from diverse backgrounds and was assigned to menial jobs such as cleaning the public toilets. Once inside the prison, the particular ward, barrack, or cell in which a newcomer was to be lodged was the prerogative

of the warder and his personal assistant, the convict unoffi-
cially assigned to him. A bribe could alter the placement at
any stage of lodging.

Within a barrack or dormitory, the prisoner was allotted space to keep his belongings and to sleep. There were
no beds. The majority of the dormitories were like big plat-
forms. A few of the older dorms had raised black cement
beds, called *phattas*, 6 feet by 3 feet, and 2 feet off the floor,
which were available for a price or a favor. Usually, a new
inmate was assigned the sunken space between two phattas. The most dreaded sleeping place was the one located
immediately outside the barrack toilet during lockin time.
The barrack munshi wielded enormous clout and decided
the allocations.

The sudden unannounced relocation of individuals was
a threat that loomed large over the inmates. Although security rules recommended occasional shifting of the dormitory
inmates, it led to intense insecurity and acrimony. When the
order came to relocate, there was a mad rush to grab the
most desirable locations, and in the process essential items of
personal property were lost or stolen. The old and the sick
always lagged behind. Sometimes individuals were hand-
picked to be relocated. Here again money changed hands for
the transfer of barracks and wards. Relocation was a punishment as well as an incentive based mostly on monetary con-
siderations under the guise of security.

Another area of rampant corruption was visitation
privileges (*mulaqaats*). Relatives and friends were allowed
to visit twice a week. This was an important occasion for
those who had visitors. Every visit usually brought not only
news, but also cooked food, clothing, medicines, snacks,
fruits, and even pocket money for buying essentials from
the prison canteen. The money received during the visits
was converted immediately into coupons to check the sup-

ply of cash inside the prison. Money could also be directly deposited into the prisoners' property account. Such arrangements work only when the system has an inherent integrity. Unfortunately, this was not the case in Tihar.

A visitor who wanted to visit an inmate first logged in at the entry gate. Only two visitors were allowed per inmate. Invariably more than three showed up. Many of them did not have an official identity card, without which entry could be refused. But for a price, the gatekeeper allowed entry. Having crossed the first hurdle, the visitor was faced with giving the jail official a percentage cut to convert cash into coupons, and often watched the jailors filch the food and other items meant for inmates. The chain of thefts did not stop here. There were frequent complaints that money deposited in the bank never reached its destination. Visitors inserted food and other items into a chute for the inmate to collect from the other side, as physical contact was prohibited. Due to the large crowd in the visitors' gallery and the presence of so many inmates on the other side, there was a two-yard gap between the iron grill mesh separating the inmates from the visitors. The chute was the only way to deliver things.

These visits and the food and essential items brought by friends and family were enormously important to the inmates, and the denial of this legitimate visit created much agony. At times inmates were not notified when they had visitors because they had failed to gratify the munshi or the warder. However, unauthorized or unannounced visits were available for money or other favors.

As the staff took advantage of visitations to make money, the thugs inside the prison used violence to ensure extra and longer visitations. The staff was afraid to enforce the rules, as the gangsters threatened them and their families with assault or kidnapping. The bullies in these gangs flocked together and also ate together. They rarely consumed prison food, as they managed to arrange the sequence of their visitations to keep a continuous supply of home-cooked food. Some members of the staff had the gangsters return favors at their individual residences for this luxury.

Survival centered on food. Although large quantities of it came from homes, it required heating, and the prison barracks had no heating arrangements. The prison food was carried from the kitchen to the barracks where inmates lined up to receive their portion. But it was lukewarm or frequently cold. Therefore, heaters were prized possessions, even more so since they were banned. Interestingly, the staff brought in heaters, confiscated them per the rules, and then resold them to the inmates. Then they allowed selective use of heaters, again at a price. For many, heating food was a must. They resorted to any possible means, such as burning rolled-up newspapers or plastic or even dry chapatis. The staff looked the other way while smoke spewed out of the barracks and cells.

Since the prison food was so bad, it was also necessary to purchase bread, biscuits, fruit, and salad ingredients, such as onions, carrots, radishes, tomatoes, and lemons. The prison's mobile canteen sold these items at exorbitant prices, and had an irregular supply. There was no price list; the whim of the convicts in charge determined the price. Sometimes they created an artificial scarcity to drive up the price. The authorities had no control over canteen activities. Even the warder had to pay a "service price" to use the canteen for a period of time. The powerful prisoners purchased most of the canteen merchandise and then sold it themselves at a still higher price by means of an internal dormitory canteen. Again, the staff took a cut for allowing these unauthorized canteens to function.

Every inmate coming into the prison was entitled to a few essential personal items, such as a soap cake, a towel, a *neem datun* (a twig from the neem tree used like a toothbrush), a postcard, utensils for food, and blankets. But actually getting these items was like a lottery, and the price varied from person to person and from one staff member to another. It was the minority of the staff who did their duty sincerely; others merely granted misplaced favors.

On a daily basis, Tihar received a large number of drug addicts who were involved in one crime or another. Obviously, such an influx created a pressing demand for drugs inside the prison. The addicts were willing to hawk anything to indulge their habit. Both inmates and the staff stepped in to meet the demand, and charged heavily for this favor. They would offer either narcotics or drugs picked up from the dispensaries inside the jail. Some staff members were suspended for drug peddling, but many managed to stay in business. Thus, the drug trade not only survived but also flourished.

The inmates formed their own security caucuses to protect their networks of supply and demand. The warder closest to the inmates looked the other way. Under such circumstances, how could the doctors and medical staff buck the trend? They charged fees for providing bed rest in the hospital to inmates who wanted to avoid court appearances, or to create evidence of a medical ailment, or to prepare false medical certificates. They also schemed not to report the loss of medical papers, and sold hospital medicines meant for the prisoners and pocketed the cash. For years the prison staff pilfered prison property—lightbulbs, soap, wood, gas cylinders, carpets, blankets, phenyl, food rations, milk—the list was inexhaustible.

From what I gathered from the staff and the prisoners, the role of the upper management could at best be termed indifferent. It was like that of a distant examiner, neither a provider nor a participant, and certainly never an inspiration or reformer. During all public functions inside the prison, the senior officials would invariably appear to be photographed. But if there was an epidemic or a riot, they ordered enquiries, postmortems, suspensions, or dismissals from a distance.

The prison history, I was told, was replete with more sad memories than good ones. The gastroenteritis epidemic of 1988 was still fresh in the memory of the staff and the prisoners. It broke out from contaminated drinking water from a hand pump. After a number of deaths, a team of officials initiated action against the prison staff, without making a simultaneous provision for sufficient water for the inmates. The superintendents received threatening directions to ensure that no prisoner drank water from the hand pumps, and if they did, the responsibility would lie with the staff. Since there was a serious shortage of potable water, this order should have gone hand in hand with the sanction of at least one water tanker to fetch water from the outside municipal services. The prison was dependent on erratic and expensive water tankers supplied by outside contractors, arranged by the municipal corporation at an exorbitant rate. The severe shortage of water was a serious problem.

Another incident, which was still vivid in prison memory, was the riot of 1990. Nine inmates were killed after a four-hour battle between the prisoners and the security staff. Prisoners used LPG cylinders as bombs against the security guards. In return, the guards opened fire. According to the prisoners, the cause of the riot was administrative apathy toward an inmate who had fallen seriously ill during the night. Despite an uproar by the prisoners, no doctor responded. The inmate died. Worse still, nobody came to remove the dead body until the next morning. The prisoners went berserk. Much later, when ten prisoners were already dead, there was a visit by a VIP who subsequently announced punishment for the guilty. But there was no commitment for improvement in the medical services, and it was business as usual.

Interestingly, during my tenure, we nearly lost even the minimum facilities we had. Let me explain. The Delhi Health Service (DHS) with the approval of the Health Secretary, Government of Delhi, posted the doctors to Tihar Jail. Once appointed, the doctor was supervised by the prison administration, which also controlled the budget for medical facilities. However, exercising our discretion to remove a dangerously incompetent doctor from his post could and did result in vituperative action from the Delhi Health Services. A few weeks after this incident, the Secretariat decreed that the medical dispensaries inside Tihar from now on would fall under the direct supervision of the Delhi Health Services. The budget was also to be controlled by the DHS, but the overall responsibility for the functioning of the medical system would continue to rest with the Inspector General of the prisons. The bottom line was that we were responsible for all that went wrong, while someone else controlled the infrastructure and the money. The decision reflected a basic lack of understanding of the challenges inside Tihar. Had we faithfully implemented the written order, the repercussions would have been serious. Prison officials would have been helpless to provide treatment because the resources were under the control of the DHS and not necessarily made available. The resulting struggle to justify decisions and actions would have resulted in a nightmare of corruption, delays, inquiries, bureaucratic haggling, bad press, potential riots, and a painful lack of medical attention to those who needed it. Anticipating the potential crisis, we fought the order, pointing out the implications, and referring to the prison manual, which confers total supervisory responsibilities on the Superintendent of the jail. It took much time and energy, but we were finally successful in having the order rescinded.

We received frequent calls requesting special favors to well-known prisoners. Thinking it was their privilege, government officials would ask the prison officers and staff to ignore the rules for certain prominent prisoners. If their requests were turned down, the officer concerned would become vulnerable. To cite an example, we had declared Tihar Jail a no-smoking zone. This rule was applicable to all, including the staff. No one was permitted to smoke inside the jail. A popular activist farmer's leader, Mahendra Singh Tikait, was incarcerated in 1995 for rioting and assaulting policemen. In Tihar he was not allowed to smoke his *hukkah*, a long tobacco-smoking pipe, popular with the rural masses in India. This became a political issue. The matter turned serious and, in fact, was brought before the highest echelons of the government. Since I was out of the country on business, Sarangi, the Deputy Inspector General was called to explain why Tikait wasn't allowed to smoke his hukkah. He explained that the Inspector General had issued the no-smoking order, and if any inmate was to be given special treatment, the written order would have to be either amended or withdrawn. Since the government was legislating an anti-smoking bill to ban smoking in all public places, and Tihar is a public place, amending the order didn't appear appropriate. Sarangi was accused of not obeying the orders of the Prison Minister.

In another instance of overruling a right decision, a jail employee who had been dismissed was reinstated. The employee had been dismissed in the mid-1980s for gross misconduct, but afterwards he continued to live in the government housing within the Tihar complex. There he associated with local political figures and, over a period of time, grew in stature and importance. He campaigned among the employees of the Tihar residential colony for his political friends. One afternoon, we were informed by mail order that he had been reinstated.

The impact of this order on the whole prison staff, and the message it sent to the rank and file, proved to be demoralizing. To the prison administration, this person was a liability. Worse, because of his connections, he had access to places he should not have had and defied the orders of the Deputy Inspector General. So much for encouraging and ensuring professional management.

In my view, the role of management is that of a facilitator. In other words, it is management's duty to solve problems and not create new ones. It is my firm conviction that if we do not solve problems, we become part of the problem ourselves. In many cases, in government service, we can become part of the problem by the way we choose to function, exercise our authority, and utilize our discretion.

Prison Gangs Rule

Motley groups of thugs had virtually converted Tihar Jail into several fiefdoms. The gangs flourishing behind the bars in Tihar were named after their leaders—the Tyagi gang, the Gujjar gang, the Satpal gang, and, to top it all, the Dawood gang. The gang members hailed from different parts of India: Uttar Pradesh, Haryana, Rajasthan, Punjab, Jammu and Kashmir, Gujarat, and Maharashtra. The various gangs vied with one another for asserting their supremacy on the basis of their reputation in a field of specialization, be it murder, terrorism, mayhem, kidnapping, or extortion. The specialization list also included vendetta, caste wars, gang wars, mercenary activities, and trafficking of narcotics. Over the years, the gangs had developed a highly efficient and useful information network. They made huge amounts of money that they invested shrewdly to acquire color television sets, comfortable bedding, and other personal conveniences inside the prison. One of them had a brood of over thirty white pigeons. The high priests of crime had also built a retinue of personal attendants from the inmates who were at their beck and call.

Ashwini Sarin of *The Indian Express* wrote on May 25, 1986, of his experience infiltrating the jail:

On April 18, 1979, I was jailed and lodged in Delhi's infamous Tihar Jail for disorderly behavior in a public place.

In the years since my investigation into life in Tihar, nothing much has changed, except for a periodic whitewashing of the facade, an occasional strengthening of the barbed wires and the erection of the odd watchtower along the 4-kilometer-long prison wall.

However, outside the jail and near the lockups in city courts, there are touts who promise good care inside the jail. One can still send in money, drugs, and a recommendation for special care. Every service has a price tag.

When the Janata Government came to power, Indira Gandhi was jailed in Tihar. She, too, was perturbed by the mismanagement and the treatment of prisoners. A number of women prisoners met her during her brief stay in jail and apprised her of what was happening inside the jail where they were living, supposedly in safe custody. When Mrs. Gandhi came back to power in 1980, she appointed

Justice A. N. Mulla to head the Jail Reforms Committee and also asked Zail Singh, then the Home Minister, to personally visit Tihar. A tipsy inmate offered the Minister liquor as officials were conducting him around.

In its report on Tihar, the Mulla Committee had noted: "It was alleged (by prisoners) that certain prisoners enjoyed special confidence of the authorities for which they were allowed extra privileges, including free movement all over the jail compound. In matters of basic amenities, like diet, clothing, interviews, letters, etc., prisoners were being discriminated against. The allotment of labor was also not based on any fair criteria."

Most jails in the country are housed in dilapidated old buildings with little or no maintenance for decades. The Mulla Committee has described Tihar Jail as the best architecturally planned and functional jail in the country. Tihar was planned in 1952 with the help of a United Nations consultant, Dr. W. C. Reckless. Senior officers say that over the years Tihar Jail and its administration have lived up to its planner's name.

There is no denying the fact that the government has been concerned about the deterioration in jail conditions and the treatment being meted out to prisoners. But the concern seems to have remained confined to the setting up of committees. "In fact, the jail is a haven for hardened criminals who live a comfortable life within its safe precincts," a senior official of the Welfare Ministry's National Institute of Social Defense said. "Most notorious criminals use prison as a safe abode for some rest after a spell of crime outside. The need for prison reform cannot undermine the aspect of safe custody in jail."

Officials admit—and jail records corroborate—
that all punitive action in the form of solitary confinement and extra labor for indiscipline and other
acts in jail have been used only in the case of hap-
less inmates who were not in a position to bribe jail
officials or threaten them with legal action.

The gang members had a regular stream of visitors
without any annoying restrictions on either their number
or on the duration of their stay. The jail staff members
never dared to interrupt, for fear of violent retribution.
During long meetings both in the prison and in court,
these gangsters ran their nefarious businesses. Incidents of
murder, kidnapping, and extortions organized from behind
the prison walls occasionally reached the media.

The typical gangster was dressed like a villain in
a Hindi film. He wore dark blue jeans, a dark shirt, sports
shoes, dark glasses with golden frames, and a mane of flowing hair. He sometimes acted like a perverted Robin Hood
by pretending to be concerned about the welfare of the poor
prisoners. For instance, he would ask the Superintendent
for 100 kilograms of ice so that not just he but the entire
population of his ward could drink cold water.

In August 1993, an evening daily, *Sandhya Times*,
reported that a member of the infamous Tyagi Gang had
threatened to extort 700,000 rupees (about US$14,000)
from someone over the telephone from the jail. The Superintendent of that prison, Tarsem Kumar, called the gangster to his office and asked him:

"Is it true that you have telephoned from the jail?"

"No, sir," replied the gangster.

"Have you tried to extort 700,000 rupees as reported in
the newspaper?"

"Sir, I am not someone who would ask for only 700,000 rupees. I have never asked for that small an amount from anyone so far."

"Oh! You call 700,000 rupees a small amount?" exclaimed the Superintendent.

"Yes, sir, I do. I never ask for less than 5,000,000 rupees (US$100,000)," he boasted.

"And what about the phone?" asked the Superintendent.

"I swear I have not telephoned from the jail. I made the call from the court," he clarified.

Wealthy inmates at Tihar were particularly vulnerable to extortion demands from professionals inside the jail. They had to find huge sums of money within a stipulated time frame to avoid dire consequences, like getting maimed. Some inmates who refused to comply were beaten and forced to seek an exemption from a court appearance where the truth might have been revealed by a medical examination. Moreover, the thugs ensured that the doctor provided the required medical certificate—either out of fear or connivance, or both.

I recall a visit to the prison hospital my first week on the job. I was alarmed to see a lone doctor surrounded by burly and ominous-looking inmates. The sole representative of the medical profession seemed to be under tremendous duress. The Rambo-like thugs had cornered the doctor to extract whatever they wanted from him. They demanded medicines, prescriptions, medical certificates, medical files, or admission forms for referral to an outside hospital. The doctor had to comply as he was in no position to refuse their demands. At the hospital, I came across very few people who actually looked ill—most of the patients appeared as if they were enjoying a break. At the slightest opportunity, they would create a ruckus to have some noise and fun. A few prison officials wandered around looking helpless. Some of the staff members were pushed around and taunted by the bullies. These gangsters were virtual dictators whose realm extended from the jail barracks to the hospital, and also beyond the prison walls.

Handling the gangsters in Tihar Jail was the most important challenge for us. A particular episode at the beginning of my tenure stands out in my memory. One evening I was informed that a prisoner in Jail 4 had been badly beaten. More than ten officers of the jail staff were reportedly involved in this incident. It took place in the afternoon when the prison was officially closed after the midday roll call. While 2,000-odd prisoners of Prison 4 were returning to their barracks, one inmate was taken from his ward and beaten by the officers, individually and collectively, at the *chakkar*—the center point of the prison. I was told that during visiting hours the previous day, this inmate, a notorious gangster and a bully, had hit one of the assistant superintendents. The officers perceived this as a challenge to their collective authority, which could only be answered by collective revenge. They were afraid that if the new Inspector General with her non-violent philosophy was allowed to have her way, their machismo image would be shattered and their authority seriously threatened. They were convinced that the status quo could not be disturbed and that I needed to accept this fact. It was a collective beating for displaying collective power. It was also a display of official unity in the face of the power of the ruthless gangsters. Through their collective action, the officers also implied that I, as an officer, would need protection from the gangsters and I had better learn my Tihar lessons early.

The news of the event spread quickly throughout the jail. Both prisoners and staff waited with baited breath to see what I would do. I asked the Superintendent of Jail 4 how the officers were able to enter the jail in the afternoon since it was officially closed. And where was he when the incident occurred? I did not get a satisfactory answer. Next, I called in the medical officer on duty and asked him to examine the inmate thoroughly and submit a detailed report specifying the nature and causes of the injuries inflicted on the beaten prisoner. I kept up the pressure during the following days, for expediting the medical report and for an explanation from all the concerned officers. Not a single officer responded.

I asked Sarangi, the Deputy Inspector General, to tell the officers that I was waiting for the medical report, and that if it established violence, no one would be spared. I sent out the signal, categorically and unambiguously, that I would not tolerate the culture of violence fostered by staff members. Eventually, the standoff ended. The medical report clearly showed the injuries to have been caused by beating the prisoner with *lathis* (sticks). The officers realized that they had been squarely indicted and approached the Superintendent to arrange a meeting with Deputy Inspector General Sarangi. One by one, they met with Sarangi and apologized for what had happened. Each of them asserted that he, personally, had not wanted to beat the prisoner but was compelled to do so by official solidarity. It was a Saturday and I was at home. Sarangi telephoned to convey the message that the officers were anxious to meet with me. I did not think it proper to make them wait until the coming Monday, so I drove straight to Tihar.

All the officers were waiting outside my office, looking tense and apprehensive. I called them into my office.

"Madam, we want to say something."

I said, "Yes, what is it?"

"We beat up the prisoner because he was a bully and abused and threatened an officer and tore his shirt. He is a gang member, and if we hadn't beaten him, we would be beaten every day. We do not have any protection while on duty or at home. The gangsters regularly threaten our families, and the department has never offered us any protection." They put forward various other arguments to justify their stand.

After listening to their explanation, I posed some counterquestions: "The gangster became abusive and violent and beat up an officer. But what about you? You officers? Didn't you do the same? Is there no difference between custodians of law and prisoners? How did you differ in conduct? The prisoner is in prison for violation of law, and where are you? What entitles you to behave like him? Were there no other means of controlling the prisoner concerned? Was resorting to retaliatory violence the only way?" Before I could conclude, they offered a collective apology. I decided to move on: "You have made me aware of the lack of security you live with. There will be no delay in setting this right."

And set it right we did. Most of the staff members were surprised to see the attitudes of the inmates undergoing a marked change for the better as a result. The file of this incident remained in my personal custody, to be opened only in the event of a recurrence of misbehavior. They did not give me an opportunity to write it up again, but such a mind-set revealed how completely the system needed an overhaul.

Security or Insecurity

The Tihar Jail complex has a three-tier security system. The watchtowers and boundary wall surrounding all four prisons comprise the outermost ring. The second ring is the area between the walls of the wards and the main wall. The third ring is at the ward gates to the barracks. Each ward is a walled enclosure containing a few barracks or group of cells. The number and size of the wards varied, due to additional construction over the years since the original prison was built in 1958.

During my tenure as Inspector General, a battalion from the Tamil Nadu Security Police (TSP) guarded the outer perimeter. The Security Police were armed and deployed on the outermost security ring along the high prison walls and on the watchtowers. The prison staff manned the second and the third rings. The members of the TSP reported directly to a Commandant, who was invariably a young Indian Police Service officer. He did not have an office within the Tihar premises and visited the prison only occasionally. He had six other officers, including a Deputy Commandant and Assistant Commandants, all of whom had been in the police force for many years. These officers were further assisted by 10 inspectors, 26 sub-inspectors, 1,100 head constables, and 1,016 constables.

The entire battalion, which consisted of over 1,200 men, did not stay on the Tihar premises, although Tihar had space to house them. They had pitched their tents about 20 kilometers away in a field temporarily assigned to them by the Delhi Police Headquarters. They had been there since they were first posted to Tihar's security in the mid-1980s. The exorbitant cost of their deployment was drawn from the Delhi Police budget. They spent much time and fuel by traveling but were unwilling to give up their foothold on the Delhi Police land even if it meant compromising the real purpose of their posting in Delhi.

Since the battalion was from south India, hardly any of them spoke Hindi. Only the officers could speak English. Their diet was also different from that of their north Indian counterparts, and their culture and habits were strikingly dissimilar. Moreover, they followed their own regimen regarding training, use of weapons, and change of duties. All these factors contributed to their alienation from the rest of the staff and the prison administration. The lack of communication with the jail staff was an ongoing problem. The policy was to move the whole battalion out every three years and replace it with a new battalion. During these three years, there was a lack of discipline, inappropriate relationships, and confirmed reports of some TSP borrowing money from one of the most notorious Tihar inmates. Not a reassuring picture as far as security was concerned.

The TSP was in charge of perimeter security and keeping watch on the activities inside the prison. Their shifts changed every two hours so that the person on duty could remain alert and vigilant. Yet there were occasional instances of a guard switching off the floodlights to avoid attracting mosquitoes, or turning around the light near his post so that he could take a nap. One such nap resulted in the escape of a prisoner who sneaked out right under the nose of the security men at the watchtower.

The physical condition of the watchtowers was pathetic. The agency responsible for their maintenance was none other than the Public Works Department (PWD). The railings around the watchtower were crumbling. The staircase was a mere a skeleton of a structure since the concrete filling had fallen off in many places. The power outlets had not been grounded, leading to the danger of electrocution, especially during the rainy season. The TSP men complained about these abysmal conditions but to no avail.

Guarding the inner perimeter was the duty of the Delhi jail cadre. Due to severe shortage of staff, the warders responsible for security on the wards were on night duty from 10 p.m. to 6 a.m. daily for weeks. During random night checks, most of the staff members were found asleep. Realistically, each ward needed at least two warders, one inside the compound and the other outside. However, most of the time there was only one, and sometimes he was responsible for several wards due to the acute shortage of manpower.

All four prisons with over 8,000 inmates were at times left under the supervision of one Head Warder and one Assistant Superintendent. There was no provision for a trained senior officer to be on duty during the night. In fact, a low-ranking officer was in charge of the entire prison for the night. According to the rules, one Deputy Superintendent had to be on duty all twenty-four hours. However, a single individual could not fulfill this stipulation. At least four deputy superintendents were needed to share the duties on a rotation basis. Instead, there was one who reported for duty at 6 a.m. to open the prison. Then he went back home and returned at 9 a.m. He ordered an afternoon closure about 1 p.m. and the final closure at 6 p.m. In fact, the rule was to open at sunrise and close at sunset. After completing all the paperwork, recording the entries of new inmates, ensuring the correct release of those whose orders had arrived, and ordering the closure of the prison, the officer was free to leave for home around 9 p.m. How could the same Deputy Superintendent possibly come back for night duty after working for over fifteen hours?

Due to the absence of proper supervision at night, Tihar's nefarious nocturnal activities never came to light. Unauthorized interviews or visitations, smuggling of prohibited articles, and forced homosexuality and sexual abuse became routine affairs.

In Tihar, all records related to security were written laboriously by hand, and mostly maintained by poorly educated warders. Due to staff shortages, literate convicts did the clerical work. The presence of convicts in the record and administrative sections gave rise to an environment where those "in the know" could sell confidential information. All sensitive information as well as policy amendments and orders, which arrived in the Superintendent's office, reached the entire prison population before they reached the Superintendent. The Superintendent's office was located within the administrative block where the convicts were employed for secretarial and other duties. In fact, even the water carriers on the Superintendent's staff meticulously observed the nature of activities in his office. These vigilant insiders knew exactly who visited the Superintendent's office, the purpose for which they came, and what transpired during the meeting. Many of these convicts-turned-clerks charged money to the inmates for providing them with vital information. Prison security was virtually compromised every day.

Tihar Jail's one concession to modernization was closed-circuit monitors with seven remote cameras in each of the four prisons. One TV camera covered the area between the two iron gates at the entrance and a second just outside this area. A third covered the visiting area. Four cameras were focused on the internal precincts of the prison. None of the cameras was focused on the wards or barracks or even at the chakkar, where crucial activities took place. The cameras fed to a 21-inch television screen inside the Superintendent's office. He could view ongoing activities or he could record footage for later viewing. The quality of the cameras and their maintenance were nothing short of dismal. They were mere showpieces. Sparrows and pigeons had even built their nests in the cameras. Questioned in the Parliament about security, officials claimed that the video equipment in Tihar was state-of-the-art and more such equipment was needed all over the jail. However, for lack of resources, this need was still under consideration.

Another major security lapse involved identity cards

for individual prisoners. There were thousands of inmates inside; moreover hundreds came and went daily. But there was no photo identity system. Thumb impressions were taken during entry and exit. An age-old method of identifying individuals by body marks was often employed. If these marks matched those of inmates scheduled for release, the staff set them free.

The prison storehouse was the dumping ground for thousands of records. The chance of retrieving a specific document was very remote. The storehouse benefited only the ants, rats, and snakes that lived there, further discouraging human entry. Due to the accumulation of huge volumes of manual records, court warrants were misplaced. On queries from the courts of whether or not a particular person was inside the jail, sometimes even if he was, the prison authorities could not give an accurate report. When the misinformation came to light, the courts would haul up the Superintendent and severely reprimand him. The superintendents of Tihar Jail were regular visitors to the courts because of these frequent botch-ups. They were a harassed lot. Physical headcounts and name verifications were often used to avoid such blunders. But, the entire process involved tremendous effort. Most Indian institutions and offices were computerized during the late Prime Minister Rajiv Gandhi's tenure in the 1980s. But Tihar, the largest prison in the Asia-Pacific region, was not destined to join the electronic age until 1994. Even then the jail staff resisted computerization because it meant learning something new.

A totally rudimentary security system prevailed. Yet there was a tremendous outcry in the name of security. No academic or social researchers were allowed inside, due to reasons of security, although they could have been of enormous help by identifying emerging problems and helping avoid major mishaps.

I vividly remember the day when I asked the then Inspector General of Tihar for permission to interview criminal addicts for my doctoral dissertation, *Substance Abuse and Criminality*. Since the prison had a large number of criminals who were addicts, and hopefully had accurate records of both their medical history and criminal cases, it was perfect for my research. But my application did not receive even an acknowledgement. I redesigned my research project and completed my doctorate without Tihar.

Media Spotlight

Tihar was in the headlines whenever there was a riot, an escape, a death, an epidemic, or disclosure of an extortion racket. Otherwise, the official system decreed the prison out of bounds for the media. The Prison Administration obviously wanted to keep certain activities away from public scrutiny, although their reticence forced investigative journalists to snoop around and then spice up their stories. With substantial evidence, such stories raised issues that put the administration on the defensive and caused the government a great deal of embarrassment. These expositions activated public interest groups and the courts.

The prison authorities did their utmost to maintain the shroud of secrecy over Tihar. Whenever they sensed the threat of revelation, they promptly pre-empted the journalists and ordered a judicial or departmental enquiry (or both) into the incident. While the media, for its part, felt that it had performed a service to society with these exposures, the outside community was fed distressing information that regularly depicted the prison system as evil and beyond correction and redemption despite the occasional efforts made by the government to reform the system. This had some negative consequences: the community distanced itself from the system; the prisoners saw themselves as incorrigible outcasts; and prison service became an ignominious position in which no individual with a choice would serve.

Those who were permanent fixtures in the jail became invulnerable to any sort of investigation, for they knew that they were irreplaceable and indispensable. They also mastered the art of protecting themselves by destroying or creating evidence, depending on the situation. In reality, the sensationalism in the press was just a flash in the pan as far as the prison officials were concerned. For them it was business as usual. Nevertheless, whenever any scandal rocked Tihar, the government machinery tried its best to control the media.

Other organizations, such as Amnesty International, People's Union for Civil Liberties (PUCL) and People's Union for Democratic Rights (PUDR), and even the Ministry of External Affairs (MEA) were also keenly interested in Tihar's affairs, each with its own reasons. While the watchdog agencies were on the lookout for human-rights violations, MEA's objective was to defend the jail in the foreign media, since many foreign inmates were incarcerated in Tihar.

Tihar had developed a tradition of discretionary and discriminatory dissemination of news. Those media persons who were not "friends" of the prison officials were not given access to Tihar. To gain entry, they had to seek court orders or permission from the Union Government, both of which were equally difficult to get. Friendly journalists had merely to ask and they were duly escorted into Tihar. The top brass knew they would not embarrass them, and they would write safe stories.

To beat the system, an ace investigative journalist, Ashwini Sarin of *The Indian Express*, got himself arrested on

April 18, 1979, and was duly sent to Tihar Jail. He wrote an eye-opening firsthand account of all that he saw. The explosive exposé ran in a five-part series titled "Getting Into Tihar." Here is part of his story:

> I still shudder to recall the experience. "Never again," I prayed as I stepped into the waiting taxi on the night of April 20 after my release from Delhi's Tihar Jail. I had been lodged there two days earlier, charged with disorderly behavior in a public place under the influence of alcohol.
>
> "A day more here and I would have turned mad," I told B. M. Sinha, my Chief Reporter, who came to take me home from an assignment, which turned out to be something I had not bargained for.
>
> The idea was to know firsthand what exactly it means to be an undertrial in Tihar Jail. Our earlier efforts to penetrate the secrecy behind the high walls through official and other sources had failed. I was to get myself arrested on a trumped-up charge and then refuse bail.
>
> My first effort to create an unruly scene, without consuming liquor, at the Delhi-Haryana border on April 17 was futile. A burly police sub-inspector gave me a long lecture on cultivating good habits. "You seem to come from a good family," he said. "Care for their honor if not your own." He hailed a taxi and put me in with instruction to the driver to unload me safely at my house.
>
> I left the taxi at Kalkaji, tipped the driver, and took a bus home.
>
> The next day, April 18, I left home after a hearty breakfast of boiled eggs and toast. "Have your fill because there will be little to eat for the

next three days," Mr. Sinha cautioned me. About 11:30 a.m. we took a taxi and headed toward Badarpur. The arrangement was that Sinha would shadow me after my arrest.

This time I chose a spot very near the Badarpur Police Station. I abused a shopkeeper with an empty beer bottle in one hand and using the other to stop the traffic trying to enter the old Badarpur settlement from the historic Agra Gate side. My torn, faded jeans and the aging checked shirt with the upper two buttons missing suited my role nicely.

The word soon reached the police station, and within minutes I was dragged into it. The lanky old subinspector and the baton-wielding constable were not too rough. Sinha was watching from a distance.

They put me under arrest. Within half an hour the papers charging me under Sections 93 and 97 of the Delhi Police Act were ready. A police pickup took me to the magistrate, who remanded me to jail custody till Monday, April 28, if I failed to produce a bail bond. The court allowed me to take 20 rupees (about US$0.50) to jail.

Outside, some touts offered to get me out on bail. "This is a very minor offense. Why are you spending five days in jail? I will get you bail for 20 rupees," one said. I thanked him as the cops took me to the lockup room of Patiala House.

Two armed cops, Ranjit Singh and Raghubir Sharma, frisked me roughly with a shower of choice abuse. One of them, after counting the two 10-rupee notes repeatedly, put the money back in my pocket with an endearing pat on my back. The other one opened the lockup door and I was in.

Outside, another constable was heard arguing

with Sinha about my food. After some time someone called out, *Hai Koi Ashwini Kumar L. C. Sarin Ka* (Is there any Ashwini Kumar, son of L. C. Sarin)? I came closer to the heavy iron door when the constable hurriedly handed over something wrapped in newspaper. I opened it and found four chapatis, stale and dry.

Sinha later told me that he had paid two rupees for the meal that I never ate.

Inside the lockup, not more than 10 feet by 15 feet and stinking like an overcrowded third-class railway compartment, I found myself among 32 others.

In 1993, Tihar was no different. The secrecy in Tihar created a fertile ground within the jail for the sale of news. Prisoners and officials both acted as agents for scoops. Sometimes the underlying intention in an exposé was noble, but nefarious factors were involved. At times, the media was used to defame either the system or certain individuals, to settle scores, or to derive sadistic pleasure. Sometimes the media exposures threw the prison system into further chaos and undermined its functioning.

In the name of security, Tihar was kept away from social scientists, researchers, and the media. The real reason for secrecy was fear of exposure. That fear fed a hostile relationship between Tihar and the press. On my daily jail visits, I wondered about this obsession with secrecy. Maintaining security ought not to lead to gagging or throttling the organization. As I understood it, Tihar was a correctional institute. Should it hide its problems—excessive overcrowding, inadequate medical system, languishing undertrials, near absence of civic services, outdated kitchens, etc.? Should it not provide visibility and access for community audit? Until I saw the prison for myself, I understood nothing about it. How could we expect anyone else to understand its strengths and weaknesses unless they too could visit the prison and have the information they needed? After all, it is the whole society that sends offenders to prison and receives and also absorbs those who are released. Therefore, doesn't society have the right to credible professional communication and evaluation of the prison? I wondered if there was a vested interest in perpetuating ignorance. Or perhaps it was only fear of exposure that kept Tihar so closed and secretive. Nevertheless, the consequences were the same.

The challenge was before us. What did we want the prison as an institution to be? Isolated, secretive, and unaudited? Or participative, contributory, and socially audited?

special prisoners: women, adolescents, and foreigners

Women in Tihar

Indian society has long been the victim of overpowering gender discrimination. The most degrading and dehumanizing aspects of such discrimination manifested itself in Tihar Jail. In Tihar, women prisoners were subjected to humiliating experiences, which robbed them of whatever little dignity and self-respect they had left. It is a miracle that these women managed to cling to their sanity. Like their male counterparts, the women were victims of overcrowding. Around 280 women were herded into a facility built for 60. Shockingly, only 20 of them were convicted criminals. The rest were waiting for trial. There were 40 children, including newborns and toddlers. The prison rules permit children up to the age of five to stay with their mothers in jail. Huddled together with their mothers, these children had become an integral part of the prison population.

The majority was in prison for theft, drug trafficking, murder, swindling, and prostitution. A few had been arrested for terrorist activities. The foreign women were imprisoned primarily for drug trafficking offenses. Although the foreign women hailed from almost all parts of the world, they maintained a reasonable degree of harmony among themselves within the sordid confines of the prison. The foreigners were kept away from their Indian counterparts in relatively small cells of 8 feet square. The Indian inmates were allotted spaces in the dormitories along with their children.

The grim and forbidding atmosphere of the prison is revealed in the mind-boggling tales narrated by some of the women prisoners. Here are some verbatim reports of women in Tihar:

I came here on October 2, 1990, three days before the big riot in the jail on October 5. This was a few

days before Diwali and I was new. I was arrested
for a narcotics offense. The police concocted a long
story and fabricated the evidence so that I could be
arrested.

When the siren went off on the day of the riot
at about 10 or 11 in the morning, they (the jailors)
locked us all up. There were about 200 of us. We
could hear noises like the walls crumbling and the
matron shouting, "The men have arrived." The
woman Assistant Superintendent in those days was
very mean; the men were looking for her, so she hid
herself in the toilet. She was always mean to us and
constantly demanding money from the women
prisoners. So, the women prisoners were also very
annoyed with her. The men who were rioting had
plans to escape and they were coming to the
women's ward to take their mothers, wives or sisters with them. So, the women too were yelling and
screaming. That was a serious mistake the rioters
made because the authorities could turn things
around and claim that the prisoners had come
there to assault and molest the women prisoners.

The rioters took the keys of the prison from
the staff and then proceeded to open the locks of
the women's barracks. They abused the head matron though they did not manhandle her. We then
saw the riot police coming. The riot police started
shooting, and the open compound where we used
to have daily prayers became a battlefield. Dead
bodies were strewn everywhere. The Deputy Superintendent was among those shooting at the
prisoners. Since I was new, I did not know or recognize many officers, but I believe the shooting
was started by [name withheld]. A British prisoner,

Michael, rushed to our ward to protect the foreign women. He locked us up in a separate cell and positioned himself outside. An African had also joined the mob of rioters. He and a Frenchman were beaten very badly. They broke the Frenchman's arms. He lost his senses and became crazy afterwards. His name was Christian Joseph. His arms were twisted and he was always dirty and unkempt. I think his cast was badly applied and that is how his arms got twisted. Nobody would clean or dress his wounds. He is still in the prison as a convict. [This man later died while still in judicial custody.]

All the men were kept locked in for three days. The next thing we heard, the prison authorities had released a statement to the press saying that the men prisoners had attacked the women's barracks because they wanted to rape the women. They made a similar accusation about Michael who had come to protect the women. They said that he had gone to the women's ward so that he could take a woman called Helen to another room for his pleasure. This is absolute rubbish. Imagine all this happening at a time when shooting was already going on and people were dying.

At the inquiry, they would not allow anybody to speak and locked us all up. If anybody dared to talk, he would be beaten and severely punished. It was horrible. Even the medical side was so bad. Several people died because the doctors were not there. I remember one day an old Sansi woman died in the ward and another was very ill and needed to go to a hospital. This happened at midnight and no doctor appeared until the afternoon of the next day. They said it was the second Saturday of the month, so no doctor was available. They wanted us to go to lockup, but I refused to go until a doctor came to attend to the sick woman. All the other women then joined me in voicing a demand for a doctor. They told me to mind my own business. But we were doing exactly that because any of us might be seriously ill and die for want of medical attention. I was brought for punishment the next day. I admitted to the Superintendent that I had refused to go to the lockup because it was a matter of life and death, and if I had not done that, nobody would have listened. The punishment imposed was that I would have no visitors. I was not expecting visitors anyway.

The Superintendent was very unreasonable at times. He used to lock us up by the inner door of the cell, denying access even to the little courtyard within the cell. It was hell. The lights would go off and there would be four or five women in an 8-foot-by-8-foot cell, which also included the toilet. The situation improved only when K. R. Kishore became the Superintendent. He was a refreshing change for us. The previous Superintendent used to sneak in once in a while in the middle of the night and would shout at the matrons if he caught them talking to any of the prisoners. Many of the Deputy Superintendents also had the same attitude. The staff was only interested in extorting money from the prisoners. There were other horrible people. One was a man who used to come into the ward and paw the women. He is gone now. He was also in the habit of calling some of the women prisoners to his office even in the daytime. No one reported him. Though the Superintendent was very strict and

would not have approved such things, he did not
know what exactly was going on. Some of the officers, who are still in the prison, behaved very badly.
One in particular we called Bindiwala because he
had a *bindi* (round dot) on his forehead. He was
a major extorter of money from us. One day, Maria,
a Spanish woman prisoner, was lighting a *chulah*
(earthen stove) in her cell when he came. The lighting of chulahs in the barracks was against the rules,
but the staff allowed it as long as they got money or
something to eat. They would come and order the
women prisoners to make tea for them. He made a
big fuss about it and shouted at Maria. She apologized. He looked around, and seeing no one there,
asked her to kiss him. She ran away screaming, and
then he also ran away. Before I came, there was
a prisoner called Dumdum who arranged prosti-
tutes for the staff members and others. Even after
her release she continued to provide this service and
that is why the officers were scared of her. She could
do whatever she wanted.

The matrons were also afraid of Dumdum. She
used to deal in drugs, alcohol, women, and stolen
property. She was a pickpocket and a thief. She
would share expensive saris and other stolen articles
with the staff, so they were happy and never said
anything to her even if she got drunk. If staff members tried to discipline her, she would beat them.
When someone from her group came to the prison,
she would give them tea and food. Then she made
them work for her, washing her clothes and dishes,
giving her a massage. She also demanded and got
a share of what they got from the *mulaqaat*.

The male officers made frequent visits to the

women's ward, often without reason. They would come and call anybody. Dumdum would be clad in her undergarments in their presence, and they would openly demand money from her, as did one of the women Assistant Superintendents. Another Assistant Superintendent conducted herself much better during the first month of her posting but she was suspended.

Five of us, Glory, Chakki, two Muslim girls, and I, were staying in Barrack 1. The husband of one of the Muslim girls had four wives and used them all for smuggling gold. When this man came for mulaqaat, he would bring money to smuggle things, which was forbidden. The Muslim girl would arrange to meet her husband in the hospital. She then started going out with the husband and boasting about it. We objected to these incidents and made a lot of noise. Glory said she was going to tell everybody about it, so the woman Assistant Superintendent beat her up. Even Maria and myself were not spared. It was inhuman because Glory's leg was broken. The same officer brought Dumdum's women and a male *lambardar* (errand boy with a specific responsibility) to beat her but she broke their stick in two.

While this merciless assault was going on, Darshan Lal, the Deputy Superintendent, came along and asked us what had happened. We were all crying and told him what had happened. He went and reported to the Superintendent. Later on the same woman officer abused us vulgarly and suggested that I was having an affair with Darshan Lal, who was like a father to us. The Superintendent then suspended the woman officer. She used to threaten me but I refused to give her any money, so she hated Maria and me. We never paid her anything while other foreign inmates bribed her to arrange meetings for them on Saturdays and holidays even though Saturday meetings were meant to be only for blood relations. Money made blood relationships and she arranged the meetings even between jail inmates.

She also acted as a go-between for prisoners who were jailed for terrorist acts. One day, one of the terrorist women tried to assault a meek woman convict and I intervened. Meanwhile, a warder named Anand came by. He was a nice man and I asked him to take me to the Superintendent. The Superintendent, K. R. Kishore, heard me and then asked what I thought was the reason for the terrorist inmates behaving in this manner. I told him the two reasons: they were paying the same woman officer and were keeping the other staff in check by boasting about their outside connections to some important persons. He immediately ordered those prisoners to be separated and changed the Assistant Superintendent.

A sort of Mafia ruled the women's ward roost. These gangsters extorted money from people with big cases, and then they bribed the staff so that they could have visitations every day. They could buy everything since they were able to pay for it.

The food in the prison was very bad. The rag used for mopping the floors and left lying out in the courtyard for hours was used to wrap the chapatis. This was a routine practice. One day the rice contained pieces of rusted wire. I asked a Warder to call the duty officer to see this. She did not want to call him and wanted the rice to be thrown away, but

I told her if she didn't I would take the matter to court. Magisterial inspection of the prison used to take place once a month. At that time all the prisoners were locked up. Only one or two prisoners were brought out to speak to the magistrate. Since the prison food was so bad, the prisoners had to light chulahs to supplement their dietary needs. They would buy vegetables through the staff, which charged triple the market price. I had no visitors, and never had any money, so I helped others cook to earn a little money, or to be able to share their food. Another inmate, Poonam, and I used to write applications for prisoners and charged 5 rupees per application. This money made it possible for us to buy essential toilet items.

The lawyers were on their own moneymaking trip. The free-legal-aid lawyer might as well not have been there. She was such a useless lawyer. The lawyer I engaged duped me after charging an enormous amount of money. He had assured me that he would get me bailed out. When I attended court I realized to my horror that he had made an application in the court to summon all my witnesses. So, instead of trying for a speedy disposal of my case, he was suggesting a fresh trial. He had also lied to me about moving the high court to grant me bail. His plan to dupe me for more money thus came to light and I dissociated myself from him. Shortly after that the court of S. M. Aggarwal honorably acquitted me. One of the prisoners who had been released earlier helped me with the money to pay for the legal expenses. Had it not been for her, I would still be in jail.

And here is an account from the other side of the fence—a woman officer:

I have been in service for over six years and have seen the conditions in the women's ward of Tihar Jail from the closest quarters possible. There was no work for women and they would waste the whole day quarrelling among themselves over trifles. Their idle minds were truly the devil's workshop. I spent most of my time resolving these petty disputes at my level because I did not want them to get into trouble over nothing. I also felt very sorry for their children whose ages ranged from infants to four-year-olds. There were no facilities for special food for them. After considerable effort I was able to arrange *khichri* (a kind of rice and vegetable broth) for the little ones. I felt so concerned for them that sometimes I brought fruit for them from my home.

There were no educational facilities for either women or children. I would sometimes overhear the children say, "Tomorrow is our court date, perhaps we will be convicted." I felt really bad to hear these tiny tots speak the language of the prison. I mourned the loss of their childhood and their innocence. I often wondered what I could do for them. I talked to my Superintendent who gave me money to buy toys for them. I motivated an inmate named Poonam to look after them and try to teach them.

Some of the women wanted to learn to read and write, and those who were really keen somehow managed, but I couldn't motivate all of them. I could have established a *crèche* (nursery) for the children and provided writing materials for those who wanted to study, but I did not have the resources.

Many women expressed great anxiety about their children being left unattended outside the prison while they were serving time. I tried to arrange for these women to have their children with them, and also to get them work in the prison so that they could earn money to look after their children. If one child got something to eat, those who saw it would ask their mothers for the same thing and a mother who didn't have money would beat the child out of sheer frustration. Some women prisoners had no visitors at all. I tried to counsel the prisoners according to the situation, but we barely had time to attend to our daily duties and no time to pay any attention to the welfare of prisoners. There was a vocational school run by the government to teach stitching and tailoring, but no one was inspired to attend it. It was a situation of complete disinterest.

Yet another officer in the women's ward recounts her experiences:

Some women prisoners spent all their time gambling. They were abusive and even threatened the staff. These women convicts were called *bees saali*, or twenty-year-termers. In 1971, the women's ward had barely 30 to 35 inmates, mostly imprisoned for involvement in incidents of theft or prostitution. Those convicted in murder cases were sent to Ludhiana Jail. In 1986, the composition of the women's ward underwent a radical change and women began coming in for dowry and narcotics crimes. There was also a steady increase in the number of cases waiting for trial. At one point of time, the number of inmates exceeded 300, including 60 children.

Regarding milk for mothers in the prison, one of the inmates revealed the following state of affairs:

Each child was entitled to 400 grams of milk. It was to be given to their mothers. Breast-feeding mothers were entitled to milk for drinking depending on what the doctor prescribed. Any ailing woman could get milk as a medical diet. All this was good in policy, but only if there was implementation. The milk that reached the inmates and children was nothing but white water. The so-called milk reached the women's barracks before daybreak. It was handed over to a woman convict, who was a well-educated foreign inmate. She withheld a good amount for herself and her boss, the Head Warder, and sold it to the inmates. She then shared the profit with her boss.

She was not alone in selling milk. The mothers of the children who got the milk traded it away to earn coupons. Many never gave the milk to their children. Some women, who had more than one child, sold the share of the second child. Hence milk was a commodity on which all cheated.

Another prisoner had this to say:

Dried prison chapatis were the favorites among women inmates as fuel for cooking, heating food and making tea for themselves, the staff, and the doctors. In winter, since more tea was required, dried chapatis sold for 10 paise each (one-tenth of an Indian rupee). But while the staff enjoyed the tea, they would often confiscate the *chulahs* (stoves) to show a raid was made. All these would come back again as favors, or at a price.

One of the officers described the sordid living conditions:

The women inmates who were convicted or being tried for nonviolent crimes, and had some education and financial standing, were assigned "B"-class facility. This enabled them to live in cells 8 feet by 8 feet while others lived in dormitories 50 feet by 40 feet. Most of the foreign women were granted "B" class by courts to help them stay together due to the cultural and language similarities. The women in cells maintained themselves better than the ones in the dormitories. In the dormitories, there were all kinds of women from all strata of society, including those who had no idea how to use a flush toilet. For them it was just another drain to throw all the muck.

Once, four foreign inmates were punished by sending them to the dormitory. This is what one of the women said of that experience:

To add insult to injury, we were given the side of the dormitory right next to the open drain flowing outside the barrack. Cockroaches were plentiful and we couldn't sleep the whole night. In the morning we decided to make the best out of the worst situation. We cleaned the whole drain ourselves. We scraped the layers and layers of grime off until we reached the floors and walls of the drain.

We got fellow occupants to join us and bring water. Those who wouldn't help asked to pay others to bring their share of water. We formed a group to take turns cleaning every day to keep cockroaches and the stench away. When it was realized that we in fact were settling down there, we were relocated yet again. But the truth was that most of the women in the dormitory lived in filthy conditions because they had no sense of personal hygiene.

Staff Vandalism

Regarding the upkeep of clothes and personal appearance, one of the prisoners went on record describing the harassment:

We had no laundry system. There were no irons to press our clothes. We folded our washed clothes while they were still slightly damp and put them under our heads. Of course many of us wore crushed clothes. We could get mirrors for 30 to 50 rupees from a warder. But she could confiscate these mirrors whenever it suited her, and then would break them to show her official power. Then all paid her again and she brought another mirror.

On medical care, a poignant disclosure was made on record by an old hand:

We women could get a referral to a general hospital or a medical certificate for a price. The money was delivered to a particular woman doctor outside the prison. She would not collect it herself but tell us where it was to be delivered. It was typically in the Bollywood style. Usually, the places were bus stops where a man would be waiting to pick it up. Once, my roommate was desperate to apply for medical bail. She was suffering from severe asthma attacks. She approached this doctor but was refused. Then my friend asked the doctor what she wanted. She quoted a price. When she received the money, the certificate followed. My friend got bail on that basis.

When I was arrested I did not have eyeglasses. I am almost blind in one eye. At my appearance before the court, I asked the court to direct the jail doctor to send me to the eye specialist. The judge issued the order. But when the doctor saw the order, she told me, "You are very smart but the order does not matter, I will not send you." I again applied to the court. The court again issued an order. The doctor still would not send me and said, "You will go only when I want you to go." I gave up. Finally, after a few weeks she allowed me to go.

The Delhi policewomen who escorted prisoners to various hospitals clearly knew the malingerers and those who had come only to meet friends or relatives. They knew escorting them was no work for them, as it didn't involve doctor visits or laboratory tests. For them it meant sitting around and getting a lot to eat. Many times during the allocation of guard duties, the policewomen would fight for these hospital-escorting duties.

Certain doctors, court guards, prison guards, and lawyers acted as illegal couriers, delivering letters and messages to prisoners. These people met regularly at a particular government hospital, all through managed referrals. It was through such means that Jacqueline, a woman inmate, and Charles Sobhraj, a high-profile male inmate, exchanged love letters, and finally went public with their engagement.

While the medical facilities existed, the medical practitioners seemed seldom inclined to use them. Doctors were frequently absent during crucial emergencies, such as childbirth. An inmate vividly described the pathetic conditions:

> Even in delivery cases, if the woman happened to give birth while she was still in the barrack between 1 p.m. and 10 a.m., there was no medical help available. This was because the lady doctor came to work at 10 a.m. and left at 1 p.m. So it was we who assisted the woman. We had no help, not even a first-aid kit. In one case a woman delivered her baby but we had nothing with which to cut the umbilical cord. We desperately searched for something, but we found nothing. Finally we got a small piece of blade from a woman in the same dormitory, but it was too many hours after the delivery.
>
> In another case, a woman delivered at night during the lockin period. No medical attendant came for her. In the morning when the barracks opened we went inside and saw her lying in all the blood and outflow. No one had washed the child. We women bathed the child; another one of us cleaned up the woman; another one, who was known for never helping anyone, made tea for the mother, for she was not lactating yet. The fellow inmates of her dormitory had left her on her own in a corner of the barrack.

A woman inmate, talking about the sensitive subject of sanitary napkins, stated on record:

For some time we received napkins but suddenly the supply stopped. We were then given a coarse gray cloth with instructions to wash it for reuse. But a lot of women, not knowing how to use a flush toilet, would choke it by dumping the cloth in the toilet, and we had to wait forever for the gutter cleaner.

Regarding sleeping tablets, one inmate remarked:

We could ask for as many as we needed and that is how we could manage some sleep. Some of us got addicted to these tablets.

On the equally sensitive subject of lesbianism, one of the women prisoners was forthcoming in her observations:

The prison did have a few incidents, and one such, which became very well known, involved a foreign woman and a south-Indian lady. She was the same woman who had been entrusted with milk distribution. She also had other foodstuffs and articles for distribution, such as oil, soap, sugar, towels, and cloth. But she would always cheat. Her other fellow foreign inmates never liked her. Therefore, she had befriended the Indians and was closer to them. She learned Hindi, wore a sari, applied bindi on her forehead, and declared herself to be Hindustani. She had a boyfriend whom she had long declared to be her husband. Both had been convicted and sentenced to ten years for a drug trafficking offense.

Then suddenly in jail, she stopped meeting with her declared husband on permitted family visiting days and said he was nobody to her. She developed a strong lesbian relationship with another woman prisoner. Both of them were staying in the same barrack and all the women knew of their relationship. When it became better known, one sensible officer, Darshan Lal, came and separated them and lodged them in separate barracks. She created a lot of noise, but then it was done. Meanwhile, when her husband heard of all this, he was enraged and tried to forcibly enter the women's ward to give his wife a bashing. The situation was somehow saved by all of us.

The prison atmosphere, with its undercurrents of violence, tension, bitterness and distrust, had an adverse psychological impact on the children staying with their mothers. The claustrophobic conditions drastically curtailed their natural instincts to play and run about. One official, who worked closely with these children, said:

They were not children; they were little monsters. They were abusive like adults and spoke the language of violent criminals, saying, "I will kill you," "I will murder you," or "I will shoot you." One day we overheard two children talking with each other: "Let Chandni come out and I will stab her in the stomach." Even at less than four years of age, they were committing homosexual acts and making sexual advances. On being scolded they would verbally abuse us and throw stones at us. They were even violent toward the insects and frogs they found in the jail. They would crush them, tear them, burn them, and squeeze them alive. They would pick up live frogs and throw them at us. No one could handle them.

Adolescent Prisoners: A Class Apart

One of the saddest aspects of Tihar was over 1,200 un-supervised young boys. They were a diverse group: scared, introverted, bullied, terrorized, fun-loving, indifferent, and homesick. They had nothing to do the whole day, so they gambled, fought, abused and bullied each other, smoked, and gossiped. There was not a single recreational activity in their wards.

Often boys looking older than twenty or younger than sixteen found their way into the adolescent ward. Both created problems. The youngest were in danger of being exploited, and the older boys tended to become bullies. To compound this difficult situation, the staff on these wards had no training for their special needs. Like their elders, these boys essentially administered themselves. The senior-most, biggest criminal among them was in charge. He and his cronies took roll calls, extorted money, allocated sleeping space, and controlled all other activities of their idle lives.

Those not part of the in-group had no recourse. The staff was not receptive. There was no outside help in the form of a counselor or a psychologist to listen to them. Many lacked the resources to make bail; the families of some were not even aware that they were in prison. Help was available only for a price, and for the poor there was none.

About 80 percent of the youngsters were nearly illiterate. Most of them had dropped out of school for lack of interest. None of them, including the literate, had any respect for school. In fact, they had nothing but contempt. There was no educational material in their barracks and no concept of schooling them inside the prison. They had no idea of what was happening in the larger world, and their world was a hellhole of illiteracy and ignorance.

The adolescents were in jail for a range of crimes, including murder, kidnapping, stabbing, drug peddling, burglary, street thefts, household thefts, and even rape. They were also in for minor offenses such as ticketless travel. While the ratio of those officially accused of violent crimes to lesser offenders was one to ten, in fact about 80 percent admitted committing thefts or violent crimes. It is worth noting that 30 percent were habitual drug users. Some had been shoved into jail for vagrancy or insolent behavior toward the police. Others were mere accomplices to seasoned criminals who managed to elude the long arm of the law. Further statistical analysis disclosed that one out of ten adolescents appeared to be innocent but had been hauled in along with others, paying the price for keeping bad company.

The majority of adolescents tended to justify their misdeeds. Emotions like remorse or repentance did not exist in their psyche. One of the more competent superintendents, Tarsem Kumar, conducted a survey that made some startling revelations. The study revealed that 90 percent of the young inmates had only one goal: that is to be rich. They wanted to make money without working for it; and they wanted entertainment without any work or responsibility. The magnitude of wealth and the nature of the accompanying trappings desired by these adolescents varied from one to another. The pinnacle of success for one was to own a fabulous house, luxurious furniture, electronic gadgets, and a chauffeur-driven limousine. Of course, they wanted all this to be showered from heaven. They were not particularly interested in achieving their goals by studying or any kind of hard work. They seemed to believe that the only important thing in life was to make money by any means—legal or illegal.

A random group of teenaged inmates was given three options: (a) they would be given work and paid double the market rate for their products or services; (b) they would have no work but would be paid 10 percent more than what they needed for a living; and (c) they would be expected to work hard and get paid according to their output. True to form, 93 percent of the respondents chose the second option where they would not be given any work but would be paid 10 percent more than what they needed for a living. Only 3 percent went for the third option, where they would be required to work hard and be paid according to their output. The rest preferred the first option.

All the adolescent prisoners were ready to do anything for 100,000 rupees, even commit murder. These youngsters displayed shrewdness and fast thinking. They stated they would take the money, but instead of murdering the victim, they would claim that they tried their best to kill him but failed. Such tactics, they claimed, led to crime prevention.

In answer to the question would they like to be Superintendent, Deputy Superintendent, or Assistant Superintendent, they chose the Assistant Superintendent, the lowest of the three posts of prison service ranks. This preference, according to them, was because the Assistant Superintendent wielded the maximum power that could be used or rather misused to make money for himself or to seek favors from the gangsters. Being closest to the prisoners, the Assistant Superintendent had the most opportunities to take advantage of situations. Finally, on being asked to choose between money and mental peace, the adolescents replied that money and mental peace were inseparable. They asserted that without money there could be no mental peace.

On the playing field, none of the adolescent prisoners could bear the thought of losing. They tried to win by any means. Inevitably, brawls occurred, which in turn created an atmosphere of tension and distrust. Nevertheless, sports were always preferred to the dull academic grind.

Most of the adolescent prisoners came from rural backgrounds and had migrated to urban centers like Delhi.

Dazzled by the glitter and glamour of high society flaunted in films and on television, they dreamed of gaining entry into its hallowed precincts of wealth and power. They were overpowered by desire for the latest status symbols, such as fashionable clothes, trendy cars, and cellular phones, and with a bevy of beautiful girls in tow.

About 10 percent of the adolescent prison population stated that they did not have any relatives or friends in the outside world who could provide for them. They felt that they were permanently trapped in the vicious cycle of crime-arrest-jail-release-crime. Of those who had families, many were willing to give up even their parents if a rich man agreed to adopt them and provide them with all the luxuries of life. About 20 percent blamed their parents for their wrongdoings and for bringing them into a world of poverty, hunger, and deprivation.

Almost 80 percent of the adolescent prisoners were slum dwellers. Such juveniles harbored the illusion that after being released they could make a massive one-time strike and accumulate a lot of money. Even if they were caught, they would be able to afford to purchase their release. If that was not possible, they could at least lead a comfortable life inside the jail just like some resourceful adults had managed to do.

Many adolescents were apprehensive, and quite genuinely so, about having a reputation as a jailbird. They felt they would be convenient scapegoats for the police, who could charge them for crimes that they did not commit. Most of the adolescent inmates declared that they would definitely prefer to be rehabilitated outside Delhi, where they could begin a new life with a new identity.

On the whole, most adolescent prisoners were basically hedonistic in their outlook and prepared to indulge in illegal activities to fulfill their sole objective of making fast money. They were also not inclined to give up their addictions, be it drugs or gambling. They were unwilling to accept any argument, however cogent, that was contrary to their views. They idled away their days in gossip, and there was no prison schedule to educate or reform them, no outlet for their adolescent energy and no schedule of physical exercise or yoga.

There were very few female adolescent prisoners, only 1 to 5 percent of the total population. Their crimes were sex trafficking and street theft. While the girls were more inclined to feel shame and remorse, most of the boys boasted shamelessly about their crimes. The boys were on the road to becoming professionals.

The young offenders had suffered from a life of neglect, and the prison environment aggravated this problem. A consistent, positive environment, based on discipline, hard work, and proper usage of time, was the only hope for reform. And that required a whole new mind-set in the prison regime. To bring about a change like that was a huge challenge.

Foreign Prisoners

Foreign prisoners in Tihar hailed from the United States and various countries of Asia, Africa, and Europe. Like the women, the foreign inmates in Prison 1 were a picture of neglect and apathy. Dumped in an alien and hostile environment, they were woefully short of the basic essentials. At least the United States and European embassies showed care and concern for prisoners from their countries, and those prisoners had visitors once a fortnight. Others were hardly ever visited.

Many foreign inmates were unconvicted prisoners in cases relating to drug trafficking and were stuck in the judi-

The inmate population of Tihar included a significant number of foreigners from all over the world.

cial tangle, often for five to seven years. Ironically, the maximum sentence for drug-related offenses, if declared guilty, was ten years plus a fine of 100,000 rupees (about US$2,000). Here is what Syed Zubair Ahmed of *The Times of India* had to say about his visit to the prison in early June 1993:

> Many undertrials of foreign nationalities are languishing in Tihar Jail for several years while their cases drag on in courts. Of the 100 foreigners, including 30-odd women, only a few have been convicted. In most trials, witnesses have not even been cross-examined. In some cases, trials have yet to begin. These undertrials belong to various countries, including Nigeria, the United States, Spain, Afghanistan, and Germany.
>
> What makes their plight grimmer is the fact that most of these undertrials have been charged with committing non-violent crimes. A large number of them are facing charges of peddling narcotics. Some have been put behind bars for overstaying and some for traveling on forged passports.

Foreign prisoners were lodged in Ward 9 of Jail 1. There were 10 convicted prisoners and about 115 waiting for trial. Convicted prisoners were lodged separately from the undertrial prisoners. The undertrial foreign prisoners were in no better condition than their Indian counterparts as far as their lodging was concerned. The only difference was that Indian undertrial prisoners languished in big barracks housing about 200 people while the foreign inmates lived 5 or 6 together in 8-foot-by-8-foot cells. Blacks and Caucasians were housed separately to avoid conflicts. Most of the foreign convicts and undertrials spoke broken Hindi, which they had learned in jail. Drugs were available for the rich, and the poor paid for drugs with labor. The verbal credit system for drugs was in vogue. Interest on borrowed drug money varied with the nationality of the inmate and the color of his skin. Prepayment for drugs, non-delivery of drugs, and quality of drugs was the major causes of scuffles among the foreign prisoners. These fights were never reported to the administration and were sorted out by the prisoners themselves. A part of the money collected by the sale of drugs paid off the lower-ranking security guards under whose protection this business flourished.

The foreigner convict *munshi*, like his Indian counterpart, patronized the jail officers and used his position to extort money and articles from the foreign prisoners. Barring a few exceptions, the foreign prisoners readily appreciated the value of services and paid to buy comforts. The marketing of services was well established. If a newcomer had a couple of dollars he could have two to three paymasters as his servants. The financial aspects of such services were better developed in the foreigners' prisons. Retail loans, leasing, and credit were available in the foreign prisoner culture in contrast to the Indian prisoners' culture.

Foreign prisoners were better disciplined than their Indian counterparts. The foreigners, however, questioned the validity of each decision made by the administration, while the Indians usually accepted whatever came. The Indian prisoners looked for escape while the foreign prisoners looked for ways to free themselves for good by legal means.

The foreign inmates particularly suffered from the prison food. Many found the diet totally inedible. A South African inmate told a tale of woe in a recorded conversation:

The food and environment were not at all congenial
for human beings. The round roasted bread, which
I later came to know as chapatis, were like paper and
could not be consumed. The vegetables were watery
and absolutely insipid. There was no potable water to
drink. Even drinking water had to be bought. Three
people died of cholera and one died because medical
facilities were poor. The attitude of officers was very
bad. They would beat me on trivial matters, like why
I was standing somewhere. I would be humiliated at
the slightest excuse. The jail officers indulged in extortion and harassment.

J. O. of Africa, an inmate since March 1991, described
Tihar as "a Nazi camp," where torture, beating, and extortion were routine. He further stated that the food was
awful but even that was being sold from the mess hall.
When someone did not pay or could not pay, he was beaten
and kicked around like an animal. Organized gangs, with
the connivance of authorities, did the extortion. Living
conditions were inhuman, and many died due to the sheer
carelessness of the authorities.

The fact that authorities did not provide even drinking
water spoke volumes about Tihar's condition. It was a training ground for crime. The officials, on any trivial pretext,
would spark off fights by provoking the members of different gangs. No Inspector General or, for that matter, any officer, came to see us or to speak to us about our problems.
Many were tortured or humiliated because of their religion.

Another inmate, Francis Ortega, from France, recounted
his experiences:

Since November 5, 1988, I have been working in the
prison canteen. Very few things like sugar, biscuits,

and oil were readily available. Raw vegetables were sold to the privileged few who had the money. If you had money you could get anything—good food, bedding, or even drugs. If you did not have money, you would often be beaten. The food was simply not palatable or adequate, but no one could dare ask for more, for he could be beaten or kicked. The jail officials knew there was organized extortion by *goondas* and inmate gangs for they also shared the booty.

The prison warders constantly reminded the foreign inmates who tended to complain that "this is India." One of the inmates named Nigel had been languishing in jail for eight years waiting for trial. He was finally acquitted and left for the United Kingdom. He gave this interview after his release when he came to say good-bye to me:

> I could not reconcile myself to the fact that I had to suffer because I had a different color of skin. I was shoved into prison with only the pants I was wearing. The customs officials kept all my clothes at the airport. They did not let me take even a T-shirt with me. When I came here to Tihar there was no soap, no toothpaste. I had nothing.

The foreign inmates' plight was no different from that of their Indian counterparts. But their agony was magnified due to problems of communication, food habits, cultural differences, lack of visitors, and in some cases, a shortage of money and shabby clothing. Foreign inmates were confronted with several seemingly insurmountable hurdles as far as the legal aspects of their detention were concerned. The gravity of the situation was intensified since most lawyers fleeced their foreign victims to the maximum extent possible. The Indian prisoners could some-how get a relative or friend to persuade, coax, or follow-up with their lawyers to fulfill the contractual obligation of appearing in court on their behalf. But the foreign prison-ers were on record saying that some lawyers just pocketed their money and deserted them. One inmate named Con-way complained:

> I was legally looted by proficient practitioners of the profession. Nine lawyers took me for a merry ride, and, in the process, I lost thousands of rupees, but I still could not get bail. Eventually, I argued my own case before Justice Arun Kumar of the Delhi High Court, despite my lawyers' efforts to prevent me from doing so. They insisted that they alone could put my case before the court, and that the court would allow me only three minutes. Since I had no trust left in them, I wished to plead my case in per-son. I was fed up. To my pleasant surprise, Justice Arun Kumar gave me 75 minutes of hearing.

In the course of his revelations, Conway described in graphic detail how the Crime Branch of the Delhi Police had extorted money from him and how the prosecution had demanded an enormous sum to remain silent.

While Conway was in custody, his father died; but it was two months before he was told. When he learned of his father's death, he wanted to make a telephone call, but even this basic courtesy was denied him. Apparently, his embassy had been instructed not to tell Conway about his father's death until his release. Conway said bitterly, "You pay 500 rupees (about US$10.00) to the police and you can make all the calls you want. Why wait for court permission which will never come?" The court gave Conway his freedom.

In a catalogue of woes, foreign prisoners could add infighting to the list. They had, over the years, succeeded in developing a peculiar subculture, which engendered a malignant form of apartheid. They had developed their own power structures, which had spawned their own brand of prison politics. For instance, a gang of Muslim and Christian blacks ran a flourishing drug trade. They had developed their own network and maintained a record system and even offered credit to each other.

If the unofficial leader of this group was released or transferred, he handed over charge to a groomed successor, and the network continued to function with professional efficiency. Those staff members who had been enticed onto the payroll of the drug pushers were instructed to protect their financiers. However, everything was not smooth sailing. Under the influence of drugs, the inmates sometimes went berserk and committed violent acts. Drug deals also generated violence when too much money was demanded, credit wasn't forthcoming, or when account books were fudged to force addicts to pay more for their fixes. Obviously, the addicts didn't keep track of the transactions, as they were floating around in their own oceans of fantasy.

Foreign prisoners belonging to the affluent countries possessed money, which was kept in their prison property account. They withdrew whatever amount they wanted whenever they wanted under the pretext of paying the lawyers. In reality, this money was siphoned off for promoting the lucrative drug-smuggling business. The drug suppliers ran a sophisticated enterprise.

The drug trade tended to thrive after sunset, under the cover of darkness. The inmates had devised ingenious ways to bring in drugs. The human body was used to the maximum advantage. All possible orifices were employed to conceal the drugs, however filthy they may have been.

Swallowing and regurgitating was another method. The ubiquitous toothpaste containers also came in handy for hiding drugs. The foreign inmates were far too ingenious for the warders, who were in fact ill equipped to staunch the inflow of drugs.

four pillars of reformation

On the Rounds

New to the job, I needed to find a management style. A number of options were obvious to me. One was to ask for situational reports from the respective superintendents of the four prisons in the Tihar complex. On the basis of such reports, we could plan strategies for damage control when trouble erupted. I could conveniently use these reports as a legitimate reason to delay making any plans of action. And if anything went wrong during the probation period, I could defend myself by claiming that I was still new and that it was my predecessors and juniors who were responsible. However, I was eager to address the problems I saw, and I didn't take this approach.

A second option was to hold the Deputy Inspector General and the four superintendents of the jails responsible for everything and make it clear to them that I would haul them up if anything went wrong, since they were the real technical experts of prison management. I could require them to send me daily reports to ensure that everything was going smoothly. I could keep demanding explanations, and passing the buck. I refused to adopt this harassing approach.

The third option was the method former Inspector Generals used—the avoid-involvement-and-know-nothing approach. A former Inspector had instructed the jail Superintendent to carry on with his work as though the office of the Inspector General was "in a distant town outside Delhi." Such a method would have enabled me to claim that I did not know what was happening and that I had sought a report, thus absolving myself of blame if the situation so demanded. This method also was unacceptable to me. One of the officers told me that their main problem was fear of negative publicity, which forced them to give cogent explanations to their superiors, including the court of law. Consequently, they followed the law of minimum intervention and left the day-to-day management of the prison in the hands of the lower ranks, to which they could pass the blame in the event of an error or problem.

A fourth option was to take a great deal of interest in my work and call for daily written reports, but to make an occasional surprise inspection and punish or reward the persons involved accordingly. This method, too, did not seem comprehensive. It is important to mention here that the staff members, barring a few exceptions, were immune to punishment by divulging their confidential reports. Most of the officers had already faced court cases and departmental inquiries, without much effect.

As I saw it, the whole system needed a new approach based on creative understanding, which would evolve as we proceeded. I started by making the rounds, that is, walking around the jails every day along with the Superintendent so that we could see the existing conditions for ourselves. I reached my office by 8:45 a.m.; dropped off the files that I had taken home, and began my rounds by 9 a.m. My schedule exposed those who were habitually late to work, including the doctors, and imposed a new standard on the staff.

The daily morning rounds gave me a unique opportunity to see what was actually happening in the prison. I began to record what I saw and report it to those who were involved. Here are examples from my first formal round of the prison:

> Boards in the Mulaqaat Written Window should be repainted and rewritten neatly.
> (*Action, Superintendent Jails*)
> Clear instructions for frisking visitors should be written on the Notice Board near the Mulaqaat Written Window.
> (*Action, Superintendent Jail 1 and TSP Comdt*)

Toilets, benches, and drinking water must be made available to the visitors.
(Action, Superintendent Jail 1)

Computerization of convict records should be introduced.
(Action, Superintendent Jail 1 and Deputy Inspector General)

Fireproof cabinets for maintaining records should be introduced. Also place fire extinguishers at crucial places for use in emergency.
(Action, Superintendent Jails and Deputy Inspector General)

Issue directions to all superintendents regarding a list of convicts who have served more than half of their sentence. This information is to be compiled by Legal Branch.
(Action, Legal Branch)

Repair of water cooler near the Legal Branch.
(Action, Jail Superintendent 1)

Social Welfare Branch should submit a performance report for 1992–1993 within a week.
(Action Social Welfare Branch)

Provide a yoga teacher for the Women's Ward in Jail No. 1.
(Action, Superintendent Jail 1)

Call the officers of Adult Education Center for women prisoners.
(Action, Superintendent Jail 1)

Prepare a list of teachers among the women prisoners.
(Action, Superintendent Jail 1)

Reconsider time of lockup and lockout at Women's Ward, Jail 1 on Sundays.
(Action, Superintendent Jail 1)

Nursery school should be provided for children.
(Action, Superintendent Jail 1)

Film on Adult Education should be shown to the female prisoners.
(Action, Superintendent Jail 1)

Prisoners in Ward 4 of Jail 1 should be provided medical facilities immediately. Hereafter, the Superintendent of respective jails should take the doctor on duty along on the rounds to attend to the patients and address their grievances.
(Action, Jail Superintendent and Medical Officer)

All Jail Superintendents should start a Rounds Observations Register of their jails. This register shall include the time of visit observations and instructions. They shall also initiate a briefing register for the warders of the respective jails. The briefing registers will include roll call of staff, the briefing, and any specific instructions.
(Action, all Jail Superintendents)

The Tamil Nadu Security Police have been asked to submit a security map and checklist of the jail, and a training program for his battalions.
(Action, Commandant, TSP)

As I entered the prison every day, I encountered groups of prisoners waiting to board the jail van to go to the courts. This was an opportunity for informed conversations. I could ask whether food had been served on time that morning, whether they had water to bathe, whether the bread was fresh, whether the tea served was hot, and whether the doctor was easily accessible in case of an emergency. Many times, I had to resort to a bit of goading and cross-examination to elicit the truth. On the basis of my morning rounds I could detect the changing conditions and whether reforms were taking hold. The groups waiting in the waiting area were representative samples of the whole prison, including inmates from different wards. The news of these conversations circulated through all the wards on their return from the courts. A typical sample of follow-up action from one of these encounters is included with documentation of the daily round:

> The Inspector General asked the prisoners who were waiting to go to courts if they had any problems. They had no complaints about the food or water. Spiritual lectures and physical exercise started in the Women's Ward of Jail 1. There are no water taps in twenty-five cells for B-class prisoners, Jail 1. The Superintendent must install one tap in each cell.
> *(Action, Superintendent Jail 1)*
> Some prisoners denied permission to purchase a wristwatch, radio, newspaper, and magazines. Superintendent, Jail 1, is directed to give them permission to purchase newspaper, magazine, small transistor radio, TV, and wristwatch at their own cost.
> *(Action, Superintendent Jail 1)*
> A call for the medical report of Vinoda Nath Jha has been pending since June 13, 1993. The Resident Medical Officer should explain why this request hasn't been addressed.
> *(Action. RMO-Hospital)*
> Inspection of the kitchen of Jail 3 revealed that the dal was not cleaned before cooking. This is a serious problem and the Superintendent has been asked to meet with kitchen staff of all four jails to put a stop to this unhealthy practice.
> *(Action, Superintendent Jail 3)*

As I walked around the prison, I asked questions and ensured the implementation of earlier decisions. My ongoing presence and follow-up compelled the staff to solve problems. I recorded the results of each round:

In Jail 4, a large number of drains were not covered. The Public Works Department needs to cover them.
(Action, PWD)

Many toilets in Jail 4 are stinking. There should be a system for regular cleaning of the toilets. The sweepers must clean the toilets before the inmates are locked in after the evening roll call.
(Action, all Superintendents)

A number of fans and power outlets are not working, causing hardship to the inmates at the peak of summer. The PWD, Electricity Wing, is requested to provide staff to check for and solve problems.
(Action, PWD, Electricity Wing)

There were many complaints about the misbehavior of Ranjit Singh. The Superintendent should call the Assistant Superintendent to discuss this problem. Misbehavior with inmates is not to be tolerated.
(Action, Superintendent Jail 2)

Ward 4 of Jail 1 is extremely crowded. The Deputy Inspector General should please plan a redistribution of inmates to relieve this situation.
(Action, DIG)

Inmates need exercise. Provide them with volleyballs, tennis balls, cricket bats, carom board, and other sports equipment. The Assistant Superintendent on duty was already instructed to do this. The

superintendent should follow up on this.
(Action, Superintendent Jail No 1)

The inmates asked for a proper letterbox to post outgoing mail. All Superintendents should examine the system and advise the Deputy Inspector General.
(Action, DIG)

News traveled in Tihar like wildfire. The prisoners passed messages or exchanged notes via this "Tihar Express" when they happened to meet one another in judicial lockups. The prisoners from all four prisons mixed in judicial lockup at the courts, which further facilitated inter-prison communications, for better or worse! Hence, day-to-day situations reported and corrected made good news for the prison without any extra effort on our part. It also emboldened inmates to come forward with problems that needed attention, such as patients suffering from serious ailments. They also told us of small covert matters, such as personal items like wristwatches, wallets, belts, and ballpoint pens not being returned by the Delhi policemen who frisked them at the judicial lockup. We found that the police kept no record of such items, which facilitated their misappropriation. Such reports indicated the prisoners were beginning to trust us and expect fair treatment.

For me every round was precious. It made each day more meaningful. My rounds revealed the realities behind the facade and made me fully aware of the challenges I faced. I could see instant solutions to some problems. The heartening fact was that with our encouragement, the mass of prisoners started to provide the answers to their own problems.

Running a prison proved to be a massive exercise in housekeeping. Taking rounds of the prison helped to identify recurring problems. The staff members were on their toes because they didn't know when the management would turn up for a visit! We wanted to make the entire system transparent so that no wrongdoing could be hidden or glossed over.

I recorded my day-to-day observations, both good and bad, on the notepad that I carried with me. After my rounds were over, these observations were typed or photocopied for circulation among all the officials in various prisons. One copy was posted on the prison's notice board. Thus, anyone coming in or going out of the prison could read the observations of the day. The notes truthfully reflected the realities of the prison and were a kind of catalogue of events as they actually were, be it complimentary or embarrassing. Everything was on record and spoke for itself. This proved to be a powerful means of communication and an effective tool for change.

The on-the-round approach greatly increased the degree of accessibility at all levels. The officers who rarely visited the jail were now brought face-to-face with those persons who had to bear the consequences of their policies and decisions. To some extent the red tape vanished! The officers viewed this state of affairs with trepidation. Their actions or inactions were being constantly evaluated by my on-the-rounds observations. I reproduce below a page from my notepad:

- Blackboards need to be provided for proper teaching.
- Strict supervision needs to be kept at study time.
- Bleaching powder needs to be sprinkled regularly in all wards. In case the stores are unable to meet the requirements, jail superintendents may purchase on their own and claim reimbursement from Headquarters.
- Meetings between schools and jail superintend-

ents need to be held. Each school can adopt a ward and provide education, library magazines, and books. In this way each ward could have its own library and educational support and move toward self-sufficiency in educational activities.

- Class examinations are to be held by the end of this week. (All prisons)
- In Jail 4, the pen-making industry should be relocated to the Vocational Wing.
- All staff of the rank of assistant superintendent must be in uniform in the forenoons.
- Garbage in Jail 4 should be removed regularly.
- The courts are to be informed of the request for new trial dates for all who have signed up for the *vipassana* meditation course.
- There was a complaint that the doctor on night duty did not attend the call promptly last night. Jail Superintendent is to look into this and report the reasons for delay to me in the evening.
- I visited the canteen of Jail 1. Canteen operator complained about the scarcity of water. The Administration Officer is directed to issue a tank to the canteen to store water and to ensure that the tanker fills it up on a regular basis.
- I also visited the kitchen of Jail 1. It was clean and better kept.

The basic objective of the rounds was to find practical and realistic solutions to specific, tangible problems for all categories of prisoners, keeping in mind the ominously rigid prison hierarchy. Appropriately, many such decisions and the implementation strategies were modified on the basis of the feedback given by the prisoners or the staff during my rounds.

For example, during one of the morning rounds, I noticed an inmate with rashes on his face. When I questioned him, he said the blade used by the prison barber was rusted and caused the irritating rashes. We re-evaluated the entire system of personal hygiene. We decided to introduce twin-blade cartridges and encouraged the inmates to shave by themselves. We also decided to make antiseptics more readily available and went on to install plastic mirrors for the inmates in suitable places where they could not be removed and used for other activities. Further, to ensure personal cleanliness, we launched educational programs. It did not take us long to open a barbershop in each prison.

During another round, a prisoner complained about a doctor who was asking more questions about the crimes committed than the medical problems. An order followed, "Henceforth, no doctor, while examining or treating the patient prisoners, will ask about the nature of crimes the prisoner has committed." The prison had no official psychiatrist, psychologist, or counselor, so what business did the physician have with the crime committed?

Another beneficial result of the rounds was a reduction in the number of court appeals. Inmates were more confident that their pleas and entreaties would be heard within the prison, so they didn't need to rush to the court for redressal. Previously, prisoners frequently petitioned the courts, sometimes on farcical grounds, and the superintendents and other officials were compelled to appear regularly before the magistrates and judges. In fact, the jail officials ended up defending themselves against various allegations made by the prisoners. Now, the officials were present in the prison and used their time for better supervision and positive intervention.

When we detected prisoners needing immediate medical attention, they were rushed to the prison hospital. If we came across ill-clad or shoddily attired prisoners, we found better clothes for them from community donations. If prisoners needed legal assistance, they were referred to the appropriate legal aid cell, which visited the prison regularly. The list could go on. We wanted prisoners to trust the administration for their genuine needs, and we wanted the system to respond with compassion and sensitivity.

One of the most visible benefits of the rounds technique was the restoration of security. Inmates began to feel that the administration of Tihar cared for them, and they would not let them be victims of negligence and apathy anymore. From the observations of September 9, 1993:

> I visited the women's ward and saw the handicraft work. The teacher needs more machines, clothes, and other supplies. The Superintendent should arrange these supplies.
> *(Action, Superintendent Jail)*
>
> I visited Ward 5 and inspected the cells. We need to arrange regular canteen visit here as discussed with the Superintendent Jail 1.
> *(Action, Superintendent Jail 1)*
>
> I saw the adult education class in Ward 6. The prisoners asked for more books and pencils.
> *(Action, Deputy Inspector General)*
>
> From the visit it is evident that the staff, particularly the Assistant Superintendents, are taking interest in their work. This is a very good trend.

By now, the prisoners knew that we meant business on the rounds. Their appreciation and enthusiasm gave us our first crucial breakthrough in restructuring the internal environment of the prison. Gradually the prisoners appeared happier and more relaxed.

Potential brawls and riots were nipped in the bud. We could gauge volatility in the prisoners fairly accurately after the rounds, and if necessary, we could quickly intervene and defuse the situation before it got out of control. During my two-year tenure at Tihar, there was not a single case of organized violence except for a couple of minor scuffles, which were instigated by a few officers opposed to the transformation taking place in Tihar. As a result of our persistent endeavors, we could isolate individuals who were hostile and try our best to help them. Many problems were addressed on the spot during the rounds. Only my observations were circulated, since these had policy implications.

I held my daily meetings with the Deputy Inspector General and the Superintendents over tea during which we discussed our observations. These observations also dominated our weekly meetings with assistant superintendents. Since the recorded observations provided irrefutable evidence of the activities in the jail, the officers were open to explanation and correction. The corrections led us to an exchange of ideas and greater understanding of each other's viewpoints. The resulting team spirit became a powerful force to motivate the lower-ranking staff to accept innovative and reformative measures.

I cannot imagine how such an institution could be run with a hands-off approach. Even with the state-of-the-art gadgets, such as video cameras at every nook and corner to monitor the prisoners' activities, or robots to cater to the prisoners' needs, direct intervention is absolutely necessary to make an institution serve as a reservoir of hope and reassurance. In my close observations of jail systems in different parts of the world, I have found that wherever management is interactive, the institutions produced better results. Wherever remote control was the norm, there were frequent brawls, riots, and attempted escapes. Direct human interaction during the rounds of the prison was the road to reform.

Championing a Cause: The Petition Box

Effective as they were, the rounds had limitations. Above all, we needed to ensure that we controlled the system, not the other way around. The prison management did not have a reliable operational system of communication with inmates to counteract the gossip network. Management's habitual attitude was marked by secrecy, callousness, and indifference. Therefore, inmates were unlikely to confide in officials. Inmates had no means to air their grievances, or a forum where they could collectively bring their difficulties to the notice of the authorities. Although complaint boxes could be found hanging on the prison walls, hardly anyone used them.

Not understanding how the cumbersome jail system functioned, I introduced a prisoners' complaint register within two days of taking charge. One register was to be available in each ward for recording the inmates' grievances. This meant that each superintendent would be responsible for twelve to fourteen registers. Eventually, I realized that this was an unrealistic expectation and I would have to check the forty-odd registers everyday myself, which was physically impossible.

Moreover, a large percentage of the prisoners were either illiterate or poorly literate and could not put their grievances in writing. Finally, we introduced the mobile petition box. Each prison had an 8-inch-by-4-inch green box, which was carried to the inmates in their barracks. The box was locked, and the key was in the custody of my office. Four constables were assigned to take the petition box to the four prisons and into the wards at scheduled times.

We introduced this system with an explanation of its importance and asked for prisoner input so we could address genuine complaints.

The mobile petition box system went into operation on June 1, 1993, exactly thirty days after I came to the prison. The petition officer was not part of the jail staff; he hailed from the Delhi Administration Secretariat Services. Therefore, he could be objective and fearless in pointing out problems that might concern his prison colleagues. As the petition officer, he alone had the key to the box. His job was to log the petitions, categorize and prioritize them, and bring them to me personally. He and I discussed the contents and decided on priority action. This could mean an urgent personal search of a person or a barrack. It could also mean immediate help to a prisoner, be it medical or otherwise; putting a staff member under watch; visiting an inmate who was depressed; or move to prevent an imminent breach of peace within a barrack.

All the petitions except those that were confidential or needed immediate emergency action were sent to the Jail Superintendent. He handled them personally and asked the ward officers to address the complaints, which ranged from the irregularity of barber's visits to the misbehavior of staff or inmates, water scarcity, and lack of medicines or doctors.

During the daily tea meetings with the senior officers, we briefly discussed trends in the petitions. Each Jail Superintendent was eager to hear the observations of the morning rounds as even a single petition could lead to collective problem solving with prisonwide implications. The other staff waited for policy announcements after the tea meetings. They knew that these were team decisions and that implementation was mandatory. The petitions became in many ways the basis for continuous correction and innovation.

The first month we received 231 petitions about medical problems, 68 on staff corruption, 23 on inmate corruption, 25 on problems concerning food, 19 on shortage of water, 13 on electricity, and 134 on miscellaneous matters, such as the need for police protection for the families of the inmates, welfare needs, and transfers between prisons. These petitions, along with rounds, became the basis for reforming the prison. Here is an excerpt from a report that appeared in *The Hindu:*

> A prisoner in Jail 4, Ward No. 3, in Tihar wants a fellow prisoner to be shifted elsewhere as he was "fomenting communal tensions." The man claims to be a leader of Hindus and is always fighting. "Please, madam, do justice by transferring this person. Everybody fears him, so no one wants to report." The complaint, which was put in the mobile petition box, has now been entered in the Prisoners' Grievances Register and has been brought to the notice of the Inspector General, Prisons. An enquiry is on.
>
> Another prisoner, a woman, requests in writing that her husband, who is also in the jail, be shifted from a particular ward because "smack was being sold there and he might become an addict." Not only is the person shifted, the Jail Administration takes steps to ensure that contraband is not sold.
>
> A convict under the NDPS Act has a suggestion on how to stop the use of narcotics inside the jail. The suggestion is simple, he writes. "Just remove the silver foil from the cigarette packets that are sold in the jail. Without the foil, the addict cannot light up." The suggestion is taken and the Inspector General recommends a reward for him. Another prisoner is rewarded with an extra cake of bathing soap and washing soap for his suggestions

on how to save on electricity and vegetables.

Nothing unusual about complaint chits and applications put in the petition box. The unusual part is that every complaint or grievance is now brought to the notice of a gazetted officer in the jail administration.

The petition box became a spotlight on the problems in the prison. In the first six months, we attended to 2,279 petitions. Each petition was carefully scrutinized, and I expected appropriate action for each. Also, I personally acknowledged and replied to each petition before the respective Superintendent followed it up. Here is an order I issued:

> In the officers' meeting today it was clearly evident that Jails 1 and 4 are not paying adequate attention to the petitions and redressal of grievances. Hereafter all Gazetted Officers, including superintendents, must read the petitions sent to them and devise a method of prompt disposal. Consider using the procedure of Jail 3. Improvement in this regard will be discussed in the next officer's meeting.

I insisted the superintendents take the petitions seriously. It was important to win the trust and respect of the inmates for the system. It did not matter what kind of paper they used or what language they wrote in or who they were. What was important was how much confidence they had and how willing they were to share grievances and provide us with valuable and sensitive information.

We devised a system of sending printed reply cards as proof that I had read the inmate's petitions. These reply cards were usually sent to the petitioners the next day through the constables or clerks who went to the various prisons with the petition box. The card carried my personal observations in response to the inmate's petition and a suggestion for action by the inmates and the staff. In this manner, the petitioners knew that their complaints were heard. For instance, if the petitioner stated that he was not getting proper medication, I would write on the card: "Please go and see the doctor and show the doctor this card." On the same card, I also wrote a small note for the doctor to ensure that the inmate's problem was solved. The concerned inmate would go to see the doctor, and the warder would not stop him from going because he had a card. The doctor gave special attention to the inmate in view of the instructions. The same inmate, if still not satisfied, could write again through the petition box. This usually led to intervention at a senior level. Sometimes, I asked the doctor why the patient was complaining repeatedly.

Confidential petitions remained in my custody or with the petition officer. We used confidential information very carefully to ensure that the informer was not exposed. We verified and cross-checked this type of information on the rounds or in some other way. Through this confidential method, we obtained useful information about staff behavior and the corruption patterns. This system eventually resulted in exposing corrupt members of the staff. Some were forced to retire. Some others were arrested and became inmates in the same jail!

When the follow-up action on the petitions proved adequate, it enhanced hope and respect for the system and it also simultaneously reduced the number of complaints. Previously, loss of hope and faith reduced the number of petitions, but with due attention paid from the entire hierarchy, one could conclude the decline in number of complaints was genuine. Similarly, a jump in the number of petitions required urgent analysis and attention from the administration. A comparison of the number of complaints received in June 1993 with November 1994 petitions shows a marked decline.

	June 1993	Nov. 1994
Medical	231	13
Staff misbehavior	68	4
Inmate misbehavior	23	7
Food	25	1
Water	19	3
Electricity	13	3
Miscellaneous	134	52

Without the petition box, we would have been unable to remove apathy and negligence. We also would never have been able to get the inmates to participate in a system for which they had no respect.

The mobile petition box was like a mirror that reflected all the activities within the jails. Any nefarious or underhanded activity was brought to light. I was aware that the box could be misused, but this did not happen at Tihar. As the system stabilized, we received about thirty petitions every day. We used the box to evaluate our work as to whether we were making progress or had regressed. The petitions also became the focus of the evening congregation of the prisoners, provoking discussions about hygiene, sanitation, storing and distributing food, and sharing books.

The staff also joined the prisoners in voicing their grievances through the petition box. A security guard wrote to me, saying, "My neighbor has six buffaloes, which he ties in the garden in front of my quarter. The garden should have been a playground for our children and a place of recreation for the residents, but no one dares to enter it. The accumulation of garbage has made it a breeding place for mosquitoes. We are all suffering because of him. Madam, we are sure that you will help us." In response I initiated a survey, which revealed a total of forty-two buffaloes, sixteen cows, and thirty-eight instances of unauthorized construction in the government living complex. We discussed this matter in a staff meeting, and the security guards who kept the buffaloes and cows requested time to move their cattle. We settled on a deadline of August 15, 1993. After that the Municipal Corporation of Delhi would confiscate their cattle. They removed the cattle but not the unauthorized construction. A bulldozer was arranged and the constructions were demolished.

But the scope of the petition box was not restricted to complaints and grievances. The petition box also brought letters of thanks from the inmates and served as a means for expressing feelings through prose or poetry. Such constructive activities instilled a sense of participation within the prison life. As the box moved closer to its first birthday, poetry reached us almost daily. We compiled poems by Akram Chacha, *Tanhaiyon ke Jungle (Jungles of Loneliness)* and *Dukhtar-e-Hind (Daughter of India),* and published them with the help of India Vision Foundation, an organization involved in prison reform.

The petition box became an information box. It revealed contraband entering the prison, the price at which it was being sold, and the players and names of the staff members believed to be involved in this racket. It became an audit box, for it exposed hypocrisy and misbehavior and divulged the names of the offenders. It became a response box as all that came in was carefully documented and the writer received an acknowledgement. Nothing was hidden anymore! Finally, it became a magic box without which Tihar prison could not have evolved into a place of reformation. But Tihar was still far from being an ashram.

Creating Security: Internal Management

Within a week of assuming charge of Tihar, I called for a meeting with all the staff of all ranks not on duty. I shared my views and explained the rationale from what I had done in this first week. Also, I encouraged the staff members to express their opinions freely and frankly. In the first week, the observations noted during the rounds had made a difference, especially after they were prominently displayed on the jail notice board. I also circulated my observations to the various prison superintendents and to the Secretariat, including the office of the Lieutenant Governor of Delhi.

The first five days of these observations carried instructions to the staff concerning different aspects of prison administration, like guidelines for visitors and providing essential facilities such as seating arrangements, toilets, and drinking water. The observations also carried instructions to urgently identify teachers to start literacy classes, especially for women and their children; to improve medical facilities; to propose a plan for time management of the prisoners; and to arrange for clothes to be distributed among poor inmates. One of my first orders was to require the superintendents to maintain a daily work diary.

The work diary was to indicate the wards visited in the morning and evening, the petitioners heard, other inspections, staff briefings, meetings, night rounds, and other activities. The daily work diary was submitted to my office, where it became part of the superintendent's performance file.

On my rounds, I had also recorded the gross inadequacy of essential amenities for the staff members. I came across the practice of subletting government quarters. It was important for me to inspire and motivate the staff to do their best to improve conditions in the jail in spite of various constraints. I also set deadlines for meeting objectives. Some of the staff members were cynical, and felt that my actions, including calling an all-staff meeting were unacceptable. These conservatives thought that the status quo had to be maintained at all costs. The staff became nervous about my daily rounds, fearing exposure of their misbehavior and loss of their control. However, they all attended the staff meetings, perhaps more out of curiosity than cooperation.

The first meeting turned out to be more than well attended; in fact, nearly 500 people were there. In addition to the regular staff members, the Tamil Nadu Special Police contingent, the Public Works Department officials, and an assortment of other individuals came. A feeling of bonhomie charged the atmosphere. Everybody anticipated winds of change, but no one knew how powerful these winds would be. In my first few days in office, I had challenged the timeless traditions of Tihar. Naturally, not everybody was amused. But everyone was curious about whether the changes would continue. Consequently, I could sense both excitement and anxiety.

The Deputy Inspector General set the ball rolling by describing two kinds of major problems faced by the jail administration. The first set of problems related to career advancement, shortage of security guards, and low morale of the staff. The second category of problems included the unhygienic and subhuman living conditions of the staff, and lack of space in the government-provided accommodations. Then Superintendent K. R. Kishore suggested that Tihar should work toward becoming a role-model prison. Kishore's suggestion gave me an opportunity to expand on this theme. During the course of this meeting, it was obvious that the staff was eager to participate. The general mood indicated that many of them would welcome a change in the functioning of Tihar. I noted the experiences, opinions, and suggestions of the staff members and then explained my own views.

Apparently, it was the first time in the history of Tihar that the mission, goals, and objectives of the institution were stated, and steps to achieve the goals were defined. We also discussed strategies. "The use of force," I explained, "will only increase hostility and anger. The collection of a few currency notes by illegal means will continue to demean Tihar as an institution. We need to conduct ourselves in a manner that increases honor and respect for the work we do. Each one of us shall have to work hard as a team. From merely keeping security we must create security. From watchmen, we must become educators. Above all, we must set about improving communication among the staff and officers." We were like relay runners that had to pass the baton efficiently to the next runner, for the entire team had to win the race.

We resolved to meet at regular intervals to review the progress toward our goals. During my remaining tenure at Tihar, many more fruitful meetings were held. Some meetings were formal, but many were informal and included families of the staff who were staying within the jail's residential complex. Family gatherings usually took place during religious festivals or social events. Sometimes, specific issue-related meetings were held, for example, to discuss the welfare of family members or education for the children. Within a few months, we set up a children's library within the staff residential complex. The Delhi Public Library generously provided the infrastructure and the books, and the children enthusiastically used the library facilities. Later, we also set up a toy room for the younger children.

The residential complex had a double-story built-in community center, which was lying abandoned. We asked the Public Works Department to make essential repairs and restore the lights, fans, and water. In this building we later brought in a women's vocational training center, a dispensary, and a counter of the Indian Bank. We also cleared the jungle around it to make a children's park within the residential complex and persuaded our friends in the Rotary and Lions Clubs to donate sports equipment. This was just the beginning.

We developed systems to help those whose performance was not up to mark. We tried to inspire the staff. For example, we decided that warders, including head warders, who were closest to the prisoners all day, would serve not only as security but also would organize various activities such as prayer, yoga, exercise, gardening, and education classes in their wards. To encourage performance, the daily reports from each of the wards were displayed on the jail notice boards. These reports revealed the progress in each ward. The individuals responsible were rewarded, others felt compelled to change, and still others were motivated to experiment.

Eventually, the performance of all the warders and head warders improved despite the absence of financial incentives. This change at the grassroots level signaled a revival. I still remember how each of the security staff would come to the *deodhi* to see if his name was on the notice board. Whenever someone's name appeared on the notice board, he felt proud and told all his acquaintances and family members. The news spread in all the prisons through the "Tihar Express."

Other changes in management involved regular evaluation at four levels. The first was the level of the Security Police. The head of the police and I met daily for a short working lunch in my office to solve personnel problems. The second level involved tea sessions with the DIG and the superintendents. These meetings focused on what was happening inside the prisons. Since I was inspecting all the prisons, I was in a good position to compare notes, participate in discussions, and suggest improvements. The third level was that of the deputy superintendents and ranks below, whom I met over a cup of tea in the afternoons in their respective prisons, rather than summon them to my office. These sessions were used to discuss and review strategies. Here is an example:

> Applications from visitors for mulaqaat with men after 10 a.m. and women after 11 a.m. will not be entertained. Only applications coming from outside will be entertained until 11:30 a.m. with proof of travel.
> *(Action, Superintendents)*
> Start the construction of visitors' waiting room. Executive Engineer, PWD (Civil) is requested to start the waiting room as soon as possible.
> *(Action, Executive Engineer [Civil])*
> Shortage of sweepers. Administrative Officer to make a proposal to increase the number of sweepers and barbers for all jails as per requirements of each ward.
> *(Action, AO)*
> Sports complex for staff. Administrative Officer to make a proposal for a sports complex in Jail Training School.
> *(Action, AO)*

The fourth level was our weekly review, in which all officers came together to assess the week. As an example, here is the outcome of one such meeting:

- The night round of the officers should begin from 11 p.m. and continue until milk distribution in the morning.
- The room of Mr. Garg, DS-II, Jail 1, will be the

night officer's room. When the officer is not on his job, he will be available in Mr. Garg's room.

- All Deputy Superintendents will briefly report on work done during the week in the next Monday meeting. A proforma is circulated with this order.
- In the weekly meeting with Assistant Superintendents, they will also report on their work during the week.

During the course of all the foregoing interactions, discussions were free and frank. Many suggestions and innovations emerged, some of which led to policy formulations. This was one such order:

I get a large number of complaints daily concerning unjustified detention of inmates despite the receipt of release orders. It is hereby directed that no inmate whose release orders have been received will be detained on technical grounds without the specific approval of the Jail Superintendents. The Assistant Superintendent will send the case to the Deputy Superintendents and the Deputy Superintendent will correct the situation if he can and then place the case before the Superintendent of Jails for orders and information. To expedite matters, any release order that the office thinks cannot be executed on technical grounds will be put up to the Jail Superintendent through the Deputy Superintendent at the earliest possible time so that the decision can be made without delay. It is also expected that the Jail Superintendent will send the concerned court a photocopy of the defective release order encircling the error committed. This will enable the Magistrate to know the kind of errors their staff are committing, and how those errors are causing undue hardship to inmates waiting for release. The above orders may be kindly and strictly complied with.

We enjoyed these sessions because they eliminated lurking suspicions, nagging doubts, and latent bitterness. All decisions, which were worthy of further review and implementation, were recorded. These meetings and the resulting interactions guaranteed implementation of decisions because they emerged after a thorough discussion with all of us in total agreement. Within a few months, we had a comprehensive and workable communication network and a progressive and professional management. We tried to create an environment where work was both challenging and fulfilling. Informal lunch and tea meetings with my officers helped create a relaxed environment for vital reforms. A feeling of mutual trust traveled from the top down, making each employee understand that he was a crucial part of the whole system. Each member of the organization was of equal importance to us.

We also did all that was possible to upgrade the skills and broaden the capabilities of the staff through systematic training programs and varied work experience. The superintendents and deputy superintendents conducted in-house training programs for the staff up to the level of assistant superintendent during the quiet period between 1 p.m. and 3 p.m. when the prison was officially locked. Occasionally, I went to class to see for myself how the training was progressing. I was thrilled to see free discussion. This was the only training for some officers. Our resources were so scarce, we couldn't afford to send staff away for training.

We were, however, able to send a few assistant superintendents to regional centers outside Delhi for training in modern penology and criminology. Assistant superintendents, deputy superintendents, and the superintendents were sent to the headquarters of the vipassana meditation center for courses in vipassana meditation. They shared their experiences in our weekly meetings. It was a source of great joy for me to see growing self-confidence and self-esteem among my staff members.

The sensitivity level of our workforce also increased with self-evaluation tests on the basis of the information received through the petition box. The staff members were told about the petitions referring to them, and then I waited for their responses without giving them a deadline. Within a few months, a questionnaire evolved, which the petition officer gave to randomly selected prisoners. The questions were as follows:

1. When did you last see your Superintendent doing a round of the prison?
    i)   a month ago
    ii) 15 days ago
    iii) a week ago
    iv) yesterday
    v)   this morning

2. When did your Superintendent invite you to a group discussion or seminar?
    i)   15 days ago
    ii) last week
    iii) not yet
    iv) What is this group discussion or seminar?

3. When did your Deputy Superintendent last visit
   your ward?
   i)   7 days ago
   ii) 3 days ago
   iii) yesterday
   iv) this morning

4. When does your Assistant Superintendent check
   the morning educational classes?
   i)   He does not come at all.
   ii) He comes once a week.
   iii) He comes two to three times a week.
   iv) He comes daily.

5. How does your Warder/Head Warder treat you
   when you go to him with a problem?
   i)   I don't go as he uses abusive language.
   ii) He is totally indifferent and does not listen
        to our problems.
   iii) He listens to the problems but provides
        no solution.
   iv) He not only listens to the problems but also
        provides reasonable solutions acceptable to all,
        and his behavior is good.

We strengthened this open audit with team inspections
of each prison and by circulating the results to all. The result? Each superintendent along with his team was trying to
be the best. This positive competition made them responsible, built teams, and brought about compassion in dealing
with problems of the prisoners. It also brought attention to
personnel problems and the needs of the workforce. The superintendents were advised to maintain a cooperative attitude at the workplace. Though we encouraged a healthy
competition between prisons, it was clear to everyone that

the spirit behind this endeavor was a collective cooperative.

I was also aware of financial costs of forced honesty. Thanks to a counseling volunteer, S. K. Sikka, who responded to our television program on Tihar, a filter-manufacturing unit opened in an abandoned but safe building on the periphery of the complex. Over sixty women and wives or daughters worked in the unit to supplement their household income.

The staff started coming up with innovative ideas. For example, an assistant superintendent introduced the concept of *prabhat pheri* (morning round). A team of 10 to 12 prisoners circled the entire inner periphery of the jail in the early hours of the morning with soft musical instruments, singing devotional songs at the crack of dawn to wake up sleeping prisoners. Contrast this with the previous practice of waking up the prisoners by striking a heavy bunch of keys against the iron grills.

The warders, who were in direct and constant contact with the prisoners through *panchayats,* or prison councils, reported to the assistant superintendents who reported to the deputy superintendents. The deputy superintendents also made their own on-the-rounds observations, which enabled them to accurately assess the reports they received.

The prison began to operate on the principle of responsibilities prevailing over rights. It was a beautiful feeling. Innumerable activities kept all of us busy and instilled a profound sense of achievement. Our goal was to return to society individuals who were willing to acknowledge their responsibilities and obligations toward the community.

Along with the prisoners, the lower-ranking staff was turning the corner. Many warders enrolled in the National Open School, which had opened a branch inside the prison. Many officers looked for post-graduation courses, including courses in computer science, in the newly opened center of IGNOU (Indira Gandhi National Open University) within the prison. The educational facilities were extended to the families of the staff members and children as well. We coined an appropriate slogan for our staff: *rakshak se shikshak* (from protector to educator).

Meanwhile, we made huge strides at the Police Headquarters. My colleague, Jaydev Sarangi, from the Delhi Civil Services, was adept at administration. He managed the office, and I managed the field. We shared ideas and analyzed what we observed every day without fail over our brief lunch break, and subsequently followed up in the tea meeting with our superintendents of jails. We teamed up most effectively. Sarangi's excellent office management helped clear hundreds of departmental enquiry files pending for decades! He was ably assisted by a Deputy Superintendent, A. K. Purohit. Sarangi and I cleared arrears in payments, house allotments, seniority lists, issue of uniforms, personal files, recruitment, and rules, etc. The credit for this cleansing lies more with Sarangi than me because he took it upon himself to pursue these matters until he got a favorable order. It was his perseverance that brought computers and cable network to the prison. Tihar became the first prison in India to have both.

Sarangi, however, will always be remembered by the entire staff for two programs he introduced. The first involved insurance coverage for the staff. It was due to Sarangi's unique initiatives that each one of us, with a small contribution of 7 rupees per month, was provided an injury or fatality insurance coverage of 100,000 rupees (about US$2,000). This plan went a long way in redressing the financial grievances of the staff and their family members.

Sarangi's second program pertained to the formation of the Tihar Employees' Welfare Association (TEWA). Through TEWA, Sarangi procured a gas agency for the staff, which supplied cooking gas to the prison. TEWA also ensured regular inputs to the various welfare funds.

Despite all this, we had members of the staff who continued to cause problems. For instance, we arrested a warder for the possession of drugs and for attempting to peddle them inside the jail. He spent a whole year in the company of the people he was previously guarding! A few more cases like this came to light over the next few months. Several warders eventually volunteered to undergo treatment for detoxification.

Yet others carried on their illegal activities despite our preventive efforts. Some continued to be rude and obnoxious in their behavior. The petition box revealed the names and the modus operandi of such offenders. We tried our best to reform them and even sent them for a ten-day meditation program outside Delhi. However, our endeavors seemed to have very little effect. The real remedy was to post these deviants out of Tihar and give them a different kind of work. I did not have the power to do this. We could only make proposals, which took their own time, even to be turned down. Eventually, we had to deal with the delinquent staff as firmly as possible, with warnings and suspensions and sometimes directing them to stay at home and not report for duty. They received their pay for staying away.

On the whole, the staff changed with the reforms, either willingly or under pressure. I saw a great deal of enthusiasm, zeal, and diligence. Note this report of Jail Superintendent K. R. Kishore directing his prison:

i)   Arrange drinking water for the visitors outside the *mulaqaat jungla* and for court prisoners inside the jail.

ii) Provide a tent for visitors for protection from sunstroke.

iii) Introduce a public-address system outside the gate of Jail 1 at release time.

iv) Introduce a system of prayer and yoga in each ward.

v) Distribute clothes to children of Women's Ward and saris to the needy women.

vi) Distribute *khichri* twice daily for the children of Women's Ward.

vii) Free distribution of *pudina lassi* and grams to smack addict prisoners in Ward No. 2 from the Prisoners' Welfare Fund.

viii) Isolate drug peddlers in Ward No. 1.

ix) Arrange material from the Prisoners' Welfare Fund for Adult Education for both men and women.

x) Increase the number of items in the welfare canteen according to the demands of the prisoners.

xi) Introduce hawker system for grams and *daal-moth*.

xii) Purchase musical instruments for the recreation of the prisoners.

xiii) Improve the system of distribution of milk, washing of raw vegetables, and preparation of dal.

xiv) Acid cleaning of toilets.

xv) In future, it shall be our endeavor to introduce all the reformatory systems possible within our means and there shall be a concerted effort toward beautification of the jail, for example, running of fountain, placing of Gandhiji's statue, gardening, flowering, painting, and removal of garbage. We shall prove that this infamous jail is the best model jail of India. Yoga activities will be at large in future early in the morning in the lawn near the *chakkar*, where up to 1,000 inmates can be accommodated at a time.

Tihar improved visibly each day. I knew that the staff was appreciating the change, for it was restoring dignity to their institution and enhancing their self-esteem. But the kind of environment we were creating left few choices for anyone, including myself. It was a question of grit. I knew it was still not time for me to expect a full transformation. Therefore, I had to carry on with motivation and persist ence, with selective and deterrent punishment. Here is one of my orders, which reveals the challenge of change:

> I have asked each prison to submit its In and Out statement daily. This is arriving regularly from some jails while not from the others. Regularity should be kindly ensured. The Superintendent should sign the Out statement so that he is aware of the time that is being spent inside the jail by his subordinates. An analysis of the statement indicates that some officers are not even spending the mandatory eight hours on prison work, and that many officers are taking long breaks in the afternoon, leaving prison at about noon and returning at 4:30 p.m. This is not at all acceptable. Afternoon breaks should not exceed two hours. Officers must return to their stations. Presence in the prison is important and mandatory. This is all the more necessary in view of the winter season when the day is short and the prison closes by 6 p.m. to 7 p.m. These observations should be carefully read, understood, and implemented. Serious note will be taken of officers being absent from their prison work without prior permission.

We had come a long way from keeping security to creating security.

The Media Makes a Difference

In the past the media had been used by prison authorities only when it was convenient for them. Many of the staffers had been departmentally punished for surreptitiously aiding the media, so I issued a standing order for media management to leave no room for ambiguity:

Objective

1. Tihar Jail needs to work toward reformation and correction for all prison inmates so that they can be provided with opportunities for a better future.
2. Tihar Jail has Security and High-Security zones. It also has areas that must be kept out of bounds from visitors, while others can be visited by authorized persons.
3. Similarly, the nature of work also falls into two kinds of activities:
   i) confidential personal information concerning the inmates;
   ii) activities related to prisoner welfare, development, and education.
4. Media coverage can be in the larger interest of the prison and prisoners in economic, educational, and cultural areas.
5. Media exposure will help mobilize community support in developmental activities to the benefit of prisoners and help achieve the objective of humanizing the system.
6. Media exposure will also enable an audit of the performance of the jail management.

Manner of exposure
a) *Written Material*
   Media reporting will not be permitted in the High-Security zone. Also no names of prisoners shall be

mentioned even if the prisoners so desire. Gazetted Officers will accompany the media persons on the round.

Anything reported and not found factually correct shall be promptly rebutted. A record to this effect shall be maintained.

b) Still Photography

As a policy it has been decided that the Directorate of Public Relations (DPR) will make an album of all the welfare, educational, cultural, and developmental activities so that reporters have options to select from the pool.

Any special occasion will be covered preferably by the DPR. In case of urgency a photographer can be hired. The Superintendent will keep negatives in his personal custody.

Journalists and photographers will be permitted only if he or she agrees to abide by the guidelines already issued in this regard.

c) Audiovisual

Movie cameras are permitted, but they shall not be used in any way that compromises security. All films belong to the IG office and will be kept in the custody of the IG office. No film will be released unless previewed and approved by a team of Gazetted Officers. The focus of films will be developmental activities only.

The Superintendent and the Deputy Inspector General will accompany movie teams.

d) Miscellaneous

A monthly in-house *Audio Magazine* prepared by the Jail Administration will carry messages from the Superintendents to the prisoners for both discipline and recreation.

All journalists will be encouraged to visit from 4 to 5:30 p.m. on working days except Sundays. Exceptions can be made for special reasons or exigencies.

All visiting journalists will collect instructions from the Inspector General's office and carry a visitor's pass to visit the jails. The Superintendent of the concerned jail will accompany the journalist. If the Superintendent is not present, the Deputy Superintendent will accompany them.

The intention of the media policy was to provide consistency to our response to media requests. This open policy broke the earlier nexus of buying and selling news, and placed the prison as it was in front of the government, courts, and the community, outside and inside the prison. If it was to be reported, let it be seen and reported, and not briefed or tutored.

The press helped spread the word of the reforms in Tihar, and in so doing, brought us more help and support. They became allies in the transformation process and mobilized the community, including the international community, as well as the legal and administrative systems affecting Tihar.

Bernard Imhasly, New Delhi correspondent of a Swiss daily, *Neue Zurcher Zeitung*, reported:

When Mrs. Kiran Bedi first entered the Tihar Jail in May 1993, the prison—the biggest in Asia— once resembled a concentration camp: corrupt personnel, a prisoner mafia that terrorized fellow inmates and ran a flourishing drug business, 300 children born in the prison who were given neither health care nor education, the food was the same stew and dirty water year in and year out. And what was a particular disgrace in the main prison in India's capital: of the 8,880 prisoners, 90 percent were persons remanded in custody, and many of them had been on remand for a longer period of time than the toughest sentence would have imposed on them for their crime—if indeed they had committed a crime at all.

Envious colleagues must have been pleased that for the country's first female police officer, the Tihar posting would at last turn out to be too hard a nut to crack. They had tried before to tame the woman who had made them sing small. Yet Kiran Bedi turned it into triumph. Hardly had she started the new job when she had the word *Jail* overwritten by *Ashram* throughout the prison, and within two years proved that this was no mere window dressing. She transformed the prison, which had been built for 2,500 inmates into a monastic place of self-examination, learning, and work . . . meditation courses meant to show that being imprisoned is not only a physical state but also a psychical attitude. While the authorities were able to offer material relief, meditation proved that it was up to the individual to perceive the state of incarceration as an opportunity for self-examination.

The Associated Press reported on March 2, 1994, after a visit to the prison:

A year ago, Tihar Jail was India's toughest prison, a cesspool of drugs and gang wars, of corruption and extortion by both guards and powerful inmates. Then the no-nonsense Kiran Bedi came along.

These days, thousands of inmates gather in clean, tree-shaded courtyards every morning for prayer and mediation. After that, they go to school.

By last July, when she became warden of Tihar Central, the only prison in New Delhi, newspapers were calling Mrs. Bedi the "lady supercop."

Soon, she was the "jail goddess" to many of her charges.

"I really feel like a mother to them," she said with a laugh that softened her raspy voice. "Sometimes I scold them, sometimes I pat them, and sometimes I push them." Ashish Nandy, a social psychologist, praised the warden's work in reforming Tihar and said the whole grim Indian prison system needs cleaning up, "but I doubt we can find so many Kiran Bedis." Most inmates volunteer for Mrs. Bedi's programs. "Probably I cannot solve all the problems of the inmates, but at least we can do something to make their lives better," she said.

With its dozens of sparkling clean barracks, the neat courtyards, shining kitchens and now-disciplined inmates, Tihar resembles an orderly commune.

"I have lived in jails that were like pigsties, but this is first class," said Jagmohan Tandon, sitting on his bed in a dormitory reminiscent of a student hostel. Photos of movie stars and artwork cover the walls.

"Tihar is unrecognizable from a year ago," said S. N. Talwar, a political science teacher who helped start an in-house magazine edited by an inmate. "I see no difference now in the atmosphere between my college and the jail."

A peaceful assembly of Tihar's many inmates

About overcrowding, a chronic condition in all Indian jails, Mrs. Bedi can do little. When it was built in 1956, Tihar was intended for 2,500 inmates. Today, over 8,000 are crammed into it, including 300 women. Only about 1,000 are convicts. The rest await trial, and some have spent years in the jail as their cases move sluggishly through the overburdened courts.

At the old Tihar, inmates say, the strong extorted money and possessions from the weak with threats of violent death. Knife fights were common, gambling was rampant and drugs were smuggled in with the connivance of guards. Prisoners awaiting trial, who are not required to work, had nothing to do but cause trouble.

On her first day at the jail, Mrs. Bedi said, she felt as if "the Himalayas had fallen on my head. My legs were buckling under me."

Then, she recalled, "I thought, am I going to be a part of this rotten system or am I going to change it?"

As a first step toward reform, she rounded up 400 men from one of the barracks, sang them a prayer and told them to repeat it after her. The prayer has become the jail's anthem, and inmates chant it daily.

Next came classes in meditation and yoga, isolation of gang leaders, suspension of corrupt prison officers. Inmates as well as officials say that drug use has declined dramatically.

Voluntary groups were allowed into Tihar for the first time in thirty-five years to provide counseling, meditation classes, vocational training, legal aid, even entertainment.

Educated prisoners volunteer to teach classes. Music programs, spiritual and religious lectures and sports contests are regular events.

"We have stopped being lazy," Mrs. Bedi said.

The media came to play the vital role of a concerned watchdog. They were invited to see what really existed in Tihar, and through their reporting linked the larger society with the prison. That link proved to be multidimensional. It conveyed information, but it also stimulated participation, appreciation, and cooperation and highlighted issues that needed attention. For example, media coverage of scandalous delays in bringing cases to trial finally made officials acknowledge and address this problem. *The Times of India* reported:

> A petition has urged the Delhi High Court to direct the government to prepare a plan for expeditious trial of foreigners who have been languishing in Tihar Jail for over five years and some even seven, without any trial. Mrs. Nitya Ramakrishna, counsel for the petitioner, has raised several questions of law relating to constitutional and fundamental rights of the foreign prisoners, human rights, drawbacks in procedure, and Supreme Court judgment in the context of inordinate delay in conducting trials of foreigners who have been in jail for years.

Yet another headline in *The Indian Express*, "Languishing Undertrials Congest Tihar Jail," led the Lieutenant Governor to admit that the delay in the process of law was highly regrettable:

... The matter now rests with the administration and the Delhi High Court. A move is on to set up more trial courts for expediting things. I agree such delays are unfortunate and the system needs to be set right on a priority.

And the Chairman of the National Human Rights Commission responded:

It is very unfortunate. Society has no justification in keeping undertrials in prison for so long. I fully agree that the process of law must be expedited. We must work out ways in which to speed up the judicial process for those who are lodged for several years.

An uninterrupted flow of information to the community finally led the High Court to intervene. *The Calcutta Telegraph* reported "To the Rescue of Tihar Inmates":

The Delhi High Court has directed Inspector General (Prisons), Kiran Bedi, to furnish a list of all the prisoners in Tihar Jail who had been ordered to be released on bail but could not come out as they could not afford the bail money. Usually, when an undertrial is released on bail, he or she has to give
a personal bond of 5,000 rupees with a surety of the same amount, or as the case may be. Apparently, a significant number of undertrials are languishing in Tihar Jail even after getting bail because they are not in a position to fulfill the conditions.

The Delhi High Court appointed a Commission of seven members to investigate the plight of the undertrials.

It was imperative for external agencies to clearly see conditions in Tihar and the process of reconstruction. Nothing is more authentic than firsthand information. We wanted the media to report what they saw and not what they were told.

building community
inside and outside

The Community Gets Involved

Eventually, the observations from daily rounds, feedback from the petition box, and our daily staff meetings identified special needs that were not unreasonable, but for which we had no resources. Our challenge was clear. Do we admit we have no resources, throw up our hands, and say it can't be done?

In my police work I had found the community to be a helpful resource and a great source of support. I waited for the opportunity to draw the community into Tihar. It wasn't long before I heard the knock at my door. My secretary announced visitors and I stood up to welcome them. I had been waiting for them. To my surprise, they said they too were anxious to meet me. They were the Brahma Kumaris, a national organization of women (and men) who teach the practice of ethics. The following day we walked through the prison together. The prisoners absorbed every word. There was complete silence in reverence for these sisters in white saris. For the society at large, the Brahma Kumaris are symbols of simplicity and purity in thought and deed. They practice and emphasize peace and non-violence, vegetarianism and proper eating habits. Soon the petition box was full of requests for the Brahma Kumaris to visit them. The number of sisters increased, and each prison had a schedule of visits posted for all to know. Tihar relied on their regular and punctual visits.

This report appeared in *The Pioneer* on May 25, 1993:

The maximum-security prison was virtually turned into an ashram on Monday with two *sanyasis* delivering religious discourses to inmates in an attempt to inculcate spirituality and human values among the undertrials and convicts.

"There is God inside me and you. By prayers and recitation of the name of God, you can lessen your sufferings and sorrows," Swami Jita Atamanand of the Ramakrishna Mission said amid applause.

"My guru taught me, hate the sin and not the sinner," the Swami said, exhorting his congregation to serve fellow beings as God resided in each one. The Swami told the prisoners they were in jail because of their karmas.

Nearly 1,500 inmates of the jail, 200 of them women, converged for the sermons.

"The topic was the universal religion of humanism. No particular religion was discussed," said Ms. Bedi. It was the first time when sermons were organized in Tihar Jail. Male and female prisoners jointly congregated in the jail for the first time. Press reporters were allowed for the first time deep inside Jail No. 1 to enable them to cover the function. . . .

From this auspicious beginning of community involvement, we invited a well-known yoga teacher to the jail. He and his students taught the inmates the value of personal hygiene, deep breathing, and some essential exercises to help them maintain good health under the prison conditions. The demand for yoga was so great that he started a training course for inmate teachers so the wards were self-sufficient and could have regular instruction. Over a period of time the yoga instructors became an indispensable resource for the inmates. Here is a report from *Delhi Mid-Day:*

Tihar Emerging with a New Face
Brahma Kumaris, homeopaths, storytellers, and more. They all frequent the place. . . . Tihar is in for

a face-lift, gradually replacing the brutal image with something that is more humane.

The jail covering several acres, housing the bad, the worse, and the worst of the jailbirds, now has a spate of activities, explaining the reason why its corridors remain crowded these days.

The quick change in the atmosphere of the jail and removing the aura of secrecy and silence from the jail came soon after the new Inspector General (IG), Kiran Bedi, took over.

Every day in the evening, the inmates collect in the courtyard in the ward and wait for yoga sessions to begin. The yoga sessions are very popular with the inmates, especially the foreigners. There are many foreigners who have been arrested mostly under the NDPS Act (Narcotics and Drugs). "They specially come and ask about the yoga instructor if she is late for her session," said the warder. Yoga classes are conducted at various times of the day in all four jails.

Positive activities in Tihar have definitely increased. The most eye-catching of them all, however, is the daily visit of Brahma Kumaris to the jail. Every evening at five these women in white come to speak to gatherings of the prisoners. Surprisingly, there is absolute silence during the session. "Some of them are so overwhelmed that they even cry. Others want to confess," said a jail official.

Equally interesting is the program slated for children—storytelling. The idea emanated when the jail authorities received a letter requesting permission to come and recite poems and stories for the jail's children, said the IG.

One evening Sheetal Sehgal of Mahila Pratiraksha Mandal (a women's protection group), who was a great community supporter, dropped by. She casually asked if she could be of any assistance to us. She was running counseling and legal-aid centers as well as schools for deprived children. I asked her whether she could help us. She is a woman who never says no to deserving causes. She came the following day with her dedicated team of women volunteers to start work with the women and children in the women's ward. Surinder Saini, Sonia Sharma, and Santosh Muthoo of the Delhi Social Welfare Board ably supported her. The centers and the school she set up inside Tihar are still functioning.

The introduction of yoga sessions, spiritual discourses, vocational training, and counseling for women, as well as the first-ever nursery for the prisoners' children, made headlines in several newspapers. Consequently, I got a telephone call from Mark Templer of the Hope Foundation, an international organization dealing with health matters of the needy. I invited him to come see me the following day. He and his team member, Ian Correa, offered to address the problems of leprosy and tuberculosis inside the prison. We had no provision to do this ourselves. For me this help was God-sent. I personally took them around the prison the same day. Within days, they started their program. They are still there, not only for the prisoners but also for the staff through the dental clinic they established inside the prison.

Besides them there were many other Christian groups who came to give counseling sessions and distribute copies of the Bible. One of them was Mother Teresa's Missionaries of Charity. A woman inmate even received a letter from Mother Teresa:

Missionaries of Charity
54A, A. J. C. Bose Road
Calcutta 700016

5th March 1995

Dear Shakira,

Thank you for your letter of 27.2.95. I am happy to know that Sr. Mamta and Sr. Coreen often visit the prisoners at Tihar Jail and that they were able to take care of that young girl who is mental. Here in Bengal, we have more than 200 young and old women who have been sent to us from the Jail. I am sure slowly we will be able to do this in many parts of India. In the meantime, pray for this intention.

I will surely pray that your case will be over and that you begin a new life. It is very consoling to know that your authorities, especially Mrs. Kiran Bedi, are doing so much for the betterment of the prisoners. I'm glad that she arranged for the Ash Wednesday service for you all. My prayers and greetings to all those who are in charge there. God loves you—love others as God loves you.

God bless you.

((Teresa mc
Mother Teresa

An Anglo-Indian woman from *The Family*, another worldwide humanitarian Christian organization, asked to provide musical programs for women and children. Never had the wards enjoyed this kind of entertainment. They were welcomed and imparted joy to one and all. By popular demand we had to ask them to come often and to a different prison each day. They were generous to the inmates with their time. In addition to music, workshops, and organized festivals, they planted trees and shrubs. They reached out to all, and over a period of time they developed workbooks on management of human relations. They continue to be associated with Tihar. Here is a report from *The National Herald* on September 12, 1994:

Tender Saplings on Tihar's Barren Land

Two rugged men join hands to plant a tender sapling on a stretch of barren land—one of them is a policeman, another a convict. The unlikely cooperation is yet another step toward positive changes that have swept the Capital's Tihar Jail. Thousands of tiny saplings, standing around overcrowded prisons, not only promise salubrious surroundings but also reflect the growing hope among prisoners for their future.

During this monsoon, hundreds of zealous jail inmates participated in covering about 6,000 square feet of land with 3,000 plants from an assortment of fruit, shade, and flowering trees and a variety of shrubs and creepers.

"It was just a matter of rekindling their old instincts as most of the inmates have rural agrarian background," says Ms. Sonia of *The Family*, a voluntary body organizing the social forestry project in Tihar Jail.

"They are so caring that there is no need to put tree guards around the plants, which have shown a remarkable survival rate of 95 percent," enthuses Tarsem Kumar, Superintendent of Jail No. 2.

The complex is to have 2,000 more trees by the year end. In a matter of two to three years, the jail will be lush with mango, guava, pomegranate, jamun, and lemon trees, and the prisoners will reap the fruits of their labor.

"It is accompanied by programs that sensitize jail inmates about the importance of preserving a clean environment and conveys the message that a young sapling planted by them could symbolize the new growth that their future can attain, if they so choose," elaborates Ms.Sonia.

The positive influence of the program is reflected in comments made by some old convicts who participated in one such tree planting function in Jail No. 2.

The oldest inmate, seventy-eight-year-old Pati Lal, a freedom fighter accused of murder, went on the stage to declare that he was glad to kick his old habit of smoking *bidis* and pledged to keep the surroundings clean.

One morning, as I was leaving for my regular walk, I got a telephone call from a woman who introduced herself as a retired official of All India Radio and a storyteller. She asked me if she could perform inside the prison.

My immediate response was, "Why not!"

"And when could I come?" she asked.

"Today," I said.

I took her to the adolescent wards, and over the weeks she became a fond motherly presence and storyteller for

1,200 boys. She came with books, magazines, clothes, stationery, and even a television for the adolescent ward. Today, she works for other prisons, too, and has been rewarded for her efforts. She has authored a book, *Aisa Jaise Kuch Hua Hi Nahin (It's Like Nothing Has Happened)*, narrating her story of the work she has done inside Tihar. Without her, the prison would have been poorer.

Two months after the entry of such individuals and organizations, the whole atmosphere inside the prison changed. By July, the then Lieutenant Governor, P. K. Dave, came to Tihar to inaugurate two new wards for adolescents. We launched a literacy program for these young people. Officials, eminent citizens, and non-governmental agencies in the field of education and vocational training all got interested in literacy at Tihar. The literacy movement gained so much momentum that Tihar officials felt compelled to make sure that anyone leaving Tihar at least knows how to write his own name and read numbers. The literacy program finally engulfed the entire prison. This would not have been possible without massive community support.

In addition to illiteracy, drug abuse was a major challenge inside the prison. Help came through dedicated individuals and organizations like Navjyoti. They brought with them models of substance abuse management and handled what we could not have done on our own. These individuals and organizations are still in Tihar. Without them, we could not have built the environment we envisioned.

When you are determined to find answers, you get solutions. This has been my frequent experience. Vipassana, a meditation program, was one such example. M. L. Mehta, formerly of the Ministry of Home Affairs, offered the program to us. As a result of this endeavor, Tihar housed a ten-day meditation camp with 1,100 prisoners assembled in one common place, unheard of in any prison anywhere in the world. Tihar received a gift with the opening of a formal branch of the Vipassana Research Institute, so courses would be offered at regular intervals.

By now, Tihar was attracting international attention. The message of our accessibility reached academia as well. A number of scholars in social sciences, law, and architecture came to do social research. One visit for which the prison system shall remain indebted forever was a visit by K. C. Shroff. Shroff, a grand old man with the enthusiasm and zeal of a motivated teenager, came straight to the point:

He said, "You have a garbage removal problem?"

"Yes."

"Would you like some solutions for this?"

"Yes."

He said, "Come, show me your garbage dump."

I took him inside the prison and showed him the stinking dumps.

He said, "What if we treat this right here and turn it into compost?"

I asked, "What about the stink?"

He replied, "You see for yourself."

We lost no time. He sent his team of experts to oversee the program, train us, and finally make us self-sufficient. One of the enterprising Jail Superintendents, D. P. Diwedi, printed sacks with "Green Tihar" and sold compost to earn money for the prisoners' welfare. We were thrilled at this transformation. In fact, it became a role model for others in garbage management. This report was carried on June 19, 1994, in *The Indian Express:*

Turning Garbage into Manure

Another novel experiment has started here in Tihar Jail: compost from garbage. The largest jail in Asia Pacific, which houses more than 8,700 inmates, produces 3,000 kilograms of garbage daily, making disposal quite a costly task.

The inmates of the jail are not only turning the garbage into rich manure, they are also marketing it, thus saving a massive amount of money, more than 1,000,000 rupees (about US$20,000) annually.

The money generated from the sale of the manure of jail garbage is deposited in the Prisoners' Welfare Fund. The prisoners who manage garbage earn wages as well.

About 40 prisoners have volunteered to take part in the exercise initiated by K. C. Shroff, Managing Director, Excel Industries, Mumbai. These prisoners are getting vocational training in garbage management and financial incentives for their work. They get a reduction in sentence for good conduct.

Inspector General of Prisons, Kiran Bedi, said that the marketing of manure from garbage had started weeks ago and, encouraged by the response, she would soon order a technical feasibility study of producing electricity from garbage. Bedi also plans to get in touch with voluntary organizations, like Sulabh International, to extract biogas from garbage before turning it into manure. She would like to meet all the energy needs of the massive jail through non-conventional energy sources.

Many nurseries in the capital are buying the bioorganic soil enricher, converted mainly from horticulture and kitchen waste in the prison, with the active help from the Kitchen Garden Association of India.

"We are trying to expand our market, and once the project goes full steam, it is expected to generate a return of over 1,000,000 rupees (US$20,000)

Tihar Jail's garbage became a source of revenue.

per annum into the Prisoners' Welfare Fund," Bedi said. The PWF money will be used for correctional measures, she added.

In a novel experiment, the five-kilogram poly-bags in which the manure is being marketed are printed in bright red by juvenile delinquents who are undergoing vocational training inside the jail.

"It gives their morale a boost to see their work being put to use and actually being sold," said Bedi.

In the field of legal aid, a group called Sakshi, headed by Jasjit Purewal, and scores of others came in to provide free legal aid for the women prisoners and needy men. This expedited trials and provided the much-needed sensitivity in an area that was neglected.

The health care improved dramatically due to community support for children, women, and men. A number of exhibitions brought about an increased awareness of health care. We met inmates' special needs through the support of specialists. We observed Health Care Days as part of our celebrations. On January 26, 1994, hundreds of doctors volunteered medical help. The entire prison population had access to specialist care. We later added alternative medicines. Though it didn't happen, we also had plans to sell ayurvedic medicine for basic ailments, such as fever, coughs, and colds, further reducing pressure on government doctors. I am told that Tihar now has sufficient doctors and is no longer dependent on outside help—yet community participation continues.

India is a land of festivals, and at Tihar we celebrated all of them: Hindu, Sikh, Muslim, and Christian. All insiders celebrated equally. The community from outside generously contributed to the festivities. For Diwali, a festival of lights, the Hindu community organized a traditional play.

For Gurupurva, the Sikh community gave food to be cooked inside the prison. For Id, the Muslim groups offered dates and puddings to all. On Christmas Day, cake was sent to all by the Christian groups. We were true to our Indian sense of plurality and hospitality even in Tihar.

Christopher Thomas of *The Times*, London, visited Tihar during Christmas in 1994 and reported:

Inmates Learn the Message of Christmas
The 9,300 prisoners at Delhi Central Jail, India's largest, are celebrating Christmas and the New Year with Father Christmas, who is a Hindu with the vaguest knowledge of what it is all about.

Ranjan Kumar Sinha, formerly a circus clown, received a crash course from foreign prisoners about the meaning of the Christmas message. He said he found it simple to understand and had no problem teaching it to fellow Hindus. "It is not much different from Hinduism really. It seems to say the same sort of things."

Nigel Beardsley, 31, from Maidenhead, Berkshire, who has been remanded in custody on drug charges for the past 20 months, wrote a play, *The Beginning of Life*, half in Hindi and half in English, with Father Christmas in the starring role. Most performers were drawn from the 140 foreign inmates, but several Hindus are involved.

Mr. Beardsley's Hindi, learned while waiting for a trial date to be set, is sufficient for the endeavor. "We wanted to send the Christmas message of goodwill to Hindu, Sikh, and Muslim prisoners," he said. "It seems to have gone down well. There used to be a misunderstanding between Indians and foreigners, but that has all gone."

The prison community enjoying a staged drama in Tihar Jail

The play is being taken "on tour" during the holiday period to the four prisons that make up the huge complex on the outskirts of Delhi. The pantomime particularly enthralled the prison's 40-odd children, who are allowed to stay with their mothers in jail until the age of five.

During my visits to the prisons in other countries, I did not see community participation. Perhaps it was not required there since the basic needs were met. But I am of the view that there is no substitute for community participation to forge reformation in a substantial way. Reformation and correction require integration and acceptance. A community creates the best environment for transformation, and in the case of Tihar, helped a prison become an ashram. Community involvement was the basis of prisoners' reintegration into the community that was now preparing to accept them back. Hundreds of inmates had started to express regret and began to feel at peace with themselves. The inmates had reached a crossroads.

The Community Within

With the prison staff shouldering increasing responsibilities, and the outside community eagerly contributing to reform in Tihar, how could the prisoners not respond? In fact, the jail itself housed the greatest strength—human resources. The men and women confined to Tihar had time, energy, and professional skills—the foundation of any vibrant society. Here was a waiting mass of human potential. It was only necessary to identify their talent and then give direction and guidance.

Early on, I realized a fundamental fact: the prisoners

were keen on changes in the system, and drastic ones at that. However, we had no ready-made magic formula for instant reform. Furthermore, the process required the cooperation of the entire population of prisoners. Their participation would have to be voluntary to avoid defeating the purpose of the reforms.

The daily rounds, reinforced by the parallel avalanche of petitions from the mobile petition box, along with the entry of the community, led to a pronounced change in the prisoners' attitudes. The impact was nothing short of spectacular. Within a short time, we initiated adult education programs, yoga activities, daily morning prayers, sports, and festivities. Remarkably, this was accomplished with the existing staff, which was only waiting to be properly motivated and organized. We next developed a model for reform called the Prisoners' Panchayat (Cooperative) System. The main objective was to encourage the prisoners to voluntarily take part in organizing educational, cultural, and sports activities and in maintaining discipline. The system went into practice on June 26, 1993. I issued the following order:

> Panchayat system to be introduced in all wards. Head warders will head the ward panchayats. The panchayat will regulate, discipline, and organize educational, sports, and cultural activities. The jail superintendents suggested we take time to consider details and evolve a working system in consultation with the ward inmates during the rounds of the Superintendents. The scheme will be finalized by next week.
>
> Each superintendent and deputy superintendent will fix a day and time of week to brief warders and head warders. A suitable place to be identified in each jail.

We appointed a superintendent or a deputy superintendent to ensure that the various panchayats were formed in each ward. The formation of various panchayats was preceded by an orientation program conducted by jail officials who explained the objectives and benefits of the new system to the inmates. The response from the majority of the prisoners was enthusiastic and positive. Many volunteers came forward to join the reformation program and were encouraged by their companions to take up organizational responsibilities. All of a sudden, a perceptible transformation took place. The ward inmates formed self-organized groups. The warder of each ward was the head of each group and was called the *sarpanch* (headman).

Once the individual ward panchayats were formed, the Superintendents summoned a *mahapanchayat*—a collective assembly of all panchayats. The objectives of this mahapanchayat were to (a) coordinate activities; (b) reach a consensus on acceptable methods of functioning; and (c) point out existing problems and suggest solutions.

The panchayats had several benefits. First and foremost, the prisoners felt less isolated and helpless. Second, the head warder and his deputies could mobilize assistance for organizing educational, cultural, and sports activities. Third, the panchayat system created a new positive equation between the staff and the inmates and also among the inmates. The focus was on solving problems and not merely complaining about them.

When we observed problems that ought to have been resolved by the panchayat we summoned the panchayat to explain. This brought accountability in community management. The spirit underlying the panchayat system ushered in an era of self-governance for the inmates. It encouraged them to participate in various reformation programs and engendered healthy interactions between the inmates and also between the inmates and the staff members.

The need for specific activity-oriented panchayats grew as programs expanded. The Teachers' Panchayat was formed to achieve the goal of total literacy in the jail. The teachers were chosen from the literate prisoners themselves. The chosen teachers truly rose to the occasion in a comprehensive and diligent manner. An Assistant Superintendent was exclusively assigned as head of the Teachers' Panchayat. He ensured that the panchayat functioned effectively, and its benefits reached the entire population of the prison. The Assistant Superintendent also coordinated feedback from various sources and used this information to improve the system.

The Medical Panchayat was responsible for identifying inmates who needed urgent medical help. They could inform the officers or send letters through the petition box. The Medical Panchayat members also conveyed to their ward policy decisions on medical matters and received training on preventive measures to help maintain a healthy environment in their wards.

All the foregoing developments called for regular interaction between the staff and the panchayats. Just as the daily briefing of the staff was mandatory, now it became necessary to hold a daily forum for all the ward panchayats.

I summoned a mahapanchayat on September 25, 1993. About 400 inmate members from all the ward panchayats in all four prisons assembled at the appointed hour. They represented all the various activities: internal discipline, mess management, literacy, yoga, sports, health care, and cultural activities. This mahapanchayat marked a turning point in the internal administration of Tihar Jail. It signaled the advent of a meaningful, collective, corrective community system. It did not matter that these men and women were in jail. They displayed enthusiasm, energy, and willingness to participate in a self-governance program of what was effectively a township of over 8,000.

Self-governance has led to a sense of responsibility and self-policing. In consultation with deputy superintendents, the inmates formed security parties whose main objective was to ferret out drugs. The inmates returning from court appearances were bodily frisked at various points by different teams, official or mixed, in order to detect any contraband items. Such multi-tier searches further cleansed the system. It was as if searchlights were beamed on one and all, and nobody could hide from the intensity of the glare.

With the passage of time, panchayat meetings had become a constructive way of life. We came across men and women who were not only developing self-esteem but also displaying leadership qualities. Such individuals were officially recognized and given identification badges and special seating places in all gatherings. We were constantly on the lookout for new ideas, new viewpoints, and new programs. And there was no dearth of input.

We decided on the Gandhian concept of *shram daan* (voluntary labor or service). We allotted Wednesday afternoons for shram daan, following the morning literacy classes. During this course all inmates would dust and clean their own barracks or cells and also tidy up their personal belongings. They would also brighten up the areas within the ward compound.

Here is a report I received from one of the most enthusiastic Superintendents, Tarsem Kumar, which reveals how each one of us was profoundly involved in developing, nurturing, and sustaining the panchayat system:

1. **Ward Panchayat**
   In every ward, a main panchayat and a shadow panchayat have been formed. The task of the main panchayat is discipline and cleanliness. The panchayat

Exercise and yoga classes in Tihar Jail improved the health
and well-being of the inmates.

members of the wards are authorized to settle all petty issues among the prisoners. Serious matters concerning lack of discipline and violence are brought to the notice of the officers. These ward panchayats were formed on the pattern of village panchayats. The task of the shadow panchayat is the same. It helps the main panchayat and members from the shadow panchayat replace members of the main panchayat when they are released or transferred.

2. **Mess Panchayat**
   The mess panchayat monitors the quality of food supplies and cooked food. They report problems to the officers.

3. **Education Panchayat**
   This panchayat monitors the educational activities of the prisoners. Their main task is to see that no prisoner remains illiterate and to make arrangements for the teachers. Presently, there are five teachers.

4. **Sports Panchayat**
   The main task of the Sports Panchayat is to see that sports and games are conducted in each ward. They also arrange interward and interjail matches. This jail won the IG trophy in the interjail volleyball tournament this year.

5. **Medical Panchayat**
   In case of medical emergency, the medical panchayat informs the duty officer, and takes the prisoner to the doctor immediately.

6. **Cultural Panchayat**
   The cultural panchayat sings *bhajans* (devotional songs) daily in wards and arranges cultural programs.

7. Nai Punja (Barber Team)

The Nai punja panchayat makes sure that the *nai* (barber) goes to each ward and does his job efficiently.

8. Yoga Activity

Yoga classes are taught in the jail and a number of prisoners have learned yoga. A yoga coordinator has been appointed to oversee the yoga activities.

9. Mahapanchayat

The mahapanchayats are held from time to time. The collective panchayats are briefed on instructions and policies from the Superintendents and from the Prison Headquarters, so they can update the prisoners of their wards on activities in progress and upcoming events.

10. Warder Briefing

The Jail Superintendent and headquarters issue orders to the head warder and warder for compliance. The warders pass on information to their ward prisoners, and in this way instructions are communicated to the prisoners to maintain peace and discipline in the jail.

The most significant panchayat set up in Tihar was the Legal Panchayat. This panchayat, on the basis of its remarkable accomplishments, went on to create legal history. Its basic function was to make the inmates aware of their legal rights, and then provide a way to exercise those rights. Many of the inmates were absolutely ignorant about the law. They perceived it as a legal maze from which all escape routes were blocked.

Gradually, with the help of the Legal Panchayat, the inmates gained confidence and shared their views during daily meetings or during the mahapanchayats. Newer and better ideas surfaced, and practical solutions to various complex legal problems evolved.

The core of the Legal Panchayat consisted of inmates with legal backgrounds and analytical skills who could draft petitions and affidavits. We provided them with the typewriters and stationery. Superintendent K. R. Kishore and his colleagues procured five complete sets of law books and other related literature. The costs of photocopying and paper were defrayed from the Prisoners' Welfare Fund. Each Superintendent provided a separate room for the legal experts, which could also be used for consultation purposes.

This impromptu legal-aid cell proved to be an immense source of relief for all of us. It was incredible to witness legal assistance offered absolutely free without any expectation of material gain or favors. This was a great achievement given the fact that many of the inmates openly complained of the fleecing skills of the legal profession. The entire approach was constructive and positive.

The Legal Panchayat developed a team of inside lawyers to tackle the endemic problem of inordinately delayed trials and to produce evidence of such lapses before the courts. Mufti Mirazuddin Farooqi, a former senior law officer from Jammu and Kashmir, led this team. Farooqi devised a simple but ingenious and effective court diary for undertrials. By judiciously using this diary, each inmate could keep a methodical record of the trial. If a trial was delayed due to factors beyond the inmates' control, the diary could be put before the court to document delays.

This format was distributed free of cost to the indigent inmates; those who could afford to pay were charged a nominal sum of one rupee. *The Asian Age* reported on this on May 10, 1994:

Undertrials Hold the Law to Be Guilty

The over 7,000 undertrials in Tihar Jail are taking the law into their own hands. Fed up with the endless rounds of courts that can stretch their cases to 10 years and beyond, the undertrials have decided to keep a written record of what happens in each of the interminable rounds they make to court for a hearing.

The Legal Panchayats set up among the prisoners in the last two months have hit upon a way to prod awake the judicial system, reported to be among the tardiest in the world. Last Saturday they began to keep a case diary of the proceedings of each undertrial's hearings. The jail panchayat documents the proceedings when an undertrial returns from the court, said Ms. Kiran Bedi, Inspector General of Prisons.

The hearings are classified as either effective or non-effective hearings. A list of all the non-effective hearings, and the reasons why the hearings were ineffective, will be submitted once a month to the Chief Justice of the Delhi High Court, the Minister for Law, the Police Commissioner, the Home Secretary, the Human Rights Commission, and the Delhi Legal Aid Bureau.

An overwhelming 7,114 of the 8,500 inmates in Tihar are undertrials, many of whom wait anywhere between five and ten years to get a verdict from the overcrowded courts of Delhi. According to Mr. S. Sen, Inspector General of Police in the Central Bureau of Investigation, there were 5.7 million criminal cases waiting for trial in Indian courts till the end of 1991. But according to one judge who spoke at a seminar on criminal justice that concluded in the capital on Sunday, over 20 million cases were pending in the lower courts while another 2.2 million cases were pending in the 18 High Courts in the country.

The judges say this is because of an explosion of litigation in the country in recent years, with the passing of new legislation and the population growth. But the infrastructure of the judiciary has not expanded to keep pace with this "huge clamoring at the doors of the judiciary," one judge said. But in Tihar Jail, the largest in the Asia-Pacific region, prisoners are not as despairing as they used to be a year or so ago of getting a speedy trial.

When the prisoners came to know of the easy availability of free legal aid, they swamped the inside lawyers. The workload of the Legal Panchayat was nothing short of stupendous. To streamline the activities of this panchayat, subpanchayats were formed to help the main panchayat. The members of the Legal Panchayat made a tremendous effort to alleviate the sufferings of their more unfortunate companions. They proved extremely effective in fulfilling their objectives. Depending upon the gravity of the individual cases, they petitioned the Supreme Court, the High Courts, or the District Courts. And in many deserving cases, relief came their way.

The indomitable Mufti Mirazuddin Farooqi was personally responsible for obtaining bail orders for several prisoners. In one case in which a convict had been sentenced to death for homicide, Farooqi made an appeal to the Supreme Court through the post to commute the sentence to life imprisonment. His appeal was heard and his plea upheld. Mufti, as Farooqi was affectionately known, literally worked away day and night. Mufti was imprisoned under TADA (Terrorists and Disruptive Activities Prevention Act). He is now back in Jammu and Kashmir, a free man whose profession is freeing others.

The Legal Panchayat was actively supported by an outside lawyer's forum, known as the Delhi Legal Aid Bureau. This bureau disseminated legal education in all the wards and made the inmates, especially the newcomers, aware of their rights and duties. These momentous happenings imbued Tihar with an all-pervading spirit of conscientiousness and concern.

Out of this emerged yet another panchayat, the Mulhaiza Panchayat (an Orientation Council), which provided information and guidelines to all new prison entrants on procedures, rules, and regulations. The new residents were oriented to the available infrastructural support systems and shown how to use them optimally. This panchayat could also identify on a daily basis newcomers who possessed professional skills. These individuals could then be guided to utilize their skills to improve conditions in the prison.

Other panchayats came into existence according to need. For instance, the PWD (Public Works Department) Panchayat was created because the actual PWD was invariably conspicuous by its absence, and we had to reduce our dependence on it. This panchayat organized inmates with engineering and mechanical skills. By the end of 1994, the dedicated members of this group had saved the government huge expense by taking on innumerable repairs and minor construction jobs. They performed the jobs willingly and joyously. All we had to do was provide them with tools and raw materials. Not a single person misused these items. On the contrary, they put them to maximum use for prison service. The specialists of the PWD Panchayat repaired broken doors and hand pumps, plugged water leakages, and repaired defective power points. They fixed fans, TVs, and

VCRs that had gone out of order. They even managed to set up audio installations for conducting stage shows inside the jail.

These professionals went on to design and build two open-air auditoriums with a seating capacity of 2,500 each. Had these activities been left to the mercy of government-run PWD, they would have never been constructed, mainly because of paucity of funds. Both open-air auditoriums were formally inaugurated.

Prison 1 already had a stadium, so its inmates erected a greenhouse and dug a pond decorated with lotus flowers. They planned to grow diverse varieties of plants throughout the year, encourage agro-economic activities, and impart training in horticulture to their fellow residents. This project was the brainchild of V. P. Garg, a zealous Deputy Superintendent, who was ably supported by Jagdish Chandra Pant, Agriculture Secretary, Government of India. The Ministry of Agriculture provided the material needed for the structure, but the inmates themselves carried out the actual construction job. One inmate, Surinder Kumar, was the driving force behind this venture. He held a master's degree in agronomics and was serving a life sentence. The greenhouse project brought excellent financial returns to the Prisoners' Welfare Fund.

The PWD Panchayat also supervised one of the most unique projects in the prison. Every day the four prisons generated almost two tons of organic garbage. To have the garbage off-site involved hiring trucks at 300 rupees per trip. Each truck made several trips per day. The truck driver invariably duped the prison authorities by not filling the truck to its full capacity, thereby increasing the number of trips. The Delhi State Government, in its supreme wisdom, refused to allow the jail officials to buy our own garbage truck even when we had the money in our budget.

We were instructed to continue with the traditional system of hiring trucks, which drained about 23,000,000 rupees a year (US$51,000) from the prison budget. The huge pile-up of garbage not only permeated the jail premises with its unique stink but was also a potential source of contagious diseases such as cholera and dysentery.

At this stage, destiny came to our rescue. As we have seen, K. C. Shroff arrived from Mumbai with his plan to convert garbage into moneymaking compost. The benefit to Tihar was twofold: we acquired a new technology as well as the skills to use it effectively, many inmates learned a vocational trade skill; and in the process, revenue flowed in. Undeniably, this venture was one of the most innovative, creative, and productive projects undertaken at Tihar Jail.

Another successful panchayat started a canteen containing a grocery and other provision shops: cold drinks outlets and Pepsi fountains, fruit juice and coffee counters, and a mini-restaurant that served hot fried snacks and tea. In these shops, the prisoners could buy vegetables, clothing, buckets, stationery, and utensils.

All these activities were the result of sincere, heartfelt, and invigorating enthusiasm and diligence on the part of the inmates and productive, cooperative coordination between the staff and the inmates. The earlier environment of mutual suspicion and even hostility was replaced by trust and an attitude of community service. The growing sense of community was expressed in spontaneous outbursts of joy and gaiety during the celebrations of traditional Indian festivals. The inmates set up various stalls during these festivals to serve special food and provide entertainment and games. All the activities during the festivals resulted from the combined effort and coordination among the various panchayats.

Tihar Jail had been transformed into an ashram. However, the atmosphere of ever-increasing transparency and openness called for greater vigilance and more caution. To ensure that no one misused the reform process, a patrolling panchayat was set up. Its duty was to make daily rounds of all wards to ensure that there were no loiterers, and that nobody stayed confined while everyone else was busy. Depressed individuals were identified and given special attention and treatment, if needed.

Four more panchayats were formed to meet specific needs: (a) the Insaaf (Justice) Panchayat, consisting of elders, to resolve disputes among barrack mates; (b) a Cable Panchayat to schedule the programs to be viewed on a recently acquired Tihar Cable Network; (c) a Vipassana Panchayat to oversee the organization of the meditation program; and (d) a panchayat against corruption and violence. The corruption panchayat was set up to forcefully drive home the point that corruption and violence were anathema to the new system, and had to be stamped out once and for all.

The community outside began to take note of the spectacular changes taking place in Tihar. In September 1994, I agreed to accept a medal of honor for work in the field of prison reforms on the condition that such medals also were awarded to all those inmates who were collectively responsible for this revolution. We held four separate functions in the open-air auditoriums to award the medals. Each function was jam-packed and marked by jubilation. Along with the medals, certificates were awarded to those inmates whose services were outstanding.

We had invoked the voluntary spirit among the inmates with remarkable results. Moreover, we managed to sustain the tempo for almost two years. The time was ripe to inject additional tangible incentives besides recognition and appreciation. We decided to provide financial benefits as well. For this purpose, we launched a panchayat fund.

However, at this point my posting at Tihar came to an end.

During my visit to prisons outside India, I had seen a casual concept of prison councils existing in different prisons. They would interact once a fortnight in a formal forum, or on a regular basis with their floor supervisor. The issues were rather peripheral, because the basic requirements were being met institutionally. Also, the numbers everywhere I went were small. In these prisons they were talking of 10 or 15 prisoners on a floor and not 400 in a ward as in Tihar. Very rarely in these prisons did all the floor councils get together, for reasons of security and discipline. This is what I consistently saw in my visits to prisons abroad.

The structure of Tihar was not comparable—either in culture, dimension, or infrastructure. I came back convinced that given the realities of Tihar, we were on the right path, breaking new ground and creating new systems.

The Education Process: An Eternal Journey

Each one of us, irrespective of who we are or what we are, is a product of our own time management. How an individual spends his or her waking hours determines the value he attaches to himself and shapes the present as well as the future. This was a lesson I learned early in life. The basic realization that time had value was drilled into me in my childhood. Every moment was precious, and once lost, could not be retrieved. This philosophy has been a basic motivation in all my actions, both personal and professional.

Consequently, when I took charge of Tihar, I felt personally responsible for being a timekeeper for all the inmates. When I could not afford to waste even a minute of my own time, how could I possibly preside over the squandering of the time of thousands of men, women, and children? I felt that most of these individuals (except the truly innocent ones) had wound up in prison precisely because they could not manage their time properly. Had they realized how precious every fleeting moment was, they would have invested their energy in useful and constructive work instead of activities leading them to prison.

How could this awareness be kindled now, right inside the jail? How could the inmates be taught the value of time? How could the prisoners be inspired to something new? We decided to allocate two hours of the morning, Monday through Saturday, to education. We spoke to the prisoners. We explained to them how they could utilize their time here in prison. We assured them that we would do our best to create a congenial environment for learning. We helped them form small groups in the wards, according to their literacy levels. For instance, groups were formed for the totally illiterate, partially literate, fairly literate, and graduates. The inmates who were graduates were motivated to teach their less literate companions.

Industrious inmates with carpentry skills made blackboards in the prison factory. From the Prisoners' Welfare Fund we bought slates, chalk, notebooks, and pencils. We appealed to heads of various schools for help and called them for a meeting. By sharing our literacy plan for Tihar, we hoped to motivate the principals and teachers to help us convert the largest prison in the country into an institution of learning. We asked for donations of spare educational material and old school textbooks. The response was tremendous.

We invoked among schoolchildren the spirit of community service and suggested that each of them donate a notebook, a pencil, or an eraser, which they could buy from their pocket money. A virtual deluge resulted. Scores of schools volunteered, and thousands of school children sent

in their contributions. We set up outlets for books and supplies at suitable points within the prison. Whenever we ran
short of books, we sent out appeals or purchased them
from the market with the earnings from canteen sales.
Notebooks and pencils were sold through the mobile canteens and the grocery stores within the jail premises. The
Literacy Panchayat ensured that adequate educational supplies were available and coordinated activities with the
prison officials.

We identified volunteers willing to teach regularly, and
if a teacher inmate was released, another inmate took over
until a suitable substitute could be found from among the
newcomers. Our motto was: "The school must go on." The
learning process never suffered due to lack of teachers. The
Tihar literacy centers were endowed with all the hallmarks
of any standard educational institution. We toned up the
administration, took daily attendance, conducted weekly
tests, declared the results, upgraded the students, and regularly rewarded the deserving ones. *The Patriot* reported on
June 15, 1994:

> In the mornings, the Capital's Central Tihar Jail
> turns into a school. This atmosphere will get a tinge
> of formality on the coming Wednesday, when a
> branch of the National Open School will open in this
> overcrowded jail housing more than 8,000 inmates.
>
> The entire jail population is split into more
> than 300 classrooms with educated prison inmates
> as teachers. Moral education, social studies, basic
> functional literacy, and languages like Hindi, Urdu,
> Punjabi, Sanskrit, French, Persian, and Swahili are
> taught in these classes. Education programs in
> Tihar Jail are being supported by more than 80
> local schools, institutions, and individuals.

The teachers from outside schools started to visit the literacy centers in Tihar and volunteered their services. Despite their tight schedules, they managed to find time to share their knowledge and expertise. The adolescent inmates benefited most, since their educational needs were accorded top priority. The majority of them diligently lapped up all that was taught to them by a dedicated group of Catholic nuns who were happy to come across so many eager and enthusiastic seekers of knowledge. In the outside world, they might have behaved differently. They might not have listened to anyone, least of all to their parents. However, within Tihar, through subtle persuasion, persistent cajoling, and innovative new methods, we managed to sustain and even appreciably boost their interest in education. During my rounds, I stopped to observe classes. Often both teachers and students were so engrossed in their studies that they did not notice me standing quietly in the back of the classroom. Such an inspiring and heartening sight was a source of delight and joy to me.

With the passage of time, we expanded the gambit of our literacy program. Those matriculates and undergraduates who wanted to learn other languages were given the option of doing so. They could attend classes conducted by inmate teachers to learn Hindi, Punjabi, Urdu, Sanskrit, Tamil, and Bengali. Those with a penchant for learning foreign languages could choose from French, Spanish, Swahili, Arabic, and Persian. Audio aids were brought in for teaching foreign languages, thanks to philanthropic donations. Some inmates even sat for an examination in French, conducted upon our request by a French Embassy official. Some learned more than one language within the span of a few months by studying during lockup!

One of the most satisfying experiences for the inmates was to be able to sign their name when leaving the prison, which they had entered by affixing their thumb impression. I felt that Devi Saraswati, the Hindu goddess of learning, had started to reside inside Tihar. To reinforce my conviction, Indira Gandhi National Open University (IGNOU), decided to offer of a broad range of correspondence courses for the inmates by setting up a study center within Tihar. IGNOU's entry represented a landmark in our education crusade.

An impressive array of other educational, social, and cultural organizations, evidently inspired by the reform revolution at Tihar, offered their services. For example, Bharat Vikas Parishad (BVP) adopted the adolescent wards of Prison No. 4. BVP committed to attend the educational requirements of all 2,300 inmates in that prison. Further, they organized interbarrack and interprison tournaments to encourage sports. Vidya Jyoti College of Theology sent in a team of counselors who proved to be sympathetic and understanding toward the inmates. The Urdu Akademi and the Punjabi Akademi offered an honorarium to those inmates who taught Urdu and Punjabi inside the jail. The entry of these two reputed academies represented a major breakthrough, as now Tihar could claim to house respected academic institutions. The Punjabi Akademi faculty motivated inmates to form a theater group, which staged plays with only the inmates as actors.

In a span of six months, the number of libraries in the prison increased from three to twenty-five. Many academic institutions, organizations, and individuals willingly donated books. I must make a special mention of one dedicated, outstanding individual, Saroj Vashisht, whose untiring and versatile endeavors was a constant source of inspiration to all of us. Saroj turned sixty in 1993, but she seemed remarkably young. She proved to be extremely dynamic in all spheres of community work, especially in those aspects related to ado-

One of the most satisfying experiences for the many illiterate inmates was to be able to sign their name when leaving the prison.

lescents and juveniles. She started off by telling stories to the youngsters. She instantly won the hearts of her young audience, who began calling her mother. All of them insisted that she visit the jail daily to narrate new stories. Each time she came to Tihar, she brought books on diverse subjects to supplement the library collection. The young inmates saw in Saroj an image of love, compassion, and understanding. Here is her story:

> I came to Tihar for community service in June 1993. I started as a storyteller. During my interaction with the adolescents, I found they were desperate for dictionaries and teach-yourself kits in Hindi and English. I have many interesting accounts to relate, one of which concerns Manoj (a Tihar inmate) who was twenty years old when I met him. His father was an inspector at Rajpur Road Police Station. Manoj and his brother had murdered eight people in that police station. He said his father had taught him that the *Bhagavad Gita* says that if you kill your enemy, you are not doing any wrong. His father told him and his brother that some people who had been their enemies were coming to lodge a complaint against them. So he and his brother went to the police station with their father's service revolver and killed them.
>
> When I first met him, I asked, "You are only twenty now and if convicted, you will come out when you are thirty-four. What will you do then?" He replied, "I'll kill the rest of the family." That worried me, but gradually he became a peaceful human being. Within two weeks, Manoj begged me to help him get admission to a correspondence course so that he could complete his graduation.

Later he also joined the meditation program. He said that he realized his father's mistake.

There were times when the boys would ask me if I could leave the books behind after the day's reading, so that they could read them later. They would ask for books on physics, chemistry, and other subjects. I was desperate to get them books.

For Saroj, the literacy movement within Tihar was nothing short of a crusade. She suggested that we ask various publishers to donate books to the prison libraries. She was confident of getting a positive response. In fact, the response was overwhelming. Stacks of books arrived, covering a vast range of subjects: science, computers, basic medicine, literature, history, religion, and management. Other organizations supplied education-related material such as slates, blackboards, chalk, notebooks, pencils, and schoolbags. Such institutions were genuinely interested in furthering literacy and knowledge and were eager to provide all kinds of support.

As the literacy and education drive within Tihar gained momentum, we expanded the circulation of newspapers and magazines within the wards. We also set in motion mobile libraries with the assistance of Delhi Public Library. The duty wards of many prisons now stored literary material along with essential furniture such as tables and chairs. Thousands of books were distributed among prison residents. Moreover, every time we held a panchayat or a mahapanchayat, books, notebooks, and diaries were given to the teacher inmates and other panchayat members, who would pass them on to the other inmates. We constantly endeavored to ensure adequate supplies of reading material, especially for the teachers, so that they could update their teaching material.

Another area in which we attempted to make headway, but were not entirely successful, pertained to vocational training. My unshakeable conviction was that if literacy was important, teaching vocational trades was crucial. But here we ran into seemingly insurmountable obstacles that seriously impeded our progress. The obstacles were limitations in the infrastructure and policy orientation as well as a lack of trained professional teachers. Nevertheless, we did not lose hope. Eventually, help did come our way in a small measure from the government of India. Professionals from the government's Shramik Vidya Peeth and the State Resource Center provided training to the adolescents in vocations such as bookbinding, file cover-making, *agarbatti* (incense) stick-rolling, tailoring, chalk-making, and electronic repair. Further, the Department of Technical Education of the Delhi State Government conducted a certificate course in commercial art and embroidery. Many talented inmates took advantage of this opportunity.

However, these efforts were not sufficient to cater to the needs of over 8,000 inmates. A majority of the jail residents were eager, even desperate, to learn a trade or a craft so that they could support themselves and their dependent families. This was one area that required serious attention, and here long-term policies as well as practical implementation procedures were urgently needed. It was up to the Delhi State Government to fill the breach.

Industries were keen to take advantage of the manpower available in Tihar, but in negotiations with leading entrepreneurs, they insisted that such an enterprise had to be on a long-term basis. This requirement clause led to a setback because the turnover of inmates was high, and we could not guarantee compliance with this stipulation. Moreover, these entrepreneurs wanted the commitment of the Secretariat before planning training or recruitment of Tihar inmates. The attitude of the Secretariat was officious, and since they rarely visited Tihar, they had no understanding of the tremendous changes taking place. Vocational training trailed far behind the literacy and moral education movement.

Undaunted, we concentrated our efforts on those areas that were under our control. The internal management structure of Tihar consisted of the staff officials as well as prison panchayat members. They were regularly on the lookout for new initiatives and new problem-solving methods. The internal management team organized seminars and workshops on subjects of interest to inmates such as the causes of crime, reformation of criminals, crimes against women, rehabilitation of released prisoners, and benefits of yoga in combating crime.

The mornings were allotted for literary activities followed by whatever vocational training was possible. But literacy and vocational training were not our only concern. We also offered inspiration and socialization skills. Evenings were allotted for sports and *sarva dharma sabhas,* ethical therapy congregations. These sabhas were held in the open-air auditorium of the jail for an hour at 5 p.m. The officer-in-charge, preferably the Deputy Superintendent and often the Superintendent, presided over the programs. I personally attended many such congregations. On several occasions, eminent visitors addressed the inmates on topics such as morality, peace, harmony, and good conduct. Occasionally, well-known dancers like Shovana Narayan performed, and singers like Anup Jalota sang devotional songs.

After the address or singing came to an end the inmates were encouraged to ask questions. We hoped to reorient the mind-set of inmates. Christian and Muslim priests, Sikh *granthis* (preachers), Hindu pandits, and others from the OSHO Mission, the Chinmaya Mission, Brahma Kumaris,

Ramakrishna Mission, International Society for Krishna Consciousness (ISKCON), and innumerable others addressed the inmates at evening congregations.

They listened with rapt attention to the discourses. This level of attention from such teachers would have been difficult to have outside the prison. The inmates began to express gratitude to the community at large and the administration in particular. Perhaps never before in their life had they received such sustained value-based education. These discourses led them to question who they were and why and what they could be. This was evident from the queries they were raising and the help they were seeking. Even in this field, Tihar was moving toward self-reliance. Many times in the evenings, when we did not have a teacher from outside, we encouraged an inmate to share his story. Such personal accounts were captivating and inspiring. We didn't miss an opportunity for community upliftment. National holidays (Republic Day, Independence Day, and Gandhi Jayanti) and the major festivals of all religions provided occasion for the expression of joy, patriotism, harmony, compassion, and sacrifice.

A non-government organization called *The Family* worked wonders for the Tihar inmates. They enacted value-based plays, which included a good deal of music; organized seminars on human relations; held workshops on hygiene and self-improvement; devised children's development programs; and they offered rehabilitation therapy for drug users. One of *The Family* members recalls the Tihar experience:

> Our first contact with the inmates of Tihar Jail was almost intimidating. Coming face-to-face with hundreds of human beings in captivity all at once was an unsettling experience initially, to say the least, till we realized that beneath these seemingly hard and cold exteriors were some very bitter, dis-

couraged, and depressed human souls desperately in need of understanding and acceptance. We decided not to get minutely involved with details of every inmate's individual case, but to look beyond their criminal record and treat them as human beings worthy of respect in the firm belief that if we treat people as if they were what they ought to be, we will help them to become what they are capable of becoming—good human beings.

We also treated them as equals instead of as inmates and talked to them as we would talk to friends instead of talking down at them. Some of them would initially make sarcastic remarks during our programs and try to disrupt them in an attempt to provoke us, but we found it best to totally ignore all this and continue being friendly toward them, no matter what. Gradually we started to win their trust, and before long, the barrier was broken and we were accepted as friends. As a result of this, our workshops and programs started having a deeper impact on their lives, and a number of them started acknowledging the fact that they were learning moral principles that they were totally unaware of previously.

We have found music and theater to be ideal methods of communicating concepts. These methods entertain and educate at the same time. We have witnessed lives slowly changing for the better.

The Tihar programs were unique in that everyone was required to participate. All 9,700 inmates (the prison population by 1995), including children, adolescents, women, convicts and undertrials, Indians and foreigners, participated in the morning classes and the evening congregations. Participation was mandatory. On my visits to prisons abroad I saw impressive educational programs for the convicts but nothing for the undertrials, and the educational classes were not compulsory. The teachers were from the outside, mostly on contract. Perhaps no one waits as long for trial as in Tihar and other prisons in India. But the spectrum of the program was nowhere as complete as it was in Tihar.

Lives were changing, and so was the entire institutional culture. One telling example reveals the extent of change. The inmates told me that in the past when a released inmate was re-arrested and brought back to Tihar Jail, he was given a warm welcome, and his old friends organized a cheerful reception for him. But after the reform revolution, a former inmate returning to Tihar triggered off shouts of "Shame! Shame!" The former prisoner was castigated by his fellow residents for returning to the world of crime. The jail inmates no more welcomed a repeat offender with open arms. The concluding slogans of evening sabhas were "Once we leave Tihar, we shall never come back," and "We will stay happy and spread happiness." The jail was becoming an ashram, a place for reform and correction. In fact, Tihar Jail was now referred to as Tihar Ashram.

Vipassana Meditation and the Magical Metamorphosis

On the rounds one day, Rajinder Kumar, a young Assistant Superintendent, overheard me saying that I wished I possessed a magical therapy to help the inmates rid themselves of corrosive emotions. He promptly came to me and said that he knew of such a therapy—vipassana meditation. I was naturally curious to know more about it. He said that if I wanted additional information, I should talk to his wife. So I did. His wife revealed that Rajinder had been an ill-tempered, easily provoked man before taking a vipassana meditation course. I verified the authenticity of her claim from other sources as well. Ram Singh, the former Home Secretary of the Rajasthan State Government, had introduced vipassana meditation programs into Jaipur and Baroda prisons. Rajinder was sure he would more than welcome our invitation to bring vipassana to Tihar.

As coincidence would have it, M. L. Mehta, former colleague of Ram Singh, was visiting Tihar, and he suggested we introduce meditation inside Tihar. He volunteered to speak to Ram Singh. To me, this coincidence was an instance of prayers being answered even before they were said. Vipassana is an ancient meditation technique. Its basic objective is purification of the mind. Vipassana meditation is secular in all respects, non-sectarian, and an effective tool. Ram Singh taught the technique in a ten-day residential course. During the course participants maintained silence and were not permitted to communicate among themselves or with outsiders. The day began at 4 a.m., and included eight hours of intense meditation at specified periods during the day. During the first three days of the course, participants focused on their breathing patterns. Any physical discomfort was overcome with self-control. The remaining seven days were devoted to becoming conscious of various body sensations and emotions and how to achieve control over them. This control initiated a process of purification, which leads ultimately to emancipation from anxiety, tension, and suffering, and transforms an individual's personality and outlook. This is exactly what we needed in Tihar. I invited Ram Singh to Tihar, and we began to plan the introduction of meditation.

After seeing the prison, Ram Singh suggested that the

Meditation training and retreats were popular with both the staff members and the inmates of Tihar Jail.

first training include 50 to 90 volunteers, preferably long-term convicts, and some staff members. He asked that we designate separate residential barracks for individuals in the course. He wanted a separate room for the lectures. A separate kitchen was required to prepare wholesome vegetarian food. Breakfast was served at 6:30 a.m. and lunch at 11 a.m. Evening tea at 5 p.m. included milk and seasonal fruit. Every evening, participants and also other inmates, staff members, medical staff, and security staff interested in the vipassana technique could watch a discourse on video.

We decided to conduct the first course in Prison No. 2, which housed the long-term convicted inmates. Ram Singh and Professor P. L. Dhar of the Indian Institute of Technology, Delhi, conducted the first lessons. As teachers, both of them stayed inside the prison with the life-termers. The hardened convicts, for whom affection, sensitivity, and care were totally alien feelings, initially viewed their intentions with suspicion. The two teachers were subjected to some nightmarish experiences during the first few days of their tenure in jail. They were exposed to a barrage of intimidations from professional criminals who flouted the rules they were supposed to follow during the course. They smoked, broke the vow of silence, and proceeded to mouth some of the choicest of abuses at all those around them. They hoped Ram Singh and Professor Dhar would succumb to their verbal onslaught and physical threats and quit. But they were proved wrong. The teachers handled the onslaught personally, without bothering the prison authorities. They continued to conduct the course as usual, ignoring the jibes and taunts flung at them. Their determination and perseverance, imbued with compassion, eventually prevailed, and after five days, the small gang of convicts realized their folly and begged forgiveness from their two teachers. This was a miracle in itself!

We were delighted with the result of the first ten-day training. At the end of the course, the first participant to stand up and speak was Bichittar Singh, who was serving a life term. He said, "I have been in the jail for the last nine years due to fabricated evidence presented by my parents and brothers. I had been harboring a feeling of revenge and ill will against my own parents and brothers. Right now, after undergoing this meditation course, I am feeling so light, so tension free, so happy, and so satisfied that I am thankful to my parents and brothers who sent me to jail where I have been given a chance to attend this unique meditation course which has changed my attitude, behavior, and way of thinking. I am also thankful to the jail authorities for giving me an opportunity to attend this course." And he went on to request that such courses be organized for the police, judiciary, and other government officers who make the decisions that affect the lives of so many people.

Santokh Singh, serving a life sentence for murder, stated that meditation had brought him peace of mind and contentment. He continued to practice during the remainder of his stay in Tihar and attended the course again along with his wife and children upon his release. Satbir Singh, an ex-constable serving a ten-year sentence, confessed that he had committed many offenses during the 1984 riots in Delhi. "Prior to coming to Tihar, I was under the impression that the stick was all powerful," he said. "After undergoing this meditation course, the helpful and cooperative attitude of the senior officers who were instrumental in reforming and rehabilitating the prisoners, my view has been transformed by love and affection. Now I think love and affection have greater powers for curbing negativity. I now believe that a man has to pay for his misdeeds sooner or later. I promise before all that I will not again harm anybody."

Niranjan Nath, convicted of robbery, narrated that his

mind was unstable and dwelt in the misdeeds of the past. The meditation course inspired him to pay attention to the present and not worry anymore about the past.

Om Prakash Bairwa, who was serving a sentence for kidnapping a girl, made the most startling disclosure. He asserted that his rivals, in connivance with the police, had falsely implicated him since he was the president of his community and wanted to contest the elections. "Before undergoing this meditation course, I was polluting my mind with feelings of revenge. I wanted to either kill the judge who delivered the wrong judgment, or kidnap his children, or stage an accident of the judge's vehicle. My mind was flooded with negative feelings. Consequently, I spent many restless nights. But now, after undergoing the meditation course, all my negative feelings have disappeared. Now I have become a firm believer in God. I shall not take revenge on anyone. My mind is now full of *karuna* (compassion) and *maitri* (benevolence)."

Those who had benefited the most were impatient to share the experience with all the prisoners. Consequently, we decided to celebrate New Year's Day in 1994 as a vipassana meditation course day in all the four prisons. The objective of this was to enable all the inmates to begin the year with inspiration. Guru Satyanarayan Goenka, an eminent vipassana teacher, came to Tihar to address the huge assembly of inmates and staff. I am reproducing an extract of his speech here:

> Friends, you have all assembled here to liberate yourselves from all bondage and misery. To be imprisoned in a prison like this is great agony. And to be liberated from prison is very fortunate. But besides the confinement within these four walls, there is a greater prison in which all of us suffer so much.

This is the prison of our negativity, our own mental derailments, which keep overpowering us. We have become the slaves of our own anger, hatred, ill will, and animosity. We are slaves of craving, greed, passion, attachment, and ego. Any defilement that arises in our minds overpowers us and makes us its prisoner. We start suffering immediately. This suffering is not confined inside these prison walls. Inside or outside this jail we are all prisoners of our own habit patterns, and we keep on suffering.

If we are relieved of our negative habits, we start enjoying the true happiness of liberation. We start enjoying real peace and real harmony. When our minds are freed from impurities, the habit patterns of our lives change. A pure mind is naturally full of love and compassion, joy, and equanimity. This is real happiness, real peace, and real harmony. The bondage of mental defilements is a universal bondage. And the happiness of liberation from these negativities is also universal. Whether one is a Hindu, Muslim, Jain, Buddhist, Christian, Jew, Sikh, or Parsi—it makes no difference. Anyone who is imprisoned in the bondage of defilement is bound to suffer. Anyone who breaks this bondage starts to enjoy peace and harmony.

The first day of the New Year has brought you this wonderful technique of ancient India, a technique discovered by the enlightened ones. The technique is scientific, result-oriented, and nonsectarian. It brings you the message of liberation, the message of peace and harmony. May all of you participating in this camp work diligently, patiently, and persistently to come out of your bondage and your miseries. May a new era start in your lives. May *dharma* bring you full liberation. May you all enjoy real peace and harmony.

Observing the tremendous goodwill generated by the Vipassana Program, Ram Singh and others suggested that we hold a meeting of the head administrators of prisons at the national level to introduce the Vipassana Program. We held that meeting January 24, 1994, at the Tihar Jail conference hall. The Inspector Generals from Assam, Gujarat, Haryana, Himachal Pradesh, Jammu and Kashmir, Karnataka, Maharashtra, Orissa, Rajasthan, and Uttar Pradesh attended. We presented the history of vipassana and described in detail its beneficial results. Then the officials toured Tihar. They had opportunities to talk to inmates who had taken the course.

Meanwhile, the demand within Tihar to attend the course kept increasing. We also wanted the maximum number of inmates to benefit, the sooner the better. Hesitantly, I asked Ram Singh whether it would be possible to conduct the vipassana course for a large number of inmates, say, around 1,000, in one go. He said, "Why not?" He recalled a prediction made by Goenkaji's Burmese guru, "One day Goenka will collectively teach this course to over 1,000 people." This prediction became a reality in the Tihar Jail in April 1994.

The logistical and security aspects of conducting the course on such a massive scale necessitated careful organization and a precise coordination. First of all we had to find a place that could accommodate 1,000 individuals without posing security threats. The best choice was two new buildings under construction in Prison 4. The official in charge, I. C. Kalra, contrary to the norms set by his predecessors, speeded up the construction work. In view of the cooperative spirit permeating the entire prison environment, skilled inmates assisted him, and other less skilled inmates dug drainage ditches, laid out a network of water pipes, and cleared the large area designated for the vipassana course. Soon they erected a huge multicolored open-air tent and outfitted it with rugs, cushions, fans, and lights.

When all was ready, 1,003 volunteers assembled to receive the instruction. The first vipassana course for female prisoners was held simultaneously in Prison No. 1 and was attended by 49 inmates. Most of the 1,000 plus inmates who undertook this vipassana course were waiting for trial. Twenty foreign men and foreign women also participated in the Vipassana Program. The foreigners were from many different countries, including Afghanistan, Australia, Canada, France, Germany, Italy, Nigeria, Senegal, Somalia, Sri Lanka, Tanzania, and the United Kingdom.

As each day of the ten-day course passed, the whole atmosphere in the prison improved. A sense of liberation grew. There was discipline without fear; there was devotion without coercion. Every evening, Goenkaji delivered discourses and answered questions. The session usually lasted for 30 to 45 minutes. When a journalist questioned him as to why meditation was good for prisoners, he said:

> Vipassana is good for everyone! We are all prisoners of the negative habit patterns of our own minds. The practice of vipassana liberates us from this bondage ... Vipassana is a tool that can help all suffering people: those who are behind bars and separated from their families, and those who are not. What you see in Tihar is a message of hope, which will benefit the whole world.

Goenkaji's discourses were videotaped and telecast by Zee TV, a pan-Asian television channel. Karuna Films produced a documentary, *Doing Time Doing Vipassana,* of this unprecedented program in Tihar. This film won the Golden Spire Award at the San Francisco International Film Festival in 1998 and the Finalist Award at the New York Festival.

On the last day, it was evident to one and all that the impossible had been accomplished. Over 1,000 inmates had successfully completed a meditation course. Goenkaji declared that this was the largest course he had ever conducted in almost twenty-five years of teaching. The successful completion of the Vipassana Course on such a large scale paved the way for the establishment of the first permanent meditation center within Tihar. After the final session of meditation on April 15, the congregation of around 1,100, including inmates, jail staff, and guests, witnessed the inauguration of the new center, which Goenkaji named Dhamma Tihar.

Within three weeks, the new center began to conduct two ten-day courses a month for students from all four prisons. We adjusted the housing situation to allow inmates who had gone through the course to continue sitting together in meditation. Each Prison Superintendent began to designate separate barracks for vipassana inmates and allotted open space near those barracks for meditation. We regularly held full-house assemblies consisting of all those inmates who had undergone the course. We established a Vipassana Panchayat to regularly coordinate between the prisoners and teachers and to also act as a think tank on all matters related to this program. All these measures proved to be crucial in enhancing the benefits of the vipassana course.

The collective assemblies were inspired and invigorated by one-day courses devised by the Vipassana Research Institute. Videotapes of Goenkaji's discourses were shown as well. The teachers answered questions raised by the inmates and encouraged their continued participation. The

Dhamma Tihar gradually developed into an organized residential center for vipassana inside the jail. Benefits that accrued from this center were substantial and long lasting.

Meanwhile, the impact of the program spread beyond Tihar and New Delhi, thanks to extensive and positive media coverage. The Home Ministry officials sent out a circular encouraging all the states of India to adopt meditation as a reform measure in all the prisons under their jurisdiction.

Nearer home, one of Tihar's Jail Superintendents, Tarsem Kumar, wrote a book detailing his experiences during the metamorphosis stage in Tihar, with emphasis on the remarkable catalytic effect of vipassana. When invited by the United States Congressional Executive Committee, I presented a copy of his book, *Freedom Behind Bars,* at the National Prayer Breakfast Meeting at The White House, Washington, D.C., in February 1995. I firmly believe that the West could use the Vipassana Meditation Program in criminal correction and reform.

A study of the effects of vipassana on the mental health of prisoners revealed several significant facts:

> While on the one hand, the emotional climate of a prison can prove to be destructive to most goals of rehabilitation, it can also provide a safe structure for individual growth and development. Certain aspects of the prison milieu can be utilized creatively by the correctional system. The emphasis on empathic understanding and unconditioned positive regard for each individual can reduce anxieties and foster psychological growth and self-actualization. Studies assessing the psychological effects of Vipassana Meditation carried out in Tihar Jail in 1993 and 1994 revealed a statistically significant reduction in anxiety, depression, hostility, and feelings of

helplessness, coupled with enhanced well-being and hope for the future. This study reinforced earlier studies conducted after Vipassana courses in the prisons of Rajasthan and Gujarat.

The vipassana effect was phenomenal. Within a span of a few months, vipassana had become an integral part of Tihar Ashram. When I had joined in May 1993, we had set for ourselves the goal of transforming the jail into an ashram—an institution that enables introspection by all its inhabitants, including the managers. It reinforced my personal conviction that certain duties are not mere jobs, but a whole mission by themselves, for they construct the future. *The Sun* carried this report:

Tihar Jail: The Inside Story
In the 1950s, V. Shantaram created history when he made a film, *Do Aankhen Baarah Haath*. The film fetched many awards in national and international film festivals. Based on jail reforms, the film revolved around a jailor (Shantaram) who reformed hardcore criminals and engaged them in constructive works.

Twenty years later, Kiran Bedi, the formidable, high-profile lady cop, is doing exactly the same thing. But now it's for real. Since she became the Inspector General, Prisons, Delhi, two months ago, Tihar Jail, the biggest prison in the whole of Asia, housing more than 8,000 prisoners, is turned into a virtual ashram.

healing drug addiction and the medical services crisis

Tackling Drug Addiction

One of the biggest problems in Tihar was habitual substance abuse. Tihar Jail had a floating population of around 250 new entrants arriving daily, and an almost equal number leaving the prison. Typically, the arriving inmates could be expected to be habitual substance abusers. The substances of choice ranged from narcotics to psychotropic substances. After the completion of formalities, new arrivals were sent off to various prisons according to the alphabetic order of their names. Inside each prison, they would be lodged for the night in an inspection ward for new entrants. The intention was to facilitate inspection by the jail doctor the following morning. However, due to the skeletal medical services in Tihar, even the routine formality of inspection sometimes took more than forty-eight hours. For the drug addicts, this protracted period was nothing short of a horrendous nightmare, for they were deprived of their regular fix. They exhibited acute withdrawal symptoms, writhing in pain and screaming for help. The warders invariably doped them to put them to sleep. In effect, the drug addicts were merely transferring their dependence from illegal drugs, such as opium, heroin, or marijuana, to prescription drugs.

The inspection wards never slept. The sounds emitted by the drug users were eerie and sometimes macabre. I just could not shut my ears to these sounds during my initial night rounds of the jail. To me, these sounds were similar to those heard in a zoo; the only difference was that this was a human zoo. The prime objective of all this cacophony was to summon the prison doctors. More often than not this objective was defeated.

Except for a single detoxification center located in Prison 4, Tihar had no facility for de-addiction. There was no systematic organized procedure for diagnosis and treatment. Within the prisons, the chaotic mix of drug peddlers and drug users was evident. The drug mafia's intricate web included some staff members drawn by easy money or coerced by threats to them or their family members. The prison environment, which was supposed to reduce drug addiction and the resultant crimes, was, in fact, stimulating it. All the characteristics of a successful enterprise were present: the indefatigable producer, the persevering pushers and suppliers, the retail outlets, pliable inmates and staff members, and above all, the omnipresent consumers.

Such was the situation when we launched our crusade against drugs. The objective was to initially curtail and then eliminate the influx of drugs into the jail. I relied on all the knowledge, skills, and experience that I gained over the years running Navjyoti centers, which I had set up in the community for the holistic treatment of substance abusers. I was confident of achieving reasonable success, but I needed dedicated and motivated support not only from my colleagues but also from the inmates themselves, who would be the ultimate beneficiaries. Such support did manifest itself, grudgingly at first, but later on, enthusiastically and wholeheartedly.

The first measure we adopted was to segregate known and suspected substance abusers from the rest of the inmates within each prison. The abusers were housed together in a ward in each prison. Next, we brought in a homoeopathic doctor on a daily-visit basis to provide exclusive attention to the substance-afflicted inmates. Homeopathy proved effective in controlling the painful symptoms caused by withdrawal, such as running noses, trembling of the body, watering eyes, sleeplessness, and other related symptoms. The treatment was basically holistic in keeping with the traditions of homoeopathy, non-addictive, and provided considerable respite to the habitual drug users. Furthermore, this therapy reduced the pressure on the already overburdened allopathic prison doctors. Various addictive painkillers and sleep inducives had no role to play. The doctor made his rounds morning and evening, before lockup time. The second round was essentially to make sure that the substance abusers had taken their medicine so that they could pass the night with minimum discomfort. This round also ensured that other inmates could sleep peacefully.

Apart from the inmates, some of the prison staff members were also entrapped in the quagmire of drug addiction. Along with my colleagues, I drew up a plan to identify and isolate these individuals. They were summoned to my office and asked to take medical leave and get themselves treated. They could seek treatment in the Navjyoti treatment centers or at any other medical center in which they had confidence. We were very clear that all staff members had to come clean before they could be trusted with any responsibility.

Along with medical attention, we augmented the diet of the substance-abuse patients. We sanctioned more milk for them. We added some variety to their otherwise monotonous menu by providing curd, jaggery, and dry black grams. All these measures generated a sense of optimism among the addict patients, who now felt properly cared for.

By this time, we started to monitor the inmates carefully as soon as they entered the prison. Inmates had a proper medical checkup the evening of their entry into the jail. Drug users were sent immediately to the drug wards. Early segregation enabled us to identify those individuals who served as the sources in the drug-supplying nexus of inmates and their outside connections.

While doing our utmost for the drug users both at the physical and psychological levels, we simultaneously inten-

Innovative drug-smuggling methods included hiding drugs inside books and cooked food brought in by friends and family during visiting hours.

sified the searches in all wards to cut off the supply. During one such search, we found that the inmate in charge of the kitchen in Prison 2 was running a brisk supply operation with nine other inmates. We found drugs concealed in his belongings and called in the police who instituted a case against him for the possession of drugs. In another instance, we received a timely tip that a warder was peddling drugs inside the jail. He was caught red-handed by the officers and handed over to the local police. After the legal formalities, the warder found himself back in Tihar, this time behind bars. He drew some consolation from the fact that three of his colleagues met the same fate.

Gradually, as the overall health of the prisoners started to improve, they began to support the prison authorities in their crusade against drugs. The petition box proved to be an invaluable source of information as well as suggestions in our efforts to check drug supply and consumption. One particularly useful suggestion was implemented immediately. A keenly observant inmate suggested that we remove the silver foils from the cigarette packets sold in the prison canteens. Drugs were placed on the foil and lit from below. Smoking or snorting was the preferred practice in the jail. The absence of silver foil made it difficult to smoke drugs. If ordinary paper were used instead of foil it would start burning. On-the-round observations and the panchayat system also proved effective in detecting drug problems. They provided precious nuggets of information that we may have otherwise overlooked.

Meanwhile, another disturbing aspect came to light. The only drug treatment center in the prison, Ashiana, was itself in need of immediate aid. A surprise inspection revealed that many of the staff members, whose names were recorded in the attendance register, were conspicuous by their absence. Much of the equipment, such as the X-ray machine, was not functional. Even more serious and alarming, the medicines for use in Ashiana were coming surreptitiously from another clinic and stealthily diverted to yet another center. We seized the medicines and the attendance records and reported the problems to the authorities. I was told that an enquiry was ordered, but there was no formal communication. However, once the center came under our scrutiny, it had to perform.

When all their activities were subjected to public scrutiny, the center staff realized that they would have to upgrade their performance, the sooner the better. Though a bit grudgingly, the staff began to put their centers in order. Consequently, Tihar could now proudly lay claim to drug-treatment centers with doctors and social workers available around the clock.

The difficult or problematic drug-addict entrants were referred to Ashiana because medical aid was available even at night, which was not the case in the drug-addict wards of other prisons. The patients who were admitted to Ashiana, and who were on the way to recovery, assisted us in our seemingly endless war against drug smuggling into the jail by identifying the supply points. The feedback provided by these patients was highly reliable. Thus, we could plug the supply points and further reduce the inflow of drugs.

Within a few months of this collective endeavor, the inmates could sleep peacefully at night. There were no more eerie and bizarre yells. During my night rounds, as I walked through the various prisons, I felt like a relieved mother whose children were blissfully asleep after a hard day's work. And the staff was vigilant, exactly the opposite of what I had seen a few months earlier.

In the field of drug addiction, the outside community began to make meaningful contributions. The Bharat Vikas Parishad offered to send yoga teachers to give the recovering addicts the therapeutic effects of yoga postures. Navjyoti offered counseling services, audiovisual programs on prevention of drug abuse, street plays with powerful messages against drug abuse, and group-discussion sessions. At the conceptual level, Navjyoti introduced user-accountability and self-management. A counselor helped the addicts organize their time fruitfully and purposefully. My colleague, Jaydev Sarangi, brought in the Central Health Education Bureau authorities to launch a comprehensive campaign focusing on the health hazards of smoking, chewing tobacco, and consuming drugs. This was the first-ever campaign of its kind in Tihar. Also many experts in the field of addiction—doctors, psychiatrists, and other specialists—volunteered their services. All of this was a profound change in the lives of Tihar inmates, who had been accustomed to a life of intense monotony.

All India Radio was greatly enthused by the response to our drug-treatment drive. A team from the radio came into Tihar and produced a program on this subject. Many addicted inmates were interviewed, and related the transformations in their lives. The inmates used this opportunity to make an appeal for greater help from the community. This appeal had an impressive impact. The Indian Cancer Society volunteered to conduct a campaign highlighting how the indiscriminate and uncontrolled use of drugs could lead to cancer. Another pioneering organization in the field of drug abuse and prevention, Sahara, offered to supervise an entire ward in the same manner as its sister organization, Navjyoti. All these developments substantially reinforced the concept of good health of both the mind and the body. The voluntary organizations not only provided a healing touch but also inspired inmates to adopt a new, wholesome lifestyle.

On my visits to prisons abroad, I saw excellent medical structures for substance-abuse treatment. They were full-fledged nursing wards for addiction treatment and an integral part of their health-care system. Tihar had none of this and yet made considerable breakthroughs in controlling the drug problem, with the support and involvement of the outside community. As far as infrastructure and management, we were getting better results with holistic strategies in dealing with deviant human behavior. The prison, in fact, was moving toward a holistic lifestyle, which meant treatment of the inmates in totality—environmentally, physically, and mentally.

Dr. Harinder Sethi, a reputed psychiatrist and director of Association for Scientific Research on Addictions (AASRA), made substantial contributions to Tihar's program. The details of how his remarkable therapeutic program began and how it developed are best narrated in his own words:

AASRA Parivar: The First Twenty Months

I had been waiting for 45 minutes for the group to assemble. Ward 12 of Jail 4, the addicts' ward, was a place no one in the jail was happy to be. A few weeks earlier, in a containment exercise, the prison authorities had rounded up all the drug addicts in Jail 4 and lodged them in this ward. The prisoners were unshaven and had a vacuous look in their eyes. Their clothes, and most of them in their underclothes, were a month past needing a wash. My thoughts were frequently interrupted by shouts and abuses hurled by the Head Warder as he called for order. The requests fell on deaf ears. The sound of the wooden rod on the backs of a few prisoners is still fresh in my mind. Slowly, about twenty of the 200-odd prisoners sat down to listen to what I had to say.

I could hardly hear myself over the cacophony. I tried to tell the reluctant group that I was a doctor who worked with drug addicts, and that I would like to know what their needs were, and whether I could be of any help. The few who heard me were grateful that someone considered them worthwhile enough to talk to. They were happy to have me come again after a fortnight.

I returned thinking that one Kiran Bedi per ward was needed. We just did not have sixty such persons for all the wards of the prison. It dawned on me that I had been given a big responsibility without any authority. It was a challenge.

This prison was unlike others. An overcrowded detoxification facility, Ashiana, run by a NGO under the auspices of the Ministry of Welfare catered to the overwhelming detoxification needs of the inmates of all four prisons. Some counseling and post-discharge follow-up was also a part of their program.

I discovered that 85 percent of the prisoners were under judicial custody waiting for trial, and no one in the prison had any control on the admissions and discharges. Rehabilitation programs for undertrials were an unheard-of concept. Even the law prescribed rehabilitation programs only for convicts, and was concerned only with custody of undertrials. Of those a significant number had prior convictions. Others faced prolonged stays in prison due to the protracted judicial proceedings, and if convicted, would leave the jail immediately, as they would have already served their sentence. A new design was needed to cater to this reality. This is how I went about it.

Prelaunch Stage

My second visit to the ward was less traumatic. A larger group collected to listen to me, this time without the use of the rod. By word of mouth, the previous group of listeners aroused curiosity. I saw that some prisoners showed signs of withdrawal. I asked if they needed medical aid. Some said yes. The majority did not. Some had already suffered for over two or three days without their drug. Some had chosen to withdraw from drugs without the aid of medication. Most of them had gone in and out of detoxification facilities several times. It gradually dawned on them that getting off drugs was not an issue—staying off drugs was the central problem.

I started visiting the ward twice a week and brought indoor and outdoor game equipment, clothes, toothpaste, toothbrushes, soap, anti-scabies and anti-lice medication, books and magazines at their request. I spent time playing cricket or volleyball with the prisoners much to the surprise of the others. Not fully understanding this phase of the program, my work was initially described in a prison magazine as "Dr. Sethi treats drug addicts with sports and games."

In six weeks the prisoners anxiously awaited my visits to the ward. Less time was necessary to gather around to hear "Doctor Sahib," as I was called. More and more prisoners joined the gathering. I talked about responsible concern, sharing and caring for self and others, leadership, and families. I continued to fulfill their special requests.

One day, there were objections by the group to some individuals who were taking advantage of the "good doctor." It was not acceptable that those who were well off were lining up for handouts. The group decided that from then on only those who did not have visits from relatives were allowed to make special requests. This marked the formation of group norms set by the majority. Grabbing the opportunity, I talked about "no free lunch." I stipulated that a payment was expected for the things I brought. The price was a commitment that all would be vigilant and would not allow drugs or peddlers of drugs to enter the ward.

The culture of helping the less fortunate in the ward was slowly catching on. The topics of my talks now included mutual self-help and "I am my brother's keeper" as an extension of responsible concern. Education and caring were highlighted as valuable assets. The more educated would teach the less educated. Teams were formed in each barrack to give massages to those undergoing withdrawal pains. However, the frequent admissions and discharges into this ward were so disturbing that it was difficult to sustain this environment of mutual assistance.

Several meetings of the leaders of subgroups were held. They disseminated messages to members of their subgroup. They discussed the concept of a community that looks after its own needs. The ward came to be known as the Therapeutic Community (TC) for recovery from drug dependence. Requests for miscellaneous items were now to be channeled through chosen leaders. A rudimentary feedback system was thus started. They named the program Aasra Parivar, a joint system of families. Family meetings were held three times a week where members would share their life stories and talk of their family of origin. They would also share experiences at their court hearings, and some shared the letters they had received from friends and relatives.

The family groups presented the setting for correction. When conflicts and strong emotions arose, encounter groups identified the problem and the solution and encouraged a change in behavior as the group saw fit. External pressure from family members forced an erring member to comply with the standards the family set.

In December 1993, an Aasra volunteer, Pradeep, who had been off heroin for four years, joined me on my visits. While I held meetings with family heads, he would hold meetings with the rest of the community and share his story of recovery from drugs. He motivated others to share their experiences with drugs, their downfall, and how they recovered after joining Aasra Parivar. He joined the project as its first staff member when Aasra was awarded a modest grant from Ishan Charitable Trust. His full-time involvement was a boon to the project.

Dr. Kiran Bedi's encouragement and numerous suggestions were readily incorporated into the program. Her attention and support gave the residents of this community respect in the eyes of the other prisoners. Suddenly they were no longer untouchables. The prisoner-teachers came in to hold classes. The local music group came regularly. The Superintendent, P. R. Meena, and the Deputy Superintendent, Sunil Gupta, took active interest in our community. Each of these individuals contributed immensely to the blossoming of Aasra Parivar.

The Delhi Police Foundation recognized the program in January 1994. The Navjyoti Award was presented to Aasra. I received the prize on behalf of residents of the program. Later, at a small ceremony inside the ward, I presented the shawl from Navjyoti to the man who really deserved it, Shivanand Khemani, the Head Warder. Cash awards were also given to the convict officer of the ward and other family heads. To everyone's surprise, they donated the cash to the Ward's Welfare Fund.

Launch Stage

Aasra Parivar celebrated its first anniversary in May 1994. With more staff trainees, our focus turned to training, curriculum, and shaping behavior. The behavior-monitoring system was refined, and a five-color behavior-rating code was introduced. An elaborate Shaping Pro-Social Behavior program was launched in the community after a detailed study of the Indian Prisons Act and the *Delhi Jail Manual*. We presented protocol to the Inspector General of Prisons and Senior Jail Officials of Jail 4. Rewards for good behavior and the consequences for antisocial behavior were defined with input from the inmates. The Encounter Group Process was taught, practiced, and refined. We further introduced an Incidents Register, which included not only incident reports of negative events, but also learning experiences. The records of incidents in this register provided a longitudinal history of the negative behavior of any individual.

The Aasra staff members served as the authority for enforcing rules. While bestowing consequences and learning experiences to residents for a transgression, the staff gave a reason that was consistent with the therapeutic community's views of right living.

They highlighted the effect errant behavior had on the community and the resident, and suggested the expected behavior option to be adopted in future. They also encouraged the errant resident to express his feelings and emotions. These staff members had to defend their decisions to the resident, the community, and the prison staff. Through this process, residents were guided toward greater autonomy and dignity.

The Education Program grew with the coming of our new convict officer, Rajinder Jathedar. This remarkable man took charge of discipline in the community and made the Shaping Behavior program work. With my encouragement, he even gave up his afternoon siesta in his cell. He would then be locked up with the prisoners in one of the barracks and conduct education classes in the afternoons. Simultaneously, he and his team helped drive out a major negative habit inculcated in prisons—sleeping in the afternoons. This habit was promoted by the lame excuse of the prison that the jail must be closed in the afternoons to give rest to the overworked Head Warders. This convenience for a hundred tired Head Warders reinforced negative habits in 9,000 prisoners and kept the NGO personnel idle for four unproductive hours while the prison slept. Under Rajinder's able guidance, a massive landscape garden project, including a pond with a bridge, a waterfall, an aviary, a fountain, and landscaped garden, grew inside the prison.

Training and Changing Natural Role Models
Without the other prison reforms, the drug-addiction program would have been a non-starter. The

Therapeutic Community grew in a favorable atmosphere of prison reform. However, some of the reforms were more successful than others in solving problems. In an attempt to change the relationship between the jail staff and the prisoners, the warders were transferred every day from one ward to another. Head Warders were transferred every week. Therefore, accountability, which was already low, became even lower, as no one stayed long enough to know the problems of the prisoners, let alone solve them.

The result was repeated chaos in the Therapeutic Community created by the jail staff members who didn't understand the programs and its methods. Much time and effort were wasted in educating each new jail staff member. Finally, Shivanand Kheman was posted to the program as the permanent Head Warder, and this problem ended.

Indicators of Change in the First Twenty Months
About 1,100 heroin-dependent adult male prisoners had been admitted to the drug-addiction program by May 1995. One-third of these were undertrials for narcotics possession and sale, one-third for thefts, and about one-third for violence under the Arms Act. About 40 percent had been admitted after a medically supervised detoxification. The rest had undergone peer-supervised withdrawal in the community.

Since the Therapeutic Community started functioning, the culture of the addicts' ward underwent a radical transformation. The ward was once the darkest area in the prison. The Deputy Superintendent would peep in on his evening rounds but saw very little as the inmates broke all the lightbulbs at dusk to avoid detection of drug use. Heroin use was a daily occurrence. The inmates were looked down upon as hopeless. The teachers of the prison education wing had refused to go in to teach them. The night duty officer would be called time and again as frequent fights broke out.

All that had changed by the end of the first twenty months. The prison recognized Aasra Parivar as a significant treatment program for drug addiction, and a stream of visitors and dignitaries began to visit the ward.

The residents showed a sense of pride in the jail community. They also valued the position of the big brother and family head. Where once it took forty-five minutes to collect the ward for a meeting, they now assembled in less than five minutes, showing increased discipline, a higher sense of responsibility, and respect for authority.

The number of quarrels decreased and heroin smuggling decreased. Fewer numbers of inmates were tempted to take heroin when it did reach the ward. There were longer periods of no drug use verified by regular urinalysis. The inmates were more honest and more likely to accept the consequences of their actions. Increased and voluntary participation in the workshops and projects undertaken by the community reflected incorporation of the work ethic.

In November 1994, Mr. Lee P. Brown, Director, Office of National Drug Control Policy, USA, visited our Drug Rehabilitation Center. He sent the following letter:

EXECUTIVE OFFICE OF THE PRESIDENT
OFFICE OF NATIONAL DRUG CONTROL POLICY
Washington, D.C. 20500

November 19, 1994

Dr. Kiran Bedi
Inspector General of Prisons
Tihar Jail
New Delhi

Dear Dr. Bedi:

As I leave New Delhi, I want to thank you and your staff for a
most informative morning at your drug rehabilitation center on
Thursday morning. It was one of the highlights of my visit.

There can only be one point of view about narcotics in our
societies. We must take all possible steps to eliminate them
and their effects from our midst. Efforts such as yours
demonstrate what innovation and dedication can accomplish.

Thank you again for a memorable visit. I wish you well and
look forward to hearing of success upon success.

Sincerely,

Lee P. Brown
Direcor

Reforming Medical Service

The problems with the medical service were not only too few doctors in our township of unhealthy residents, but also a lack of communication with the prisoners or prison supervisors. To begin with, we introduced mobile dispensaries. If prisoners could not reach the doctors, then the doctors had to be brought to the patients. This move initially sparked a good deal of resentment and unease among the doctors whose proclivity for immobility was renowned. They preferred to remain ensconced in the safety of their clinics rather than venture into hostile territory. Moreover, their working patterns and habits were now under scrutiny, and they were clearly troubled by visibility. However, the inmates were delighted, especially those individuals who labored hard in the prison factory and could not afford to take time off. The staff accompanying the doctors was glad to see the doctors and pharmacists on rounds, as I recorded in notes from one day:

> I visited the Jail Training Center on May 19, 1993, and met the warders who were on training after their duties. I asked them for feedback. They were happy that the doctors were visiting the wards, and reported the satisfaction of prisoners with medical services has greatly increased due to the doctors' rounds in the wards. However, due to a large number of inmates wanting to meet the doctors in every ward, it isn't always possible to visit all the wards during one shift. I explained that in case of an emergency, the doctor could always be called. The warders stated that this kind of direct medical attendance in the wards has helped medical care reach all needy patients. In the earlier system, aggressive

inmates got comparatively more medical attendance while the others were ignored. The warders
suggested a doctor on rounds could visit bigger
wards on a regular basis and smaller wards once or
twice a week.

As in other areas, the medical service, the round observations, and the petition-box revelations were eye-openers.
The reports from these two sources identified those prisoners who were suffering from an assortment of diseases.
They also brought in specific grievances or complaints with
regard to the medical situation, which were duly considered. All these developments resulted in an unprecedented
scene for Tihar: the normally elusive and inaccessible doctors actually doing rounds of the wards and examining the
inmates. The jail doctors vehemently opposed this change.
They forcefully argued against it, constantly complained
about it, and tried to devise ingenious means of sabotaging
the change. At one stage, they even threatened to collectively boycott the jail by staying away from duty. They
knew that they held a monopoly and tried to exploit the
situation to the maximum extent. They felt secure in their
seemingly invulnerable medical fortress. The doctors believed that the prison authorities would bend over back
wards to retain them.

Unfortunately for them, they had misdiagnosed the
new command. We were determined to proceed with the
process of change, irrespective of the obstacles. In this con-
text, Jaydev Sarangi suggested that we call in private doctors from outside. This suggestion was undeniably useful,
but did the prison rules and regulations permit the appointment of private doctors?

We discovered that instead of engaging doctors on an
honorarium basis, we could invite them by providing trans-

portation cost. Fortunately, we could ourselves defray the costs incurred in hiring taxis or other modes of travel, without waiting for the State Government's approval. We decided not to restrict ourselves to the allopathic system. We sought out doctors specializing in alternative medicine.

However, the first major hurdle we had to cross was the resource crunch. We had to procure the basic medicines and the equipment needed for running even a rudimentary medical system. We somehow managed to buy the required medicines by diverting money from the Prisoners' Welfare Fund and dispensed these through the new team of doctors who possessed all the hallmarks of sincere and dedicated professionals.

We provided advance warning to the external team of doctors so that they could make themselves available during the rush hours. They would visit the wards, which the regular prison doctors felt were not worth their attention. The newcomers in their professional coats and stethoscopes, both young men and women, instilled a much-needed sense of confidence among the inmates that there really was someone to listen to their tales of woe, some of which were heartrending. The very fact that a doctor had examined the inmates was extremely reassuring for them. This fundamental change in the inmates' viewpoint provided the first successful breakthrough in our attempts to end or at least curtail the prison doctors' monopoly, and gradually they realized that their strike threats were ineffective. But they were still reluctant to join the efforts of their colleagues from outside. Nevertheless, they agreed to don white coats stitched by the jail tailors and carry stethoscopes, which at least bestowed on them the unmistakable identity of the medical profession.

Our efforts to improve medical services proved fruitful during daytime and evenings. But at night it was a different matter altogether. At night, the entire prison population of over 8,000-plus was dependent on only one government-appointed doctor. The pressure on this individual was evidently overwhelming, and to cope with it he adopted the path of least resistance by prescribing the same drug regardless of the problem. All our endeavors to enlist the appointment of additional doctors for night duty failed. The Directorate of Health Services and the Health Secretary of the Delhi State Government expressed willing helplessness since they themselves were short of doctors. We had to raise more resources ourselves to meet the requisite challenges or suffer the consequences. We decided to engage the services of a private doctor who was willing to be on call in prison at night. This meant Tihar now would have two doctors at night instead of one.

While the non-official doctors went about their duties methodically and effectively, the in-house men, instead of being inspired, continued to fret and fume. Despite all our attempts to change their ways, they stuck to their traditional rigid patterns. We continued our reform effort by requiring the Resident Medical Officer to send his work journal to the Prison Headquarters on a daily basis. This step enabled us to assess and evaluate the daily health bulletin of the prison. The work journal included the daily reports of all doctors, so we could keep track of each doctor's performance. When the doctors came to realize that they were under appraisal, they decided to exchange views and opinions and coordinate their activities so that some semblance of unity could be achieved. This level of communication was unprecedented at Tihar.

We gave the medical staff all the amenities we could—transportation, better administrative facilities whenever needed, risk allowance, and reimbursement of telephone expenses. These amenities may appear trivial to an outsider, but for the doctors they held a lot of significance.

For emergency cases, we sanctioned the expenses for hiring a taxi for transporting the patients to a government hospital if an ambulance was not readily available. To introduce more logistical support and to ensure increased doctor-prisoner rapport, we appointed an Assistant Medical Superintendent and an Assistant Hospital Superintendent. Both these individuals met daily with the prison doctors in order to ensure prompt clearance of all important medical documents and other related matters. Both would attend the afternoon coordination group meetings of the doctors and note suggestions and opinions. Essentially, they acted as a link between the doctors, the prisoners, and the administration.

Meanwhile, we persuaded the government-appointed doctors to provide normal medical services during those weeks which had a string of consecutive holidays. Such breaks in service in the past had been responsible for massive backlogs, resulting in riots and violence. We also cleaned up the hospital. Essential instruments, the X-ray machine, the sphygmomanometer (a device for measuring blood pressure), and the dentist's chair were repaired immediately. Although the number of such instruments was grossly inadequate, we intended to make optimum use of what we had.

We asked superintendents to collect the medical reports from the night-duty officers and to ensure that the ambulances meant for transporting seriously ill patients were readily available and not diverted for extracurricular activities. In the inspection wards we started identifying and segregating those entrants who needed intensive and immediate medical care. Further, the superintendents devised a comprehensive medical register, which provided all the vital information about a patient at a glance. We also had to maintain a death register, but fortunately we had to use it very rarely.

One of the major projects we envisioned was an ultra-modern detoxification center with state-of-the-art equipment to combat the pernicious impact of drug addiction. This project never got off the ground due to obstacles placed by the State Government. Eventually, we ran out of patience and resolved that we would become self-reliant and self-sufficient. This objective was a noble one in theory but difficult to achieve in practice. Even a relatively trivial matter like asking a referral hospital to designate a separate custody ward for visiting inmates was not within our control.

While we were concentrating on ensuring readily available medicine for all inmates, we received an order directing the transfer of the management and control of the Tihar medical services to the Directorate of Health Services (DHS). This order effectively took away the control of whatever medical resources we had but placed the overall responsibility for maintaining the medical services squarely on us. This order also meant that in the event of any mishap, only we were accountable, although we had no control over the budget or personnel. Here is a portion of that order:

Sir,

1. I am directed to inform you that the Lt. Governor has approved transfer of all dispensaries and the hospital in Tihar Jail to the Directorate of Health Services with immediate effect on "as is where is basis."
2. Consequently all the resources, human as well as material, will stand transferred to the Directorate of Health Services with immediate effect.
3. For day-to-day supervision and control, the Jail dispensaries/hospital will be under the administrative control of IG (Prisons).

4. The additional staff as are necessary will be provided immediately.

5. All the medical and paramedical posts of the dispensaries and the hospital shall henceforth be borne on the strength of Directorate of Health Services.

6. All matters relating to transfer, posting, creation of posts, filling up of the posts, purchase of medical equipments, stores, medicines, and other matters relating to the running of the dispensaries and the hospital shall henceforth be dealt with by the Directorate of Health Services.

Yours faithfully,
Joint Secretary
Government of Delhi

Our reply highlighted the chaos such a change would create. We pointed out that supervision and control cannot be separated from the capacity for making the resources available, and that the Delhi Health Services was remote in every way from the prisons. The Delhi Health Services did not have the capacity to provide the resources, which are required on a minute-to-minute, urgent, and round-the-clock basis. Further, the delay in medical care of any kind has law-and-order and security implications inside overcrowded prisons. In the past, it has been a primary reason for riots and strikes by the prisoners. We asked for a meeting to discuss the working implications of the order to avoid jeopardizing the medical care for the prisoners and for the security of the prison.

The response to this was a modification of the original order as follows:

Sir,

The Hon'ble Lt. Governor, Delhi, is pleased to modify the earlier decision of this government regarding transfer of all dispensaries and hospitals in Central Jail to Directorate of Health Services on "as is where is basis" communicated vide this Gov't letter of even number, dated December 29, 1993, with the following conditions:

That the management, material resources including handling of budget, purchase of stores, equipment, medicines, will continue to remain with the Prison Administration. However, to draw benefit of better cadre management and share of trained manpower, it would be desirable to encadre the medical and technical staff of Jail dispensaries/hospitals is [sic] encadred in Directorate of Health Services.

Yours faithfully,
Deputy Secretary
Government of Delhi

Irrespective of the outcome of such tedious and tardy communication, we, including the then Resident Medical Officer, Dr. Vijay Kumar, and his team of doctors were determined to restore and maintain the medical services at their optimum levels. We opened up another front in our war against the medical disservice and introduced holistic health education to reduce dependence on doctors. We started with a few pragmatic tactics: segregation of drug addicts, a ban on the use of addictive medicines and drugs, and a no-smoking campaign. Declaring smoking to be a health hazard, smoking and the sale of cigarettes were totally banned in all the prisons.

We laid great emphasis on both hygiene and nutrition and ensured that clean and safe water was available. We also ensured that adequate quantities of soap, both for toilet use and washing of clothes, were available. We saw to it that all the inmates bathed regularly, wore clean clothes, and shaved daily. The inmates began to clean and clip their nails and to keep their hair clean and beards trimmed.

As far as better nutrition was concerned, we increased the supply of good quality milk, provided better-cooked and more palatable food, and added pulses and grams to enhance the nutrition. It wasn't gourmet fare, but we did our best under the circumstances to provide some variety in the menu. We also set mobile canteens rolling, mainly to provide tea, cold drinks, and light snacks. In winter, there was a special round of hot tea and hot water. In summer we set up *piaos*, places where drinking water was freely served to quench the thirst of hundreds of inmates, as they returned to the prison from the court.

But despite all the positive developments, we just could not meet the challenge of medical emergencies. The infrastructure and resources in the jail hospital were woefully inadequate. We could not grapple with those complicated situations that required specialists' skills, as these professionals were not to be found in Tihar. Again, we sought help from the community outside. Such help eventually came our way, and when it did, it was overwhelming.

It started as a trickle in the form of a wheelchair and prosthetic equipment donated by the philanthropic Bharat Vikas Parishad. A few of the handicapped inmates were fitted with artificial limbs. Some of them could now walk without support from others or without the help of crutches. B. R. Sharma, yet another volunteer totally committed to reforms in prisons, conducted a popular first-aid course for both the staff and the inmates, and awarded formal certificates on successful completion of the course. A renowned eye specialist, Dr. R. K. Bhutani, personally visited Tihar with his modern gadgets and examined the inmates with eye problems. He also arranged to provide spectacles for the needy. A stream of specialists from other disciplines began to pour in to help us. We were elated not to be abjectly dependent on the prison doctors. We had managed to effectively tackle one of the most contentious issues confronting Tihar without resorting to negative or pernicious tactics.

Among the various reputed experts, I would like to mention Dr. Kusum Sehgal of NACO (National AIDS Control Organization). She initiated an AIDS-awareness campaign in Tihar and also assessed a practical program to prevent the spread of this scourge. She made extensive rounds of the various prisons, interacted with the panchayat members and put forward valuable suggestions. Also deserving mention is the Hope Foundation, which provided full support to TB and leprosy patients and went on to open a full-fledged dental clinic inside Tihar.

In addition to treatment, we emphasized the crucial importance of the prevention of diseases through exhibitions and mobile film shows. We used any occasion to mobilize support for medical care for the prisoners. The high point of this program came on Republic Day in 1994. On this occasion, more than 500 medics and paramedics, including eminent specialists in various fields came to Tihar. Virtually all the 9,000-plus inmates, including the children, were thoroughly examined.

As the degree of community interest in Tihar increased, doctors specializing in diverse therapies such as magneto therapy, acupressure, or naturopathy rolled in. We

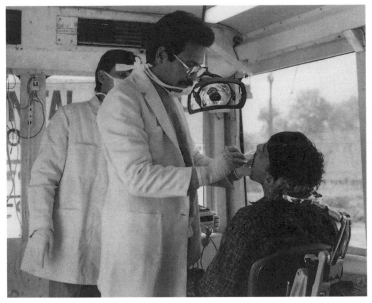

Dentists and doctors volunteered time and services inside Tihar.

announced an Alternative Medicine Day, where the inmates could take advantage of different systems of medicine. They could now choose a system with which they were familiar or with which they felt comfortable. Over 200 doctors from the alternative medicine fields participated in this. Some doctors also arranged film shows, exhibitions, and practical demonstrations, which proved to be an education not only for the inmates but also for the staff members. Also, some leading pharmaceutical companies generously donated their products.

Shifting from an overdependence on allopathic drugs to alternative medicine led to a reduction in costs and also reduced the adverse side effects of allopathic medicine. Eventually, we managed to provide outlets inside the jail for ayurvedic and herbal medicine for minor disorders such as coughs, colds, stomach upsets, and skin rashes. Such a provision instilled a great deal of confidence in the inmates, who could now self-medicate instead of waiting agonizingly for doctors.

By the first quarter of 1995, the medical reform program had produced remarkable results. Each prison could now boast of containing three separate dispensaries, one each for allopathic, homeopathic, and ayurvedic medicines. But among the most significant medical measures were the Policy Statement Document and Project Outline for HIV/AIDS Awareness and Surveillance:

Objective
AIDS education, leading to behavioral change. Preventive measures equivalent to those available in the community shall be made available to all the prisoners.

All prisoners should receive HIV/AIDS education upon entry, during their prison term, and in pre-release programs. The jail library should be stocked with pamphlets, books, and journals on HIV/AIDS. Wall charts mentioning the mode of spread of infection of HIV and preventive measures to be taken should be displayed in all the wards.

Methodology

Involve other NGOs: Train volunteers to give standardized information on AIDS. This would ensure that there is no confusion in the minds of the largest population regarding various aspects of HIV and AIDS.

Divide the jail into workable sections: Ward-wise schedule can be prepared so that groups of 150–200 inmates are formed for educational sessions. Create an infrastructure for audiovisual equipment in all the jails.

Behavioral change workshops: After the first educational sessions, initiate behavioral-change workshops.

Select and train peer educators to carry on the program: Create an infrastructure for research so that constant evaluation and upgrading of services is possible. This would be a unique research opportunity in a closed community of prisons.

Time Frame

- Education of the entire jail population by September 30, 1995.
- Begin workshops for behavioral change by December 31, 1995.
- Educational programs and workshops are ongoing.
- Continue training for peer education.

Development of Infrastructure for HIV Testing in Tihar Jail

■ Compulsory testing of prisoners is not recommended, but the facilities for voluntary testing for HIV infection should be available to the prisoners with adequate pre- and post-test counseling.

■ Follow Sentinel Surveillance methodology. The first stage HIV screening (after pre- and post-test counseling) is for persons in high-risk categories: drug addicts, juvenile prisoners, commercial sex workers, and prisoners suffering from tuberculosis.

■ **Strict confidentiality on HIV testing should be maintained.**

Tihar continued to move toward good physical and mental health. What we did in Tihar had no comparison to the prisons I visited in the West, which had adequate medical infrastructures. None of them compromised on this count. They worked constantly to improve in whatever way they could, regularly conducting surveys on health-related behavior and evaluating situations to raise health standards. They worked not under court direction but out of professional habit and public policy. In Tihar, we had to make a huge effort, for we had just begun.

women behind bars:
a new dignity

Child Care and Women's Education

The women were even more amenable to the reform process than the men. Perhaps this was due to the smaller (250–300), more homogenous population housed in the same ward. When they were not confined in lockup, they stayed together as a group. This situation facilitated communication and made it easy to convey information about our plans and programs for their welfare and empowerment.

We needed strategies to tackle those problems that were specific to women prisoners. Here again, we called upon the outside community for help, and it came in abundant measure. Before long we had a wide spectrum of corrective reforms including yoga therapy, collective prayer and meditation, a cleanliness-and-hygiene drive, a literacy program, and a forum for the expression of creative talent through literature, poetry, music, theater, and the visual arts, as well as weaving, knitting, and textile printing.

It was immediately obvious that child care was necessary if we wanted the women inmates to take part in one of the above programs with total dedication and commitment. A women's organization, Mahila Pratiraksha Mandal (MPM, a non-governmental organization), a forum for the protection of women, came to our rescue. MPM volunteered to start a nursery school for the children of women inmates and opened the school in the women's ward for approximately 60 small children. Generous donors provided a large collection of soft toys and educational games for the nursery school. Eventually we supplied uniforms and school supplies such as copybooks, crayons, and pencils. For all the programs for women and children, Tani Bhargava of the Ishan Charitable Trust, and Surinder Saini of the Delhi Social Welfare Board provided financial help.

The nursery school soon began to teem with delightful

activity. We could hear the pitter-patter of small feet and hear innocent lisping voices singing jingles and rhymes. A separate kitchen was set up to provide a more nutritious diet appropriate for growing children. For the first time in the history of Tihar, children were treated as children. Part of their education included excursions outside the prison to expand their horizons. Private buses took them to gardens, museums, temples, mosques, and the zoo, and also on visits to outside schools. The rewards of such outings proved invaluable and greatly helped in transforming the life patterns of these children. From the depths of despair and gloom they now went to seek the heights of hope and light. They gave up fighting among themselves and stopped tormenting the harassed prison staff because their energies and concentration were now focused elsewhere on creative, constructive, and beneficial activities. This was reported by the *Indian Express:*

Better Days Ahead for Convicts' Kids

Four-year-old cherubic Chandni is not an offender, but she still lives the life of a convict. Reason: she was born in the women's cell of Tihar Jail. There are eight such little ones who share her fate and are thus "convicted" by birth.

Besides them, there are 52 more small children who have been incarcerated along with their mothers as many are too small to be deprived of motherly love, and some of them have nobody back home to look after them.

But, for the radically changed jail management ever since Magsaysay award-winner Kiran Bedi has taken over, a few voluntary organizations have chipped in to take care of these children and their mothers. Sushum Lata, a counselor of Mahila

Pratiraksha Mandal, which runs a crèche there, said that the only animal these children had seen in the jail was a cat. And when they were taken to the zoo, she pointed out, they ran after a caged bear shouting, "Oh, such a big cat!"

In the last year these children have been exposed to the outside world several times. They have now learned to sing songs, recite poems, and recognize animals and vegetables. When a visitor steps into their crèche, they immediately greet her, "Namaste, Aunty."

Says Chandni's mother, Shabnam, who has been given life imprisonment in a murder case, "I am very happy for Chandni who is fortunate enough to get so good an upbringing."

But these children are not kept in Tihar for more than five years. As soon as they become eligible for formal education, they are sent to Delhi government-run homes. Assistant Superintendent Meena Lucker said that they have so far sent 16 children to the Kirti Nagar-based home.

What about those who were not fortunate enough to join their mothers in the jail and have nobody to look after them? Tears rolling down her cheeks, Mithilesh Devi, who has been an undertrial in a murder case for four years, said, "I have two children who have nobody to look after them. Their father died long back."

Ms. Lucker said that Mithilesh Devi's children—Ashok Kumar and Manoj Kumar—were living in deep misery. Often they spend their nights without food. On top of it, when they went to their neighbors for help they were taunted as "murderer's children."

We also improved the medical care of the children of women inmates. Two eminent pediatricians, Dr. Suri and Dr. Arora, volunteered their services. They provided polio and other vaccines and instructed the mothers in fundamental health care. They underlined the importance of regular bathing and keeping their hair well groomed and their nails clean. They stressed that children need to wear clean clothes and display an overall tidy appearance. The doctors also explained to the mothers how to administer basic first aid and what to do in case of emergencies. Here is a firsthand account by Dr. S. K. Arora:

> When I received the offer of an honorary Senior Pediatric Consultant, I accepted it.
>
> After my first visit I immediately realized that it was a great challenge, unlike anything else I had done in life. Here was a group of emotionally disturbed mothers accused of serious crimes, away from family members and a normal environment. My plan of action would not have succeeded had it not been for Mrs. Bedi.
>
> **Priorities:** The first priority was to create a soothing, happy, relaxed environment, which we did to the best of our capacity and stamina. Guilt, sorrow, anger, depression, aggressiveness, despondency—all had to be fought with counseling.
>
> **Infrastructure:** I requested a baby-weighing scale, benches, toys, sweets, and special pediatric cards to monitor growth of the children.
>
> **Immunization:** The schedule followed the immunizations recommended by the Indian Academy of Pediatrics.
>
> **Diet:** We changed the food to include soft freshly cooked food, porridge, fruit, eggs, milk, and

kheer. In general we tried to make sure the food was tasty and attractively served and included balanced proteins and enough fat and carbohydrates to promote growth. We made a special effort to provide clean water.

Hygiene and Clothing: We placed special emphasis on soap, towels, hand washing, and staying clean and properly dressed.

Health Survey: The common diseases were malnutrition, anemia, boils, conjunctivitis, worm infestation, diarrhea, and fever. If we couldn't properly treat the child, we immediately referred him to an outside hospital. When we noticed that some mothers did not give prescribed drugs to their children, special supervisory staff made sure the child received his medicine.

Family Relations: Some mothers violently beat their children. In those cases, we provided counseling. We also encouraged visits with the father and other family members whenever possible for the emotional satisfaction of everybody concerned.

Education: We devised special classes for the children with a curriculum designed to make study become play and play become study.

I was sad to see my visit to Tihar end.

With the children properly cared for, the mothers were free to study and work. The most important objective was literacy for all the women. We provided informal literacy classes for the totally illiterate. Those women who had some education were classified according to their level and sent to appropriate classes. Two inmates, Poonam and Shakira, worked as teachers and two more came in from outside to reinforce their efforts.

The women's literacy mission was the cynosure for
almost all eyes. The prison authorities ensured a regular
and adequate supply of study and work material. They also
made sure that the environment was clean and encouraged
the inmates to study seriously. The teachers conducted tu-
torial classes to make students eligible for examinations at
various levels. The courses covered a wide range of subjects
from basic mathematics and science to literature, grammar,
and social studies.

In addition to literacy classes, we initiated a host of
other practical and productive activities, such as typing, tailoring, and embroidery. Acquiring these skills instilled
much-needed self-confidence in the women. When a
women's social organization managed to procure job work
for the skilled women inmates, their self-confidence was
even further boosted. They were now learning and earning
simultaneously.

Another activity that helped the women inmates to eke
out a livelihood emerged in the form of spinning. The Jail
Superintendent provided five *charkhas* (spinning wheels).
The charkha had been popularized by Mahatma Gandhi,
who made it the focal point of his concentration and meditation all through his life. Provided with rolls of raw cot-
ton, the women spun cloth, which was sold outside the jail.
While they worked, they sang devotional songs to the
rhythm of the charkha.

These volunteers of the MPM also visited the relatives
of the women inmates and helped restore broken family
ties. They also worked to secure the women's release from
prison as soon as possible. They did not stop there. They
brought in women lawyers to deal with difficult and complex cases where mere counseling was not enough. The
women lawyers showed commendable zeal and enthusiasm
and were held in great respect.

A well-known musician, Vasanti Chaudhary, who was teaching in a government school, volunteered to sing *bhajans* (devotional songs) for the Tihar inmates and to educate the musically inclined ones on the finer points of classical music. K. R. Kishore, Jail Superintendent, arranged for a few musical instruments to be brought in. He had the electrician inmates set up an audio system inside the women's ward. Soon the entire women's ward reverberated with the melodious and tranquil strains of therapeutic music.

The efforts of Vasanti Chaudhuary were supplemented by the renowned social organization, The Family, whose contributions have been mentioned in various other contexts. The philanthropic members of The Family volunteered to teach music on a regular basis to all those inmates who were interested. They also conducted theater programs within the women's ward. The Family created a cheerful atmosphere marked by gaiety, and conducted workshops whose basic themes were positive communication, child care, personal hygiene, and creative activities. These workshops employed puppets, picture postcards, and action songs.

The remarkably dynamic storyteller Saroj Vashisht donated a set of about ninety religious books, which we stocked in the reading room for women inmates. Coincidently, this reading room was set up in the cell vacated by the famous Bandit Queen, Phoolan Devi, who later became a member of the Indian Parliament. She learned to write her name in Tihar.

The reading room soon attained the stature of a full-fledged library, as writers and publishers supplied books on a regular basis. A woman inmate with basic cataloguing skills was put in charge of the library.

The women's section of Tihar was a magnet for an assortment of sociologists, filmmakers, and lawyers. Their

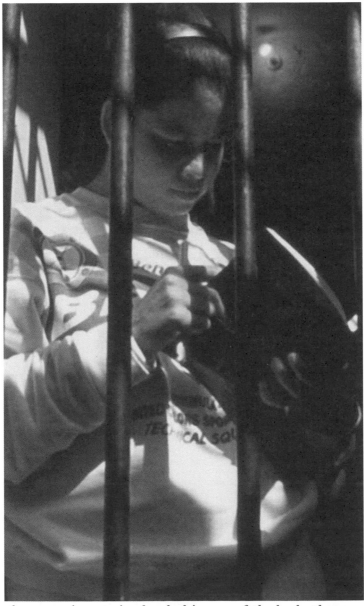

A woman inmate is absorbed in one of the books that was donated to the library in Tihar Jail.

views and impressions expressed in articles, books, or films, generated greater support for the women inmates and brought in more contributions from the community. For example, the report of the Honorable Ms. Fatima Biwi, a member of the National Human Rights Commission and a former Judge of the Supreme Court of India, galvanized the courts into releasing women languishing in prison awaiting trial. A well-known author on the subject of commercial sex, Promila Kapur, conducted case studies of women inmates accused of prostitution, and made pragmatic proposals for rehabilitation.

A women's forum of advocates known as *Sakshi* (female companion) offered its services in identifying and assisting women inmates who needed advice. These women lawyers analyzed each and every case that came their way and provided the requisite follow-up. The Delhi School of Social Work sent an eager group of students to Tihar to conduct research and work along with the women in various projects.

Another organization, Marg, held a workshop for women inmates, which can be best described as a legal literacy workshop. The Marg legal specialists made the members of their audience aware of their legal rights. They also spoke on related subjects such as legal petitioning, visiting rights for relatives and friends, and trial procedures. They enlightened the women on the laws pertaining to marriage, divorce, adoption, dowry, and child marriage. The information and data provided by Marg went a long way in redressing the grievances of women inmates and resolving their problems.

With the introduction of the women's panchayat system, the female inmates became self-governing as well. The Legal Panchayat for Women worked in coordination with the visiting lawyers and counselors. The requisite legal petitions for those inmates who could not prepare them for themselves were drawn up by their more accomplished companions or by the foreign inmates.

One day in November 1993, a sixty-three-year-old black American Buddhist nun, a saintly woman named Sister Max Mathews, came to visit the women inmates of Tihar. She became the center of economic empowerment of women inmates. A former teacher, fashion designer, and art collector who has lived in Europe, Nepal, and India, she has devoted a part of her life to helping Tibetan refugees earn a living by marketing their handicraft.

At Tihar, Sister Max used her creative energy, marketing acumen, and unwavering determination to launch self-financing programs that enabled many women inmates, most of whom were undertrials, to become economically independent for the first time. Since her arrival, almost half of the jail's 300-odd women prisoners were trained in knitting, painting, embroidery, and other artistic projects, which were marketed outside Tihar. At least 90 of these women were able to open bank accounts.

Through Sister Max, we also attracted the support of the Danish Embassy for the nursery school. Her innovative work, literacy, education, and other rehabilitation programs gave the women inmates additional tools to readjust to society.

Here are firsthand accounts of two admirable women who made the difference: Sister Max Mathews, and Danish social worker Margrete Bentholm. At my personal request, they spoke to a freelance journalist, Lisa Vanhan. Here they capture the excitement of the reforms in full detail.

Sister Max's Narration

I first saw Tihar in November 1993. At that time, I was working with Tibetans for the export of handicrafts. A Mumbai-based artisan-exporter friend, Kirit Dave, mentioned that he and his father had an exciting prospect for me. His father, Mr. K. C. Shroff, picked me up one morning and asked me to bring some of my Tibetan pieces along. I had no idea what I was in for.

When I first saw the prison that day, I thought, "What is this place?" It looked more like an Indian village than a jail. It was beautiful, with lots of bushes and trees. Its buildings were all neatly painted white, and there were barracks arranged in a U-shape around a big open courtyard. There were bars on the windows, but I didn't see any locks— nothing that would indicate at a glance that it was a prison. There was no feeling of threat or fear. The atmosphere was not charged. I was surprised.

Once inside the prison gates we walked through a large, grassy open quadrangle. As we entered a second courtyard, which I learned later was the women's prison area, I heard women laughing. There was a woman standing on a raised platform entertaining a group of women and children who were all sitting on the ground in rows. She was wearing a *salwar-kameez* with a vest, and sneakers. It was Kiran Bedi. She was talking to them as a mother, as she always did. No one wore uniforms, not even the warders. The women wore ordinary saris and salwar-kameez.

The lecture was in Hindi, which I don't speak, but suddenly I heard my name. She asked me to hold up my Tibetan things and show them to the group. Then she came over to us and explained that she had asked all the women who were interested in working to stay back. About 50 or 60 women were curious, including a number of non-Indians, and they were being interviewed about their work and skills.

Kiran Bedi's plan of reforms was based on income-generating activities. That was what I'd been brought in for, though I didn't know it at the time. She had asked the Shroffs to set up a training course at the prison to teach the women handicraft skills, but Kirit didn't feel they could manage it from Mumbai and asked me to assist. Since the prison could contribute nothing except the resources of the inmates, Mr. Shroff was to finance the project initially.

Though Mr. Shroff and Mrs. Bedi didn't really spell it out to me until later, it dawned on me after she finished speaking to the inmates what they wanted me to do. I found out that she had told the women I had come to offer work and training. Kirit called me later and gave me the details. When I first spoke to Kiran Bedi, she was open to my ideas. She didn't give me any specific charge. Her desire was to rehabilitate the women economically, socially, emotionally, and in every other way to show them that they have a resource in themselves.

That first day some of the women were apprehensive, but the foreign women positively descended on me and some even embraced me. They almost never had visitors, and for someone to express an interest in them was exciting. They were so eager. Some had tried projects before, giving money to warders to get them supplies, but nothing had come of those efforts.

Fortunately, the women who came forward had skills and talents. I found a tremendous amount of energy and enthusiasm among them and immediately felt the possibility of achieving something with their help. I might have hesitated if it wasn't for the response of the foreign women, because I wasn't initially sure how I could make a success of the project.

But after you meet Kiran Bedi, you can't say no. Several women whom I had helped joined me, and we worked under the auspices of Kiran Bedi's Non-Governmental Organization, Navjyoti. (Nav jyoti works in Delhi slums to rehabilitate drug addicts and runs programs to help street, slum, and working children.)

I hired four foreign inmates as supervisors of production units and paid them 1,000 rupees a month. Maria, a Spanish woman, organized women to paint cloth, stationery, and greeting cards, and to print gift-wrapping paper. A large-hearted Nigerian, Gloria, headed the knitting section, and she inspired women to work like no one I've ever seen before. Margo, a Dutch national from Surinam, ran the hand-stitching unit. The women hand-rolled and finished silk scarves from Tibet and crafted table runners and linens.

Shakira, an Anglo-Indian woman in Tihar, was my major coordinator and one of the most successful women to emerge from the programs. She helped the supervisors and made sure they had the supplies they needed. She worked with them, and I worked with her to train women, produce the goods, and fill our orders. When she was released she went to work at Navjyoti and made a new life for herself.

Training is very important. The majority of women inmates needed training to make the handicrafts we set out to produce. Because the prison population is always shifting, trained inmates left suddenly, and there was a steady stream of new-comers needing training, so training services had to be offered continuously. To manage this, I hired Perminder Kaur, a woman from outside Tihar, who was skilled at all crafts.

I sat down with my supervisors and made a brief outline and schedule for the projects and gave it to Kiran Bedi. We started right away with her approval.

In the beginning my limited Hindi made it hard to relate to the Indian women inmates. I was at Tihar three to four days a week, and I had to spend some time on my own projects to make a living. So the supervisors and Perminder were my links. This structure became an incredible system of group interaction. We saw a huge change in the women. When I arrived, the women always sat with others of the same caste. Once the work started, they began working together harmoniously, and the fighting and bickering nearly stopped.

We started the women knitting squares. Due to Gloria's magnetism, we soon had 100 knitters. By Christmas, I started marketing the products to the foreign and diplomatic community in New Delhi at *melas* (fairs) and special sales. The proceeds were used to pay the women for their work, pay salaries, and buy supplies.

I initiated a system for payday in which all the supervisors and women workers kept payment records in their notebooks. We took thumbprints as signatures at first, but to encourage people in the literacy classes, we decided no one would be paid if she couldn't sign her own name.

For most of these women, it was the first time that they had money they had earned. It was the first time that most of them had any money of their own at all. It certainly gave them a lot of confidence to make something someone liked enough to pay for. Once, I brought two foreign buyers who had placed orders with us to see their work, and it encouraged the women enormously to see that people were actually interested in something they had produced.

We fought to get bank accounts for the earning women. We had to put up quite a fight. We were told by the Indian banks that convicts have no rights and could not have bank accounts. Finally, we got the banks to cooperate, with the argument that 90 percent of the women were undertrials, not convicts. In the end more than 90 women opened bank accounts. Most of them had never seen a bankbook or checkbook before, nor had any savings.

I never really wanted to know why the women inmates were there. After I had been there for a while and we got to know each other, some of them talked to me about their cases. With the money they earned and saved, a number of them were able to hire lawyers, pay school fees, or send money home. There were some stories of women who were released that way.

A few months after I arrived, the women prisoners put on a fashion show for Kiran Bedi on the day she designated as Women's Day at Tihar. Jessica Lefkow, a raven-haired American actress who directed and acted in community theater in Delhi, provided the music and showed the women how to walk like models on the runway. The stuff they made, vests, sweaters, knitted mufflers, was nothing special. It was raw. But you cannot imagine the joy of the women. In the photographs taken that day, you could see the pride on their faces.

My only training has been in teaching, and my experience has been gained from running my own garment business. I ran this project like I taught, using my intuition and instinct about what might work or sell. I can see things though I can't do them myself. I'm a catalyst. At Tihar, I got people involved and brought in people from outside who had special talents. Somehow I knew what could be done. My role was to get people excited and enthused about the project and market it.

Kiran Bedi made it very clear that the prison had nothing to give but the resources of the inmates. She had trouble getting what she needed to implement her reforms. But she gave all she could in terms of support and enabled us to do our work. I had no transportation when I arrived, but she allowed me to have rickshaws to bring in supplies. We had to have tools to do the handwork and she allowed knives, scissors, and needles to be brought in. The Supervisors had special lockers to keep track of them all. In my three years, there was never an incident of misuse.

There was no hostility in the women inmates toward me. There was genuine openness, based on the fact that I was bringing them money. We developed a relationship over time. There was an exchange of appreciation and gratitude because I spent so much time there, and brought cakes, birthday cards, and other things. Many of the women in Tihar had long been deprived of attention, stimulation, or gifts. They wanted to succeed; they were excited; and Kiran Bedi's enthusiasm added to it. There was no hostility when I was late with payday, and often I couldn't pay on the dot exactly. As long as I came to the prison and brought orders and the work continued, they didn't mind.

The women crocheted sweaters, glass covers and plate covers. They embroidered cushion covers and table runners, dresses, nightgowns, skirts, and quilts. Using sewing machines they produced bathrobes, kimonos, aprons, nightgowns, children's clothes, vests, and salwar suits. We also had printing projects and used potato-printing techniques. The inmates made hand-painted greeting cards, stationery sets, and paper bags used to wrap gifts. They also hand-painted cloth for dresses, vests, and skirts. From jute they knitted bath mitts, belts, mats, and bags.

Of all the projects, our knitting project became our biggest earner. I got an order from J. Peterman, a trendy U.S. mail-order catalogue, for 5,000 pairs of long socks. These were hand-knitted with four needles using up to seventeen colors of Tibetan wool in each pair. We made them in three sizes and four styles and sewed the J. Peterman label inside. We also knitted Christmas stockings and jute mitts for them. The women received 70 rupees (US$1.50) per pair.

Madame Carine du Marche Savas, who was married to the then Dutch Ambassador to India, was instrumental in all we achieved, especially in this project. She was a dynamo, a real ball of energy. Her talent was helping non-government organizations network, and she was a great inspiration. She worked with me day and night on the Tihar project and wrote the grant proposal to the Dutch Embassy.

The Embassy approved the funding of 1,500,000 rupees (US$3,000) for this project, the first training program ever in Tihar. It involved training in knitting with four needles to fill the sock orders, tailoring, and typing, and it began in April 1994.

For the tailoring section, Carine herself volunteered as an instructor, training the women to make patterns and tailor Western-style clothing. She contributed her design expertise from study at the French School for Fashion Design in Paris. She also arranged melas among the foreign diplomatic community where goods produced in Tihar were sold. She told foreign women about our work and got them involved.

For the typing segment, we hired a typing instructor and we organized typing classes, which were especially in demand by foreign inmates. Though the classes ended when the teacher left, the women continued to use the typewriter brought in by Carine on their own initiative.

The inmates grew assertive with their economic independence. At one point they refused to make large jute bath mats, which were hard to handle and rough on their fingers, because they wanted more money than we could afford.

I worked to get Carine and others with special skills inside the prison to help the rehabilitation of women. I made a speech to the American Women's Association of New Delhi and took some women from its volunteer committee to the prison to meet Kiran Bedi.

Kiran Bedi designated December 1 as a special day at the prison to set up something new. Nanete Hulshoff Pol, another Dutch volunteer, organized craftsmen to come from Delhi's Craft Museum and set up their craft stalls on the prison grounds for the prisoners to see how the handicrafts were made. We brought in potters, bangle painters, kite makers, candle and soap makers, and a handful of others to demonstrate. Kiran Bedi told us to use the whole lawn and bussed all the prisoners from the other sections in to see it. She wanted us to set up training courses in all the handicrafts.

In December 1995, we introduced quilt making and started the production of Advent calendars with the help and inspiration of two Americans, Marilyn Edwards and Teresa Olthoff. Some of the men prisoners also worked on these projects.

I gave as much work as possible to the men's carpentry workshop. They made the frames and looms for the weaving project and made stools for the kitchen. They wanted to earn and learn too, but the prison had so few resources.

One of my two great concerns for the women inmates of Tihar was their children. Only children up to age five were allowed to live in the prison with their mothers. The solution came from a Danish social worker, Margrete Bentholm. Margrete had worked in Africa and Scandinavia, and we asked her if she could put her social work background to use in the women's prison. It was magic when Margrete and I met. We worked well together and learned from each other. I was interested in the income-generating aspects of our work and she was interested in the social, emotional, and legal aspects. Both of us wanted to help Kiran Bedi implement her reforms.

Margrete wrote a proposal for the children's

nursery school in 1994, and it began in March 1995. Our dream was to set up a halfway house for women after they left Tihar, where they could find support and transition back to the world outside. But we couldn't get the funding, and it has never become a reality.

Margrete was also instrumental in forming Concerned Women, a group of foreign women who visited the foreign women prisoners and spoke to them in their own languages whenever possible. This program still exists today.

Margrete Bentholm describes her experience setting up the nursery school at Tihar
I met Sister Max at Tihar in January 1994, when I first visited the women's prison with a Danish friend. I met several inmates that day and quickly saw what Sister Max had already accomplished with her programs there.

A woman came up to me and said: "It's so terrible. I'm going to be released next week. Here I have work and friends. But outside I have nothing. You have to help me." I've been a professional social worker and activist for twenty years. Among other things, I worked on a women's extension training program in Zambia, and I worked for the Red Cross in Malawi. In Denmark I set up crisis centers for women and children.

I've seen so many income-generating projects fail in Africa that I was skeptical at the beginning. I had no intention of working at Tihar, but after discussions with a Navjyoti social worker about the needs of women and children, I saw that I could make a contribution.

The 60 children in the prison had no special arrangements except a small half-day nursery run five days a week by a social welfare organization, Mahila Pratiraksha Mandal. It was something, but it was limited.

The social workers discovered after interviewing the women and observing the children that the children had no experience of the outside world. Many were born in jail. They didn't know or recognize any animals—only cockroaches and stray cats. When they were asked to draw a picture of anything they wanted, they didn't know what to do. Only one child drew a banana. It was clear that they had no dreams, because they were starved for social stimulation and development.

Many of the mothers were in crisis. They didn't have the extra reserves to do what was needed with their children or to give them attention. Some simply gave up. The social workers wanted us to give hope to the mothers so the children would grow and develop.

With the idea of starting a nursery school and training teachers, Sister Max and I approached some NGOs. We were attracted by the experienced people of the Mobile Crèche who had set up high-quality-care nursery schools and non-formal education for children of construction workers. They also conducted training courses and extension programs. They were just right for the women and children of Tihar.

We had to wait for foreign money to be approved before we could finally start in March 1995. The Mobile Crèche workers concentrated on language and physical development. They made the children practice singing, drama, art, and yoga. They helped the children to decorate the room we were given using their paintings or the simplest of things, such as old magazines, and we changed the wall decorations regularly. We found Rajasthani cradles for the smallest children and carpets from the Danish Embassy. We helped the children make their own toys out of waste materials. The nursery school became an oasis with a completely different atmosphere from the rest of the jail.

The workers also started an intensive training program for the prison mothers, so they could become professional crèche workers. We paid the trainee inmates a small, symbolic stipend to give value to their skills. Twenty-five women participated and 14 became certified after nine months. The rest left the prison so they couldn't complete the course.

The course focused on health, nutrition, and developing creativity. It developed self-confidence. Suddenly, the women realized they could learn, and it gave them life. The certification was the same for similar training outside the prison. They couldn't believe they had finished a proper education program with an examination. It made such a difference to them. Now they would have a recognized skill when they were released from prison.

The nursery school changed the way the women talked with each other and their children. They paid each other and their children more respect. Gradually, the atmosphere in the project changed. You could feel it, even though they spoke Hindi and I didn't.

We've seen a remarkable change in the children. It has given them a good start in life. They looked healthier and put on weight, because they now had nutritious and fresh food. They washed more regularly. The mothers started to make an effort to make their children look nice every day. We helped by bringing in donated clothes.

There was a different look in the eyes of the children. They started to behave just like any child outside the prison. Previously, they were like small wild things, afraid and full of apathy. After a while, they started coming up to adults and reciting poems. Finally, they were receiving love and care. The nursery was a safe haven for them.

The Mobile Crèche workers helped us to select women from outside the jail to run the crèche. Inmates assisted Shakira, who was known to all the women and whom the children loved, adding to the warm atmosphere.

My role was to see the need, find the money for the project, make a proposal that would fit the needs of the women and children, and work toward making things happen, with professional advice from the Mobile Crèche. We were supported in all this by Kiran Bedi.

I will never forget the first time I met Kiran Bedi. A big man welcomed me into the prison. There were flowerpots in the halls. There was no door to her office in Tihar. She wore salwar-kameez and vest, and her hair was chopped short. Her eyes were so radiant. I felt her intense focus when it was my turn to see her, and immediately I wanted to give my best. Her reaction to our proposals was "Go and do it." She helped in whatever way she could and gave us a building, and later doubled the space for the women inmates.

My second abiding concern was the food served in the prison. In March 1994, I proposed that an African prisoner trained as a chef should teach the women to cook for the children and to make healthy, nutritious food for them. With 25,000 rupees (US$555.00) donated by the American Women's Association and 10,000 rupees ($US222.00) from my own pocket, we built a new kitchen with two sinks, a water pump, marble-slab counters, dishes, a refrigerator, coolers, and ice. It was beautiful and clean.

Six inmate-trainees worked in rotation. They made everything imaginable and sold the food to the women, who were now earning money and could purchase what they liked. The women were so happy. They made cakes and bread and fruit yogurt. The new kitchen was a great success and the women bought everything.

Our chef expanded her product lines to include cold drinks, tasty snacks, ice cream, birthday cakes, and delicious milk shakes. With the money we made we brought in fresh food from outside to make more. We bought much better quality rice and ate two or three different vegetables a day.

To help the male prisoners, the women started a food service on Saturdays when prisoners were allowed family visits. The prison even let us have a rickshaw for transporting the food from the women's kitchen to the visiting area. Saturday was our big day, and we sold a lot of food that day.

That spring I initiated a poetry workshop, to give some of the more literate women another avenue of expression as an outlet for the stress in their lives.

I've been completely and totally enriched from the experience of working at Tihar. It's an opportunity to give something back, and it's a challenge. Sometimes I pay the women at Tihar before I pay my rent. Tihar has become a part of my life. It's one of the most worthwhile things I've ever done, and I'm grateful for the opportunity.

The *Business Standard* carried this report, "Poetry from Behind Bars," on December 2, 1995:

There is starkness about the title on the red cover of the slim paperback. It says, *The Tihar Collection: Poems by Women from Tihar Jail, Delhi.* Packed into fifty-odd pages are the sorrows, longings, and frustrations of the women undertrials of Tihar.

The poems offer fleeting glimpses into the poets' past. Memories—some sweet, some bitter—come alive. A home tucked away somewhere and the warmth of a family; a relationship gone awry; nostalgia for friends far away. A lot of the poems are attempts to grapple with the bitterness churning inside. But there is a strong element of hope in some poems: *Hoping that someday we might enjoy a normal life once more / Coz that is what we are living for . . .* Andrea.

The poems were written at various times in the course of the undertrials' confinement in jail. But they were put together and given a definite form in the course of a workshop held in the jail earlier this year. Of course, a lot of the participants were foreigners or Indian women who had received an English education.

After the recent prison reforms, several voluntary groups have initiated activities with the women of Ward 1 of Tihar Jail. Most of these women are undertrials charged under the Narcotics, Drugs, and Psychotropic Substances (NDPS) Act of 1985. A lot of these activities are aimed at developing skills for income generation. Their hidden agenda aims at tapping the creative potential in these women.

Concerned Women is one such group. This group of eight women, all foreign nationals, has helped bring out this collection of poems. Released in September, the slim poetry anthology has already been reprinted twice and the proceeds from the sale have gone toward the welfare of the women of Tihar. The efforts of two other ladies have also yielded results. Dolly Narang, who runs the Village Gallery, Hauz Khas, and well-known writer and painter, Bulbul Sharma, recently exhibited mono-prints done by the women prisoners at Tihar.

The exhibition was held at the Capital's India International Center and was attended by Delhi's glitterati, which included the likes of M. F. Husain and supercop Kiran Bedi. A lot of the works were sold and there were checks in the mail for some of the artists on the eve of Dial.

At Navjyoti, Sister Max Mathews put together a unique project called Weaving Behind Bars. She was appointed by Navjyoti as Program Officer for this project funded by the Dutch Embassy. The expanded project was a three-month intensive training course for instructors in artistic weaving. The immediate objectives of this course were (a) to train ten selected women inmates in the techniques of creative weaving; (b) to produce a wide variety of woven articles of first quality to attract up-market customers in India and abroad; (c) to hold a sales exhibition of the items in Delhi to develop and explore market possibilities; and (d) to ensure the continuity of the weaving and training program in Tihar.

The income-generating activities in the jail had so far concentrated mostly on women's traditional skills. The new focus on production of artistic weaving was a step away from this tendency. Weaving is an age-old tradition in India, but this project was intended to introduce artistic products for selected up-market consumer groups.

The training would include knowledge of different weaving techniques, including macramé, crochet, screen-weaving, and weaving on wooden frames with jute strings; knowledge of various raw material combinations; composition using a variety of textures, design, and color-matching techniques; quality control and presentation; finishing and framing; and marketing skills and basic presentation skills.

The Weaving Behind Bars project gave new opportunities to the women inmates. It gave them a way of expressing themselves, as well as a livelihood. The trained women trained others and sharpened the innovative techniques.

Here are some statements from the women inmates in the training program:

> It keeps me occupied and I like it—otherwise I spend my time doing nothing, just wandering around. With the persuasion of another student, I joined this program and I earn money now. It's a home product, which I can use later on, once I am released.
> *(Paramjeet)*
> Paramjeet taught me. She brought me to this class. Earlier I just sat idle and gossiped, as I didn't have any skill. There is no one to support me, so

I will have to live on my own, arrange for my food,
and earn for my living.
(Murti)
　　I am always eager to learn something new, so
I joined this program. I like to match the colors
and I like the weaving process too. Sometimes
I have some designs in mind, but it changes auto-
matically when I am working. So the final product
becomes different from what I had in mind.
(Kiran)

Besides the art of weaving, the highly acclaimed painter
and author Bulbul Sharma, along with Dolly Narang of the
Village Gallery, came to Tihar to encourage the women to
take up painting. Bulbul Sharma narrated her experiences
during a painting workshop she held in Tihar. Her account
reveals how the emotions of the women inmates swung
from apprehension to suspicion to curiosity to eagerness,
and finally, to trust:

With hesitant hands they picked up the rollers and
tried the plates. The first day of the monoprinting
workshop the Village Gallery had organized at the
jail was a day of discovery. I was unsure about the
working conditions at the Tihar Jail and also worried about the reaction of the women inmates. The
gates were unlocked and we stepped into a huge
open courtyard full of tall trees. The women inmates, equally apprehensive and suspicious about us,
watched us carefully as we unloaded our bag full of
colors, plates, rollers, and printmaking tools. "I cannot draw," said one woman. "The last time I held
a crayon was in school many years ago," said another.
But as I began to demonstrate the method of mono-

printing, the women gradually came forward, one by one, to test out the rollers and to touch the paints with their fingers. Soon we had a crowd of 20 or more women around us, each one eager to make her own monoprint.

The simple method of monoprinting, which requires no skills or any expensive materials, is an easy way to initiate people into this art. The women learned quickly and soon lost their initial hesitation. They laid out flat layers of color on a plastic sheet with the roller. We used ordinary oil color tubes instead of printing inks since they are easier to spread. Once the color was spread on the sheet, we asked the women to draw a pattern with any pointed instrument like a hairpin, a twig, or the back end of a paintbrush. The women began with tiny hesitant lines and dots but after a while they covered the entire sheet with intricate drawings. The next session was much easier for both the women and for us since each knew what to expect. The women now handled the roller with ease, used more interesting combinations of colors and searched on their own for new kinds of marking tools. They collected strings, old leaves and bits of cloth to make new designs. They experimented with various techniques, like combining crayons with monoprinting or finger painting with collage, dabbing paint on the plastic sheet with their fingers. The women made monoprints on different kinds of paper provided by the Village Gallery.

After a few sessions we found that the women were working entirely on their own with very little input from us except for an occasional encouraging remark or word of praise. There was great enthusiasm now for the drawing classes and many women who had not worked with us earlier now came to watch and then sat down to work. Gradually, as they worked on new patterns and designs, some of them began to talk to us about their past lives and their hopes for the future.

Shakira spoke about how she would like to be a professional cartoonist and made a series of portraits using the monoprinting technique. Baljeet worked quietly to create powerful portraits and a subtle abstract monoprint. Savita, Santosh, and Nirprit were curious to learn more about monoprinting and kept coming out with new ideas on paper. Sumitra Devi took to the art of monoprinting like a professional and tried various innovative ways to print. She used thick impasto layers of oil paint with torn strips of paper, rolled light colors on dark, and used strings to make unusual abstract patterns. Karpai, a shy elderly woman from a village, spoke no Hindi and communicated with us only through gestures, but she had a skilled eye for color.

The women often recalled images they had seen in their childhood and tried to re-create them in a monoprint. In the beginning they had worked spontaneously, picking up any color that was lying nearby, but after six or seven workshops, they began to think and plan ahead. Some of them, of course, still rolled out colors swiftly, drew quick patterns, and lifted the paper at once—eager and impatient to see the results. The immediate, swift flowing quality of the monoprint, which is one of its charms, can be seen in their works. Flowers and trees, strange birds from faded childhood images, portraits of unknown faces, intricate patterns from tribal art, and abstract landscapes from dreams are some of the many striking images in the mono-prints by the women of Tihar Jail. The women were surprised when we asked them to sign their names on their monoprints. "Who would ever come to see our work? The outside world forgets you very soon once you are here," said one woman as she created an imaginary world with a roller and a tube of paint. But in a few months their monoprint exhibition held at the India International Center attracted an admiring audience. The exhibition even traveled outside India.

The reformation process for women went a long way to instill self-confidence, determination, organizing skills, and, above all, dignity in the women inmates. They began to look toward the future with new hope and new aspirations, as you can see in the following statements:

> I want to be a lawyer or a public prosecutor and help innocent prisoners.
> *(Poonam Vasudev)*
> I want to run a tea stall or work in a household (as a domestic help).
> *(Johra Alam)*
> I want to work at home and make some small but attractive items, such as *rakhis*.
> *(Najma Sattar)*
> I want to start a service center for washing, re-pairing, and repainting vehicles.
> *(Lakshmi Nattu)*
> I want to, first of all, serve my father and later give discourses for the upliftment of women in-mates at Tihar.
> *(Heera Moti Mishra)*

The vision of these women inmates kept on growing. Tihar Prison was no longer a prison for most of them; it was now a center of empowerment, preparing them for their release. Harinder Baweja, a correspondent of the newsmagazine *India Today*, reported:

Tihar Jail Women's Cell: A New Dignity
We enter Tihar Jail, Delhi's top-security prison, with a great deal of trepidation. My meager knowledge of jails comes from their portrayal in films, but the focus there is always on male prisoners. Granted permission to spend time in the women's ward of Tihar Jail, my mind kept conjuring up horrific images of women chained to their cells and crying out hysterically.

One of the three men escorting us bangs on the sturdy iron gate and a frail, middle-aged policewoman peeps out of the door. She opens it immediately on noticing the Jail Superintendent, K. R. Kishore. He has just been filling us in on the assorted crimes the women there have been jailed for. Accompanied by the photographer, I enter, expecting to see women holed up in cells and wearing blue-striped prisoners' uniforms.

What we come upon is a picture in complete contrast. Inmates are sprawled in the courtyard in colorful clothes, some combing their hair, others enjoying a ride on a swing strung from a tree branch. Helen, a tall, gracious British woman, is sweeping the rainwater out, while Sarah is busy making a cucumber-and-tomato salad.

Helen, I was shocked to learn later, is an Oxford graduate and a computer analyst who even after six years in jail is an undertrial. Not surprisingly, she is completely broken in spirit, just like Maria, a Spaniard, who has also been languishing in the jail as an undertrial for the past five years.

Surprises don't cease at finding scores of foreigners in the women's ward. There are also daughters and wives of the elite and wives of terrorists as well as 40 children, all under the age of four. Not to speak of two felines, named Shcru and Chein Chein, favorites of all the prisoners.

The atmosphere in the dreaded top-security prison is not too different from the one in women's hostels with their own nightly curfews. But it soon metamorphoses into what could well be an ashram. Or even a temple.

Suddenly the premises resound with the *dhak-dhak* of a *dholki* (drum). Startled, we rush out from a cell into the courtyard. Others troop out too. Soon, the entire ward echoes with strains of a *bhajan* as almost all the 270-odd inmates sit cross-legged, heads covered, lost in prayer.

Kiran Bedi, who recently took over as IG, told us later this is a daily feature. Bedi, in fact, has been instrumental in initiating many reforms, which have made the prison a "livable place" in the inmates' opinion.

Tied by mutual empathy and a common yearning for freedom, the inmates usually make allowances for each other's moods. Each has been through the same gamut of emotions herself. Frustration. Dejection. Paranoia. Claustrophobia. Acute depression. Occasionally, fights break out over trifling matters. "Why did you step on my blanket?" They are resolved soon enough, for it's time for Maxi to appear on the scene. Chosen as leader of the recently formed panchayat, Maxi's job has been made easier, for her view counts each time a prisoner's parole application comes up.

Oddly enough, confinement has had a salutary effect on a few prisoners who prefer jail to the outside world. Like Anita, who has been in Tihar for the past twelve years. Convicted for killing her husband's first wife's three-year-old son, Anita would rather stay on at Tihar than "go back to the man who showed me what police stations and jails look like."

Sarah, a Canadian booked under the Drugs Act, is also content. Not because she has been jailed but because she hopes to get out on bail. She has been in Tihar for only a month, unlike Maria, Shakira, or Poonam, who are shattered by the legal wrangles that have kept them from freedom. Poonam is considered lucky by others, for at least 60 of them have been able to get out on bail on applications drafted by her.

Each time the pain increases and hopelessness takes over, the inmates think of one of Shakira's poems which reads: "Indira Gandhi went to jail, and so did Gandhiji. The stigma didn't deter them, why should it bother me? If they survived to challenge fate, why should I fail then . . ."

Walking out of Tihar, we can't help wondering how the miniature world within the jail comes so close to being a deceptive replica of what life would have been, were they free. But only just.

epilogue:
ten years later

Life After Tihar

A conversation with Kiran Bedi inspired author and social activist Ruzbeh Bharucha to interview a number of former Tihar inmates who, inspired by Dr. Bedi's reforms, have built lives of service in the midst of challenging circumstances.

I first met Dr. Kiran Bedi while writing *Shadows in Cages*, a book on mothers and children in Indian prisons. I asked her about the ramifications of her reforms on the lives of those inmates who were no longer in Tihar Prison.

"It's been ten years since you were transferred from Tihar Jail. Did your reforms have a lasting impact on the lives of the inmates after they left Tihar? For instance, you wrote about Shakira, whose poems have been published. I wonder where she is now and how life is treating her."

"Why don't you interview a few of the inmates and find out for yourself?" Dr. Bedi suggested.

I thought it was a casual remark. Little did I realize then that there is nothing casual about Dr. Bedi!

Months later, I had a conversation with Shakira, a former woman inmate. She now represents various social organizations that run day-care centers in prisons, and organizes vocational training courses for those living in slums and resettlement colonies.

I asked, "How did Dr. Bedi's reforms change your life in Tihar, and did they make a difference once you were released from prison?"

"Dr. Kiran Bedi has changed my life. I cannot imagine what would have come of me if not for her. Her tenure as Inspector General ensured that people like me could spend our time in prison constructively. Before the arrival of Dr. Bedi, there was nothing to do in Tihar. We were languishing every day in prison, and each moment weighed heavily upon us. Each day seemed like a lifetime."

"You mean before her arrival you did absolutely nothing in prison?"

"Absolutely nothing, and that is the greatest punishment
anybody could hand out to women like me who have lived
a life filled with activity and deadlines. After her arrival, my
days were filled with constructive activities. I began to look
after the nursery and managed vocational training and the
income-generation projects she initiated."

After speaking to many former inmates of Tihar, I came
to realize that the greatest contribution and effect of all the
reforms initiated by Dr. Bedi was to endow the inmates
with self-confidence and dignity. She made each one feel
that her existence was worthwhile and infused them with
a sense of belonging, self-confidence, and self-respect. These
qualities have stood many of them well all these years.

My conversation with Shakira continued. "When you
were released from Tihar, what was the reaction of your
immediate family and friends, and how did Dr. Bedi's ideology and reforms help you cope with the outside world?"

"The reaction was unexpected. People I did not expect
to come forward in fact accepted me without prejudice, but
my family and so-called friends, whom I thought would
embrace me with no questions asked, kept me at arm's
length. My immediate family was hesitant, and even ten
years later, some of them still find it hard to relate to my
tenure in Tihar. But distant relatives, who I wasn't in contact with for many years, came forward and made it clear
that they were there for me, and if I needed any kind of
support, I could bank on them unconditionally.

"Thanks to Dr. Bedi, I could also rely on various social
organizations. One group, The Concerned Women, com-
prised of Dutch nationals, really helped me. The day I was
released from Tihar, one of the women from this organiza-

tion drove me to Dr. Bedi's residence on her bike. Dr. Bedi welcomed me with open arms. In fact, I began to work on the day of my release. Dr. Bedi made certain I joined a reputed social organization that needed somebody who could run a nursery school and work with children in slums. Dr. Bedi's reforms and training had equipped me with those qualifications."

"I imagine that not everybody took well to Dr. Bedi's presence and the reforms in Tihar. There must have been inmates who were not interested in transforming their lives and the lives of those around them. How has life treated them once they were released from Tihar?"

"I know many of them who have gone back to their old ways. Either they have gone back to prison or they have returned to their old lifestyle of peddling drugs or associating with drug dealers or gangsters. It is not easy for a woman to live in society with the stigma of having been in prison. Many can't cope with the ridicule and taunts of their family. You don't have an emotional anchor to protect you. Your family doesn't want you. Your husband doesn't want you. Thus many women find an easy way out by latching onto somebody, or they simply return to their old ways. But those who have been touched by Dr. Bedi's ideology fight on."

"I guess the most important effect of Dr. Bedi's reforms and humane attitude must be a more positive attitude toward life and toward society at large," I said.

"Most certainly. There are very few people who come out of prison not bitter and negative toward life and society. Bitterness is natural. Everybody goes through that phase. I was very, very bitter at one time. The best thing Dr. Bedi did to help us deal with our frustrations and negativity was vipassana meditation. Yes, the reforms and her initiatives were a great help, but it was meditation that helped so many of us tremendously."

"Do you still practice vipassana?"

"I meditate. I won't say I practice vipassana. Dr. Bedi made meditation a part of our daily life, and it really helped innumerable inmates. Hard-core criminals were transformed into gentle, caring people. I only wish there were more like Dr. Bedi who would introduce such reforms in prisons. Society at large would benefit, as those who re-enter society would do so, as kind, caring individuals, not individuals filled with hatred and anger.

"It is not easy to resettle back into society. We have to keep proving ourselves. We have to work harder. We have to face all kinds of reactions, from family and friends and colleagues. I have gone through so much prejudice even while working for social causes. Prejudice exists even now in my family. One of my siblings still hasn't accepted me. She has still not told her children that I am her sister. So life goes on. It is Dr. Bedi's reforms and initiatives that have helped me to cope with life. I shudder to think what I would have done if she had not entered my life. Just the fact that she had faith and believed in us helps so many like me to move on with life in a positive and graceful manner."

A few days later I spoke with Mr. Var, a resident of Srinagar, Kashmir. Mr. Var had spent more than nine years in Tihar before being honorably acquitted. He was another ideal study of how a man wrongly accused and imprisoned, instead of becoming bitter, goes on to help others. Mr. Var and three other former Tihar residents met me for interviews.

I spoke first with Samir:

"I was released from Tihar on 29 August 1997. In Tihar, thanks to Dr. Bedi's initiative and reforms, I had resumed my education. Once out of Tihar and with a graduation degree in hand, I enrolled in a computer course and took up various other courses that would help me find employment. The fire that Dr. Bedi had lit in our hearts motivated us to walk the right path and make something of our lives. But then my struggle began. Wherever I went the doors were shut to me. For a long time I was unemployed, and you can imagine the frustration I felt. But during those dark days, all that Madam had taught us through her own conduct and attitude made certain that I did not drift to the wrong path. Luckily for me, I got a job in a Bangalore based company as a computer operator. Initially I was employed in this company as a driver. But the gentleman for whom I was driving saw my signature on the register one day and inquired about my qualifications. When he learned that I was a graduate and had done various computer courses, he insisted that I do computer work in his office. I am now an account manager in a company called Airtel."

"Tell me, how have the reforms initiated by Dr. Bedi helped you in your life?"

"It is with her help and grace that I completed my education. In fact, I am happy that I was put into Tihar when she was in charge, as only Madam could have influenced me to get a grip on my life. I now have a good job, and I am married to an educated woman. Our children will be educated in the right schools. If Madam had not been in charge of Tihar, I would have been finished. In prison, one is encouraged to become a criminal. You make criminal contacts and are assured of an income every month for criminal activities. If it weren't for Madam, I would have come out a frustrated man with negative emotions and criminal intentions."

Next I interviewed Khalikul Zama:

"I was in Tihar for five years, from 1994 to 1999. It is ironic that all my life I wanted to do social work but never had the chance. In Tihar I had the perfect platform to serve people. I taught mathematics and various other courses, including Hindi literature. After my release, I continued my social-service activities. Madam was such a motivating force in our lives. We were not allowed to sit on chairs before she arrived. If we were called to meet the jail authorities, we were asked to stand or sit on the floor. Forget talking to the Inspector General; nobody had even seen the man. But all this changed after Madam came to Tihar. She would make rounds of Tihar even at 2 a.m. Such dedication is bound to inspire thousands for the rest of their lives. Without the reforms she initiated, I am certain released inmates would become criminals again. I am sure of this. Society makes it very hard for released prisoners, or even those waiting for trial who have been honorably released, to live a respectable and peaceful life. We know the situation in most prisons. Not everyone is guilty, but society doesn't care about such things. Once in prison. you are labeled a criminal. When a person enters prison and sees atrocities, corruption, and extortion being indulged by the authorities themselves, he is convinced that this is the only way to lead life. A small-time thief becomes a bigger criminal and a criminal turns into a full-fledged gangster. Tihar was a laboratory of crime. Madam gave us another option. In jails all over the world, where is such an option offered?"

"You were released in 1999."

"Yes."

"What did you do then?"

"I was certain that I wanted to continue my social work and activity. But see the irony! In Tihar, under Madam's guidance, I could concentrate completely on social work and reform. I did not have to worry about food, clothing, shelter, and medicine. But in the outside world, especially in India, there is no Prisoners' Welfare Association to help an ex-prisoner. I faced innumerable difficulties. I did not have the money to start a social organization, but I did begin to motivate people who had money to establish schools in Delhi and Haryana. Three schools have opened with me as their Founder Principal. They are doing well. I am indebted to Madam's initiation to do social work. If it weren't for her, only Allah knows what I would have done with my life."

"How are those who were with you in Tihar and are now out doing in life?"

"When we started IGNOU there were only seven students. By the time we were released from Tihar, there were around a thousand of us. I can confidently say that at least 70 percent of those thousand people are on the right path. Yes, some have gone back to their old ways, but the majority of us are walking the path of truth and peace. Let me say, the police have a big role in forcing many released inmates to go back to the path of crime. Take Bharat Singh, for instance. He was released while I was still in Tihar. He was leading a normal and honest life. The police kept approaching him and asking him for commissions. He kept telling them that he had changed his ways and was no longer in crime, so the question of commission did not exist. One day, they levied false charges against him and he was back in Tihar. We agitated on his behalf and even wrote to the Parliament. We put so much pressure on the authorities that he was released. But in prison, he had become so disheartened and angry that he was contemplating a life of crime once again. One by one, we counseled him and made him realize the need to stay straight, and now he is living a crime-free life. The fight against prejudice and hate is always on. I think what we really need is some support once we are released from prison.

"So many of us are unemployed just because of the stigma of prison. A friend who was with us in Tihar lost his job after two years when the employer found out he had been in prison. This man worked hard and honestly for more than two years and gave the employer his very best. Now he is being punished. This makes a man wonder whether following the path of honesty is worthwhile. Having a support group would help people like him."

Next I spoke with Arun, who looked like a boy of eighteen though he was in his mid-twenties:

"I entered Tihar in 1994 and was released in 1997. I had just completed the tenth grade. In Tihar, thanks to Madam Bedi, I finished the twelfth grade and also did a course in commercial art. When I left Tihar I had one more year to get my graduation certificate, but due to monetary problems and other circumstances, I haven't finished. Even now, so many of us who have been released from Tihar are facing major issues of unemployment. I was employed immediately after my prison stint, but the moment the employers found out that I had spent time in jail, I lost my job. Society doesn't make it easy for people like me to walk the straight path. All doors for an honest life are shut for us and all the doors for resuming criminal activity are wide open. If it weren't for Madam's influence on our lives, we would certainly have drifted to crime."

"She has become the voice of your conscience."

"Exactly. She treated us like her children. She educated us and loved us. How can we let her down? I have a one-year-old child now, and I want to impart the same values to my child."

I will never forget the response of these men when Dr. Bedi later joined us. Samir and Arun immediately touched her feet, as is the custom of showing respect for millions of Hindus all over the world. Zama and Shabudin stood transfixed. There were tears in Shabudin's eyes. We sat down for a group discussion.

Samir said, "Before you arrived, every moment hung heavily upon us. We had nothing to do and this only increased our frustration and negative state of mind. The most important thing you did for all of us was to keep our time and our minds constructively occupied. By allowing us to resume our education, you not only took care of the present but also the future. You gave us the power to feel useful in life."

"Was education the key to change in all of your lives?"

"Yes, Madam. But it was not just education. After you were transferred, education reforms continued, but the attitude toward us had changed. Once again we were being treated like animals. But it is difficult to destroy a huge structure once it has already been built, and it is difficult to destroy conviction of the mind. Both external and internal structures were built by you, Madam. The transformation was real. It wasn't a farce and it wasn't meant to make you happy. Whether you know it or not, your presence and reforms in our lives still have a very powerful hold on us," Zama explained.

"What do you think, Shabudin?"

"Madam, there is no doubt that after you left, most of the authorities tried their best to break us. We were treated like animals, especially those who were active participants in your reforms. But even those prisoners who didn't participate in the activities you initiated held you in high esteem and eventually we got their support, too. You were transferred, but your presence was still very much in our hearts and in Tihar itself. I was called in and told by the then Inspector General that the Open University (IGNOU) was going to be closed. He told me nobody was interested in the program. I argued that there were at least two hundred students who were preparing for their exams. When he heard that there were two hundred of us in IGNOU, he insisted that if within a few days I did not show him a signed list of six hundred students, he would shut down IGNOU."

"My God!"

"You can imagine, Madam; where were we to get four hundred students in a week's notice? It was then that these hard-core thugs came to our help. They said that whatever you had begun was important for the future of the inmates, and even though they weren't involved or interested at all in education, they understood the need for others to continue their education. So they personally took Zama, Var, and myself to all the inmates in Jail No. 3 and convinced them to sign. We got the six hundred signatures and IGNOU continued," Shabudin explained.

"Shabudin, you were in prison for another four years after my transfer. How was that? Was there conflict in your mind?"

"Madam, even during your time, there were many inmates from Kashmir and Punjab, booked under the Terrorist Act. They kept telling me that I should be leading our movement and not a movement of reform and education. But eventually it was these people who stood by us and took an active role in the education process you had initiated. You will be happy to hear that all of us who were fighting the system and who earlier were involved in various activities against the system are now involved in helping society. I don't think any of us went back to any of the agencies that were trying to destabilize the country. In fact, most of us have begun to help people, in whatever capacity we can."

"That is so heartening to hear, Shabudin."

"Madam, you can break a building but not a mind. The staff thought that by breaking down IGNOU they would break us down, but that was wishful thinking. In fact, it was the social pressure within the prison that forced the authorities to continue with your reforms."

"You all must have gone through hell, though."

"Madam, it is better to go through hell externally than

in the mind. We are still going through hell in the outside world, but at least in our minds there is peace and the consolation that we are walking the right path. Let me give you a small example. After our agitation in jail for IGNOU to continue, we began to put external pressure on the government also. We had our sources and our well-wishers outside the prison too, and through all these efforts the government realized that the social change in the prison could not be ignored. A grant of over 5,100,000 rupees (approximately US$120,000) was sanctioned. From this grant, supplies were purchased. I was asked to sign a document stating that the IGNOU center had received these supplies worth tens of thousands of rupees. We insisted that we would sign only after inspecting the supplies. What we were shown did not match the quantity shown on paper. Obviously, we refused to sign, and all hell broke loose. I was even put into a mental asylum as a form of punishment. But once the mind is made up, Madam, it is very difficult to break it."

"You know, Madam," added Samir, "it is strange, but we miss our days in Tihar with you. I feel that if I were in Tihar for another two years I would have moved far ahead with my education and with my life. Even now when I think of the old days, tears come to my eyes for even though we were in prison, you gave us freedom of spirit and thought. You made us feel important and needed. The facilities you gave us, the environment you gave us, we can never forget, and because of all this, we are on our feet and not dependent on anybody."

"Does society still treat you badly?"

"Yes, Madam. However politely or tenderly you behave or talk, most people behave badly with us. But there are a few people who have really supported me and encouraged me. Just a few days back an old man held my hand and introduced me to his grandson. He told the little boy that if I could continue with my education even in jail and come out as a graduate, then surely he could concentrate on his studies with all the luxuries available. The old man asked the boy to touch my feet and get blessings. I had tears in my eyes, Madam. A lot of parents chide their children and point to us as negative examples. A lot of them are surprised that instead of coming out of prison a thug or a criminal, I came out as a graduate and as a responsible member of society."

"Meditation has helped us a lot, too. It has taught us to go within when the world outside becomes so spiteful and cruel," Arun added.

For a long time, Dr. Bedi and her Tihar friends sat and chatted. I sat and wondered when society would realize that every sinner has a future and every saint a past.

Mr. Var and his old friend Mr. Parvez received Saina and me at the Srinagar airport. Saina is Dr. Bedi's daughter and, like her mother, she too is engrossed in social work. We drove to the Vision Public School that houses more than a hundred children of which twenty-six are orphans. Most of them have lost their parents through the atrocities committed by political militants or various agencies of Pakistan and India. The Himalayan Institute of Honesdale, Pennsyl-vania, and India Vision Foundation support the lodging, boarding, and education of these children. Mr. Var oversees the administration.

Mr. Var spent seven years in Tihar before he was honorably acquitted:

"After seven years, I was honorably acquitted but tens of thousands of rupees had been spent on my case, and my family was by then bankrupt. It was only after I was released that my family informed me that my father had died, a heartbroken man. A big part of me wanted to seek revenge on all those who had put me in this situation. But

Dr. Bedi's influence had a powerful hold on my mind and conscience. Since my release, I have been involved in social work. First I started a college called the Dr. Saxena Vision Foundation. Now we have started Kiran Law College and Vision Public School. All these institutions make certain that a portion of those being educated get free education."

After a heartening visit to the school, Var drove us to the hotel, where he and Parvez introduced us to Mohammad. They had all been in Tihar as political prisoners due to the struggle in Kashmir.

Mohammed said, "The most important thing that Kiranji did for all of us, political prisoners as well as the other inmates, was that she treated us like human beings. That little humaneness was like a breath of fresh air. Maybe if she had not treated us like human beings, then bitterness and hatred would have ruled our lives even now, and who knows? We might have been back in prison or even dead."

"What kind of social work are you involved with now?"

"I am trying to help those who were with me in Tihar to move on with their lives in as peaceful a manner as is possible in Kashmir. You know how it is. On one hand you have agencies working from across the border, and then we have various agencies run by India. Then you have the militants, military, and the police. The common man is being trampled between all of them.

"When I was released in 2000, I did not have a penny. My family was financially finished. All our money was gone and we were deeply in debt from fighting my case. My agenda was very clear. I wanted to settle down in life, take care of my family, and then do something for the inmates of Tihar. That was the least I could do after all the love and care with which Kiranji had showered on all of us. So the first thing I did was to make certain that the ancient art of creating wooden ceilings, called *khatamband*, was revived. Mr. Var, another inmate of Tihar, who as you know is involved in social work, was starting a college; and to help me, he gave me the responsibility of working in his college. As soon as I got settled, I began to train other released inmates in this traditional art. As my work grew, I could help more inmates. Then I got involved in Kashmiri shawls. I did the same thing with the shawls. The moment I got more work, I brought in others who were really going through hell after their release. Now they are involved with my work and living a respectable life.

"Nowadays, I am also helping youngsters just released from prisons with a business venture at the powerful *dargha* (a spiritual master's last resting place) of Hazrat Bal, where people gather to pray. The youngsters sell spiritual merchandise each Friday. I bought two hundred collapsible beds that I rent to them for 10 rupees a day (about US$0.25). These beds help the youngsters set up their stalls and show their merchandise. Thus in my own humble way, I am trying to help these youngsters.

"I focus only on those who have been released from prison because they really have no place to go. They have lost so many years, often through no fault of their own. Their families are financially finished trying to fight their cases in the various courts of law. Society doesn't want them anymore. We are trying our best to help them. Also, I help youngsters who are languishing in prisons in Jammu and Kashmir either to get bail or to get a lawyer. And a few of us ex-inmates of Tihar are trying to convince the Red Cross to sponsor a trip from Kashmir to Delhi for the aged parents and family of some prisoners in Tihar Jail. These old people cannot afford the expense of the trip and the stay in Delhi.

"Kiranji has taught me that social work and helping those in need is like *ibadad* (prayer). I have seen prison life before Kiranji and life in Tihar after she was transferred.

To help humanity has been her mission, which she has passed on to us. She has changed the lives of so many people that it cannot be measured. Criminals have changed and have taken the right path due to her efforts and reforms. In my religion only an individual without character praises somebody without substance or for some selfish gain. Thus, when I praise her I do so because she deserves it. Yes, you cannot change everybody. A dog's tail will remain crooked no matter what, and many criminals are like dogs. But the fact remains that she has really changed the lives of innumerable people and thereby the lives and future of so many families.

"Now the situation is back to square one in Tihar. According to my information, an inmate was beaten mercilessly and urine poured into his mouth. Do you think that individual is going to come out a reformed man? He will come out bitter and seeking revenge and filled with hate for society at large. He becomes an easy target for agencies to recruit and use to kill and hurt the innocent.

"Kiranji allowed the Hindus and Muslims to follow their faiths. She allowed us to pray at the dargha of our leader, the great Maqbool Haq. Thanks to her, we have come out more secular in thought and reason. Now I have heard they are trying to make some building where Haq Saab's dargha stood. You think secularism is going to be nurtured, or fanaticism? Kiranji helped us to look beyond the self and try to see the larger picture. We are trying our best. The rest is left to Allah."

We also spoke with Aslam who had also been a political prisoner in Tihar:

"What were you doing before you entered Tihar?"

"I was in government service. After my release, my situation was really bad. It is with Allah's grace that I wasn't killed by one of the agencies or militants! But I was on suspension, without pay. I filed a case and after seven years won the case."

"Did you get any compensation from the State Government?"

"No compensation at all. What is worse is that though I was reinstated in my job, so many of my own people view me with mistrust. Once, I told my supervisor that 'if you do not trust me, tell me so; I will leave this job.' Frustrations are tremendous. My son has been picked up by agencies from both sides. He has been hit on the head so badly that he has virtually become a vegetable. He is twenty-one but not capable of doing anything constructive. But, we are moving on, quietly trying to lead an honest life."

"Have all of your Tihar colleagues refrained from joining radical agencies?"

"Many of our colleagues joined various agencies from outside (Pakistan) or from here (India). These people are treated with respect, and make lots of money, but people like us have realized what is going on. We want to lead a peaceful and an honorable life."

The day before we left for Delhi, Var and Parvez introduced us to Mufti Farookh. He is now one of the leading advocates (attorneys) in Kashmir and exuded an aura of confidence.

"I was in Tihar for five years."

"You were practicing law before that?"

"Yes. I was not only practicing law before Tihar, but in fact I handled innumerable cases in Tihar Jail. Kiranji treated all of us like human beings. That filled us with self-respect and dignity; something that we carried with us once we left Tihar. Not everyone, but many were touched by her reformative spirit and initiative. Another important thing, which really touched all our hearts, is that she gave us religious freedom. Hindus, Christians, Muslims—all of us were allowed religious freedom, and, trust me, that really extinguished a lot of frustration and anger within so many prisoners. Also, I have myself seen inmates who couldn't read or write leave Tihar prepared to take up jobs that required those skills. That itself changed the lives of so many inmates.

"My best law cases and noblest legal work were in Tihar. One day Kiranji asked me to review a case of Mr. Janki Das, who was sentenced to death for the murder of his wife and children. The Sessions Court and the High Court had given him a death sentence. When Kiranji asked me to take up the case, I at first told her that it was morally not right to fight a case on behalf of a man who had killed his own family members. But she convinced me to take up the case. I filed the papers for Janki Das. On Friday, I was called once again to Kiranji's chambers. She congratulated me—because of me Janki Das's execution was stayed. But most importantly, she organized a big meeting at Jail No.1, where in front of everybody she highlighted my role in helping Janki Das. This magnanimous gesture from her side won so many hearts.

"Chandra Pal was another case. He was convicted and given the death penalty. She asked me to fight on his behalf for she believed that there was something really amiss. So, I did so. One day right after my *namaz* (prayers), I was trying to sleep. I heard somebody crying, so I opened my eyes and saw Chandra Pal. I told him not to worry, as we would take care of the case. But he began to cry loudly and told me, 'No, Saab, I have been released.' I did my job, but the important thing is that Kiranji believed in his innocence and my ability to fight for an innocent man.

"Kiranji gave a signal to the world at large that all inmates, whether undertrials or convicted prisoners, could be reformed. Forget reform homes and probation houses, change and reform can be achieved in prison itself, and if such transformation can take place in prison, then it can take place anywhere in the world. She has taught us to treat all alike. In front of her, we all were first and foremost human beings. There was no Hindu or Muslim or Christian. We all were human beings, and I think she has taught all of us to think in the same manner. She has conveyed a strong message to the world at large that if inmates in one of the most dangerous prisons in the world can be reformed, then nothing is impossible."

Returning to Delhi, I reflected on how easily these Kashmiris, most imprisoned under the Terrorist and Disruptive Act (TADA) and later honorably acquitted, could easily have turned hostile and revengeful. Instead, virtually all of them have devoted their lives to social work. In these times of bloodshed and terrorism, Dr. Bedi's reforms and initiative take on an importance of epic proportions.

India's New Prison Act

A new prison act replaced the Prison Act of 1894. The new law makes the existing management practices and reforms mandatory. For the first time in the history of the Indian prison management, the Prison Bill contains a mission statement in the Preamble. It says:

A Bill to provide for the detention of prisoners committed to prison custody and for their reformation and rehabilitation, with a view to ensuring safe detention and minimum standards of treatment of prisoners, consistent with the principles of dignity.

It took the Indian prison system 107 years of "imprisonment" to liberate itself from the colonial hangover. For instance, it categorically abolishes the practice of whipping as a punishment for prisoners and the staff. In place of these barbaric measures, it provides an institutional system of grievance redressal. Under the new dispensation, prisoners have a right to legal aid. Other highlights are:

a) Regulation of community activities and visitors to the prison;
b) Provisions for undertrials to work and earn wages if they so desire;
c) Aftercare and rehabilitation of prisoners;
d) Review of cases of prisoners pending for more than one year and release of undertrials whose detention exceeds period of punishment proved for the offenses;
e) Abolition of convict officers as security guards, etc.;
f) Medical examination of a prisoner on the same day of admission;
g) Liberation in facilities of communication through interviews and letters;
h) Abolition of solitary confinement;
i) Provision for a Law Officer and Welfare Officers for jails;
j) Training of prison officials on the responsibilities and rights of prisoners; and
k) Regular audit.

It took 107 years and the sustained effort of prison officials, prisoners, and non-government organizations to see this change. Whenever determination is combined with innate goodness, anything is possible.

About the Author

Dr. Kiran Bedi, the first woman inspector general of Tihar prison, the largest prison in Asia-Pacific, was instrumental in bringing about radical reforms in the Tihar prison system. She has received numerous awards, including The Ramon Magsaysay Award (Asia's Nobel Prize), The Swiss-German Joseph Beuys Award for holistic and innovative management, and the United Nations Serge Sotiroff Memorial Award for drug abuse prevention. She is the founder of two internationally recognized organizations: Navjyoti and the India Vision Foundation, which provide education, training, and counseling services to thousands in some of the poorest sections of India.

The Himalayan Institute

The main building of the Institute headquarters near Honesdale, Pennsylvania

Founded in 1971 by Swami Rama, the Himalayan Institute has been dedicated to helping people grow physically, mentally, and spiritually by combining the best knowledge of both the East and the West.

Our international headquarters is located on a beautiful 400-acre campus in the rolling hills of the Pocono Mountains of northeastern Pennsylvania. The atmosphere here is one to foster growth, increase inner awareness, and promote calm. Our grounds provide a wonderfully peaceful and healthy setting for our seminars and extended programs. Students from all over the world join us here to attend programs in such diverse areas as hatha yoga, meditation, stress reduction, ayurveda, nutrition, Eastern philosophy, psychology, and other subjects. Whether the programs are for weekend meditation retreats, week-long seminars on spirituality, months-long residential programs, or holistic health services, the attempt here is to provide an environment of gentle inner progress. We invite you to join with us in the ongoing process of personal growth and development.

The Institute is a nonprofit organization. Your membership in the Institute helps to support its programs. Please call or write for information on becoming a member.

Programs and Services include:

- Weekend or extended seminars and workshops
- Meditation retreats and advanced meditation instruction
- Hatha yoga teachers' training
- Residential programs for self-development
- Holistic health services and pancha karma at the Institute's Center for Health and Healing
- Spiritual excursions
- Varcho Veda® herbal products
- Himalayan Institute Press
- *Yoga + Joyful Living* magazine
- Sanskrit correspondence course

A *Quarterly Guide to Programs and Other Offerings* is free within the USA. To request a copy, or for further information, call 800-822-4547 or 570-253-5551, write to the Himalayan Institute, 952 Bethany Turnpike, Honesdale, PA 18431, USA, or visit our website at www.HimalayanInstitute.org.

Himalayan Institute Press

Himalayan Institute Press has long been regarded as the resource for holistic living. We publish dozens of titles, as well as audio and video tapes that offer practical methods for living harmoniously and achieving inner balance. Our approach addresses the whole person—body, mind, and spirit—integrating the latest scientific knowledge with ancient healing and self-development techniques.

As such, we offer a wide array of titles on physical and psychological health and well-being, spiritual growth through meditation and other yogic practices, as well as translations of yogic scriptures.

Our yoga accessories include the Japa Kit for meditation practice and the Neti Pot™, the ideal tool for sinus and allergy sufferers. Our Varcho Veda® line of quality herbal extracts is now available to enhance balanced health and well-being.

Subscriptions are available to a bimonthly magazine, *Yoga International*, which offers thought-provoking articles on all aspects of meditation and yoga, including yoga's sister science, ayurveda.

For a free catalog, call 800-822-4547 or 570-253-5551, e-mail hibooks@HimalayanInstitute.org, fax 570-647-1552, write to the Himalayan Institute Press, 630 Main St., Suite 350, Honesdale, PA 18431-1843, USA, or visit our website at www.HimalayanInstitute.org.

SACREDLINK™
The Healing Revolution

The Himalayan Institute has a long legacy of global humanitarian effort in addition to its dedication to personal self-transformation. In recent decades the Institute has been instrumental in a number of projects in India, including the Himalayan Institute Hospital Trust, Medical College, Nursing School and Rural Development Institute; India Earthquake Relief; and the Himalayan Institute Indian Chapter in Allahabad. The Institute has supported numerous other worthy causes in India, including schools, a Sanskrit college, and the work of India Vision Foundation in prison reform.

To further its global initiatives, the Himalayan Institute supports and works hand-in-hand with the Sacred Link Global Humanitarian Project, an independent sister organization, conceived by the Institute's Spiritual Head Pandit Rajmani Tigunait, Ph.D., to build, fund, and manage a world-class, large-scale humanitarian effort to address illiteracy, inequality, and poverty around the world.

The mission of the Sacred Link Global Humanitarian Project is transformation of individuals, and the societies, economies, and environments in which they live. Acknowledging that our planet, society, and livelihood are all interrelated, and all in need of healing, the Sacred Link Global Humanitarian Project is the "Healing Revolution."

If you would like to support the global humanitarian projects of the Himalayan Institute and the Sacred Link Global Humanitarian Project, call 570-253-5551, e-mail info@sacredlink.org, write us at 952 Bethany Turnpike, Honesdale, Pennsylvania 18431, or visit our website at www.HimalayanInstitute.org or www.SacredLink.org.